Landscape of Hope and Despair

The Ethnography of Political Violence

Cynthia Keppley Mahmood, Series Editor

A complete list of books in the series is available from the publisher.

Landscape of Hope and Despair

Palestinian Refugee Camps

Julie Peteet

PENN

University of Pennsylvania Press

Philadelphia

10   9   8   7   6   5   4   3   2   1

Published by
University of Pennsylvania Press
Philadelphia, Pennsylvania 19104-4011

Library of Congress Cataloging-in-Publication Data

Peteet, Julie Marie.
    Landscape of hope and despair : Palestinian refugee camps / Julie Peteet.
        p.   cm.—(Ethnography of political violence)
    Includes bibliographical references and index.
    ISBN 0-8122-3893-1 (cloth : alk. paper)
        1. Refugee camps—Lebanon.   2. Palestinian Arabs—Lebanon—Social conditions.
3. Palestinian Arabs—Lebanon—Economic conditions.   I. Title.   II. Series.
HV640.5.P36 P48   2005
362.87′089′927405692—dc22   2005041612

Contents

Preface

The landscape of human history is littered with displacements, diasporas, forced migrations, treks, and flights; violence and terror form the substance of innumerable memories, silences, and nightmares. Over the course of several centuries, the Atlantic slave trade displaced twelve million Africans. In the nineteenth century, the Cherokees were forced down the "Trail of Tears," the Navajo were marched on the "Long Walk," and the Herero of Southern Africa were forced into the Kalahari Desert. In the twentieth century—dubbed the "century of refugees" (Loescher 1993)—the displaced were iconic figures evoking war and human rights tragedies.

In the first half of the twentieth century, the breakup of empires spawned large-scale displacements (Marrus 1985). The end of the Ottoman Empire was followed by the forced removal of hundreds of thousands of Armenians and the expulsion of the Asian Greeks from the emergent Turkish state. At the same time, in the southern United States, economic pressure, discrimination, and terror compelled thousands of African Americans to make the "Great Migration" to the North, portrayed in the stark yet colorful murals of artist Jacob Lawrence. The depression and drought of the 1930s gave rise to the westward movement of the "Okies," migrants from Kansas, Oklahoma, and West Texas, poignantly rendered in Steinbeck's *The Grapes of Wrath*. In Europe, the displacement of over thirty million people in World War II is unparalleled in modern history (Zolberg et al. 1989).

While these movements were propelled by violence of various kinds such as the structural violence of poverty and the threat of starvation, or racialist-driven terror and discrimination, ethnonationalist exclusions orchestrated by expanding and consolidating states have played a prominent role. Modern warfare, with its advanced technologies designed to inflict high casualties and a propensity to remove civilian populations, has produced mass movements and enabled exclusivist states to expel undesirable populations.[1] In the twentieth century, "ethnic cleansing" in emergent states multiplied in rapidity and scale.

Nineteenth-century administrative and bureaucratic interventions in the lives of displaced Native Americans (see Biolsi 1995) and their reconstitution as subjects indexed a shift to modernity and the displaced as a discursive formation and object of intervention. The relief organizations that responded to the Armenian and Greek displacements were precursors to the full-fledged institutionalized and bureaucratic refugee aid regimes that arose in World War II and its immediate aftermath. Two world wars fostered the emergence of international aid regimes and legal frameworks to manage the millions displaced by modern warfare.

The postwar period, the end of British colonialism, and the partitions it left in its wake, also generated mass displacements. The Great Partition of 1947–48, which gave birth to India and Pakistan as separate nation-states, is one such example. Subsequent Cold War conflicts in postcolonial arenas generated refugee flows from Central America, South Asia, and Africa. In the 1990s, the end of the Cold War sparked new and unanticipated conflicts as states weakened or fell apart. Despite international mechanisms of intervention, sanctions, diplomacy, and peace keeping, the last decade of the millennium brought mass displacement and ethnocide in Rwanda, Bosnia, and Kosovo. There were "more refugees in the early 1990s than at the end of World War II; the DPs [Displaced Persons] were only the beginning of a flow, not the end as had been hoped" (Wyman 1998: 3). At the turn of the twenty-first century, the world's refugee population was 13,000,000.[2] Palestinians and Afghans topped the list as the world's largest groups of refugees.[3]

This book centers on one community of Palestinians, refugees in Lebanon since 1948, and recounts how they have crafted meaningful places and identities. In 1948, around 700,000 Palestinians were displaced by the emerging Israeli state. Palestinians refer to this event as *al-nakbah*, a calamity or disaster of monumental proportions that occupies a singularly traumatic place in Palestinian collective memory and the national narrative. These Palestinians remain displaced, often stateless, while those in the West Bank and the Gaza Strip have lived under Israeli occupation since the 1967 conquest.[4]

I write this preface from a different geographical and temporal zone of Palestine, the occupied West Bank and East Jerusalem where Palestinians are undergoing what they perceive as the final stage of Zionist colonization of the land and dispossession of the indigenous population. In the Palestinian national narrative, the displacement of 1948 ranks as the beginning of the conquest of Palestine. The occupied territories are fast losing their Palestinian character as land confiscation, settlements, the policy of closure, and more recently, a 24-foot cement wall, have functioned together to continue dispossessing the Palestinians of their lands and obstructing their eventual sovereignty. Administrative measures to

strangle economic life and humiliate Palestinians are intended to transform the demographic landscape by diluting the Arab population. In
this way, Israel acquires more territory with fewer people. It will not
repeat the mistake of 1948 and produce massive numbers of refugees.
Instead, Palestinians will be displaced "voluntarily"; they will appear as
migrants rather than refugees and thus will attract little international
attention. Migrants will not have the legal status of refugees.

The current predicament of the Palestinians reminds us that, in the new
millennium, societies continue to be decimated by the expansion of
colonial states. The Palestinian community in Lebanon is a historical
and social product of a particular colonial strategy and thwarted Palestinian national ambitions. Local resistance to colonial projects, once
dubbed "savagery," is now dubbed "terrorism." In current colonial
(rather than post-colonial) situations, how does one navigate such a difficult ethnographic terrain in terms of scholarly focus and methodolo-
gies? Part of the answer consists of an older anthropological outlook and
approach. Anthropology has a long tradition of "salvage anthropology,"
describing and documenting populations and cultures disappearing
with the advance of stronger, more technologically sophisticated, con-
quering societies. The inventory and salvage approach was developed by
ethnographers documenting the decline of the Native American way of
life after the wholesale loss of their lands and forced transfer to reserva-
tions. Ethnography in general has shifted over the course of the last century from capturing cultures in their supposedly "pristine" state to
observing, recording, and analyzing the process of destruction itself.
Contemporary anthropologists still take inventory, so to speak, but they
have also carved out a role that makes them a part of the process of
resisting such culturally destructive incursions by bringing these issues
to public attention and on occasion advocating for the groups they work
among. The quarterly *Cultural Survival* is one venue for such work. Thus
the ethnographic endeavor has become much more than an exercise in
understanding and analyzing cultural difference; it is also intended as
an act of intervention. The contemporary ethnographer in a crisis situation still observes and records, but without reifying cultural traditions,
and we locate these processes in more complex global and historical
terms. Our task is also to analyze not just how violence and suffering of
refugees are enacted, experienced, narrated, and coped with, but also
the historicity and the structural conditions, local, regional, and global,
that underpin their displacement.

Anthropological scholarship on refugees faces the particular challenge
of advocacy. Refugees are one of the most vulnerable groups an ethnographer can work with and because of this raise provocative questions

about positionality. Capturing the dilemma of the ethnographer in instances of violence and terror, Warren comments that there is "no neutral subject position from which to narrate" and "no uncomplicated sympathetic position for ethnographers" (2000: 230). Journalism, which has more distance, both physical and emotional, from the sources of its information, also confronts moral dilemmas of observation, writing, intervening, and advocacy. Photographer Donald McCullin has been widely quoted for his poignant statement during the height of the Lebanese civil war (1975–90): should I take a picture of a dying man or try to help him?

Ethnographic methods developed since the era of salvage anthropology eminently position us to produce scholarship on the everyday experience and meaning of suffering and refugeeness. Increasingly we are witnesses to human rights violations and listen to harrowing tales of suffering. We become intermediaries as the people we work among plead with us to "tell." We have the capacity to extend the voices of those in pain which can, in the right circumstances, be therapeutic and empowering, although certainly not always (Hayner 2001: 133–53). However, I would caution against adopting a narrow stance as witnesses.

Another task of the anthropologist is to humanize those otherwise marginalized and demonized, giving them a voice and bringing their life experiences to others. Working with populations at risk or in a state of emergency heightens the anthropological imperative to forge beyond the constitution of the refugee by a traumatic history to explore refugee agency. Conflict and war's toll on human lives are rarely rendered in all their tragic dimensions by those on the winning side. Until recently, anthropologists assumed a moral and cultural gap between those they wrote about and these who formed their audience (Geertz 1988: 132). A committed anthropology seeks to dissolve that barrier by humanizing suffering, bringing it home, so to speak, making those who read witnesses as well.

Those writing on Palestinians often face a unique dilemma—how to avoid nativism and a nationalist historical discourse and their sometimes stultifying outcomes without however denying the national project to those who are stateless? Nationalist approaches to Palestinian history and society may be sites for critique, but we still face a central problematic. The obstruction of Palestinian national aspirations and the lack of a state have had tremendous implications for the everyday well-being and human rights of millions of Palestinians who remain stateless or under foreign occupation. In some instances, national politics can be progressive, anticolonial movements with fluid and expansive boundaries of inclusion, as occurred during the era of the resistance movement (1968–82) in Lebanon. In freeing ourselves from the nationalist paradigm which has structured scholarship on Palestine, we face the task of developing alternative approaches that recognize the Palestinian need for security, equality, and citizenship in a state. This book attempts to narrate and understand Palestinians less through a nationalist lens than through one that tracks and understands social change through the concepts of place, identity, and human agency in the face of daunting obstacles. Popular memory studies have offered one way of breaking the grip of nationalist historiography, for they illuminate the disparities in historical accounts, casting complex shadows on official nationalist discourse (see Swedenburg 1995; Slyomovics 1998). My view is that studying the crafting of place and identity offers an alternative to the nationalist focus that has enormous promise.

Fieldwork among refugees and those under occupation carries certain risks for the ethnographer, from the actual physical dangers of witnessing and recording in an "ethnographic emergency" (Feldman 1995) to the professional perils of having one's work critically examined by the academic and policy community with unusual scrutiny. My fieldwork among Palestinians has ranged over three types of violence: low intensity conflict such as the first *intifada* (uprising), to civil war; the war, invasion, and siege of Lebanon by a well-equipped army of a modern state facing lightly armed, stateless refugees; and, more recently, the violence of spatial closure and severely restricted mobility in a situation of military occupation and settler colonialism. In each of these situations, civilian casualties were high and conflict raged on a daily basis. Palestinian spaces in Lebanon and the occupied West Bank and Gaza Strip are heavily marked by the trauma of prolonged and pervasive violence. When I worked in Lebanon during the 1970s and early 1980s, the years of the Lebanese civil war and the 1982 Israel invasion and siege of Beirut, the Palestinians were at the peak of their power. In my most recent research on the West Bank (2004), the potential for physical violence was always on display—at the ubiquitous checkpoints and from tear gas and gunfire to beatings by Israeli soldiers. It was low intensity in terms of actual physical violence and the deployment of military hardware compared to the wars in Lebanon, but to my mind it was high intensity in its impact. In these three settings, dangers in the field have come from local Lebanese militias or the occupying Israeli army rather than the Palestinians themselves, who see the anthropologist as someone who will record and circulate their stories to a broader audience and whose boundaries of belonging and acceptance are expansive.

Fieldwork for this book was less volatile than during the civil war. In the early 1990s, there were almost no foreigners in the camps conducting research or even working or visiting. The on-the-ground dangers derived from simple visibility, which could call attention to families one visited who might then be visited by the Syrian army or Lebanese police to inquire as to why they were hosting a foreigner. The actual infliction of physical violence had subsided considerably by the early 1990s and given way to various forms of structural violence. This was a terrorized population living in an extreme state of fear and anxiety. My fieldwork was not done under intensive shelling and sniper fire, or the fear of car bombs, or of an invading and besieging army. The dangers in the 1990s were those more common to a postconflict situation of defeat and containment; the camps, spaces of defeat, were surrounded by checkpoints operated by the Syrian Army, the Lebanese Army, and local Shiʿa militiamen. The residents of the camps were depressed and anxious from years of warfare and living on the extreme margins of society where they had serious concerns about mass transfer and faced harassment, both subtle and overtly violent, in nearly every aspect of their daily lives. A deep sadness comes from working in a community facing a bleak future.

What connects my fieldwork in Lebanon, and more recently in the West Bank, is both the violence visited on the Palestinian people and their remarkable ability not just to survive but to do so with tenacity and creativity. I have often wondered what it would be like to do fieldwork in a noncrisis situation. The world is in a state of emergency, and accordingly many anthropologists work in conflict zones. The early salvage anthropologists also worked in conditions of both structural and physical violence, or their immediate aftermath, but often did not recognize or center in their works those historical and political processes which had rendered these societies visible, vulnerable, and open to outsiders. The contemporary anthropologist's recognition of these conditions has intensified and is itself an integral and defining part of the field.

I have not faced hostility or even suspicion from Palestinian communities over the course of three decades. Perhaps prolonged crisis and historical traumas turn some societies inward, furthering exclusivist worldviews, while others open outward, forging acceptance and tolerance of those who come to work in their midst and fostering an imagined inclusive future. Palestinians have a keen sense of who is an enemy and who is a friend and thus don't easily buy into the "foreigner as enemy" syndrome. Their brutal experiences of betrayal and assault by Arab states make them less prone to such simplistic thinking. This is perhaps why spaces such as a refugee camps, designed to house and manage those excised from an exclusivist state and have suffered prolonged assaults, sieges, and massacres, can be cosmopolitan spaces of tolerance.

Palestinian society in general is in a near permanent state of emergency, as their geographical space shrinks under the weight of settlers, closures, and land confiscation in the occupied territories and confinement in Lebanon. The closure of the West Bank and Gaza Strip is paramount to another disaster, a defining moment akin to the tragedy of 1948. As settlements expand and the wall carves up the West Bank, the shrinking of Palestinian space continues unabated. Built overwhelmingly on Palestinian land, well inside the Green Line separating Israel from the West Bank, the wall is less about security and more about a massive land grab as thousands of Palestinian acres of farmland in its path are confiscated. The fact that a strong and viable leadership is absent means that there is not a coherent strategy for resisting closure. Spatial control and management of Palestinians now includes forms such as the wall and the policy of closure, which drastically restricts human mobility. These are new techniques, harder to track and observe than the spatially demarcated refugee camps; yet they are an accompaniment to the refugee camps that resulted from *al-nekbah*, the first mass dispossession of the Palestinians. Walled-in areas and checkpoints allow for the monitoring and surveillance of Palestinians on a large scale and indeed Palestinians refer to these enclosed spaces as "open-air prisons."

The book is organized around the themes of place and identity and their contextualization with a framework of structure and agency. Chapter 2 explores briefly the Zionist discourse on place. The construction of the Palestinian refugee began at this point in time. This chapter probes the discourse of claiming exclusive rights to place and its articulation with practices designed to effect a mass dislocation of Palestinians. Chapter 3 examines the construction of the refugee as an object and category of intervention by an international relief regime, a process mediated by the refugees' creativity in constructing their own world within the limits of structural constraints. Chapters 4, 5, and 6 detail the ways the camps were transformed spatially through symbolic and material interventions, and the kinds of identities refugees claimed over fifty years divided into three periods: 1950–68/69; 1968/69–82, the era of the resistance movement and the civil war; and the post-1982 period of the camp wars and the subsequent marginalization of the refugees and the camps. The social world of the refugee camp was a highly contingent field, one tightly articulated to both local and global arrangements of power. In these three chapters, the social world of the camps unfolds across time and space. Relations with neighboring Lebanese communities, the nature of the borders between them, and their forms of authority and control form the setting for the production of identities in a wildly vacillating balance of power and violence. These chapters explore Palestinian identity as it was constructed against and within the constraints of power. Identities and place are mutually constitutive within the larger framework of spatial, institutional, and discursive forms of power and as such are always in formation.

Chapter One
Introduction: Palestinian Refugees

The refugee condition, once experienced, does not wash off.
—Charles Sternberg

This book on Palestinian refugees in Lebanon tells the story of a continuing journey through multiple places that has been propelled by intense violence. It explores how the refugees created a sense of place, identity, and meaning in new spaces, using the tools of culture, memory, and militancy. The construction of the Palestinian refugee as a category of person and an object of intervention both constrained and enabled the refugees' practice of crafting new worlds. The book's title encapsulates the contradictory meaning of refugee camps—sites of poverty, marginality, and terror as well as remarkable creativity. Thus they were places of both hope for the future and despair. I ask, What is the relationship between place and identity? In a world on the move, how is a relationship in constant motion conceptualized and negotiated by the displaced? As places signaling defeat and exile, camps spawned a sense of despair for their residents, but they quickly became places—the only possible places—from which a future could be imagined and organized for. They contained what Parmenter calls "a landscape of despair" and "a landscape of anticipation" (1994: 64), both of which she evokes by citing Rashid Husayn's poem "Tent #50":

Tent #50, on my left, is my new world,
Shared with me by my memories; . . .
Tent #50, on my left, that is my present,
But it is too cramped to contain a future.

For fifty years, the lives of the Palestinians in this book have been indelibly connected to two geopolitical and social spaces: Lebanon and

Palestine/Israel. As refugees, in the space of the state but not of it, so to speak, they navigate within the complexity of local and regional political and cultural interests and boundaries. Their presence/nonpresence and actions have been productive of space in the form of political arenas and imaginative national projects. Thus Palestinian identity formation has unfolded in a spatiotemporal framework of betwixt and between, here and there, then and now, within a local and regional context. For these refugees, identity has been tightly referenced to places of departure and new locales, connecting them in intimate ways.

The construction of the Palestinian refugee is embedded in a logic of displacement integral to a particular form of ethnonational, neocolonial state formation and consolidation, followed by international and local administrative interventions. It also derives from the spatiality of the refugee camps and the refugees' creative capacity to craft new places, social worlds, and identities. Camps can be conceptualized as spatialized forms of power and governance, whether they are used to contain and rescript refugee identities or serve as sites for launching resistance.

The paradox that human societies and individuals are products of structural and disciplinary forces, yet exercise remarkable creativity in improvising and carving out meaningful lives which then effect a transformation in these forces remains a central problematic of contemporary anthropology. Palestinian refugees constructed meaningful places and lives animated by an imagined future and a guiding narrative of the past and present that bound community across the spatial divides of Palestine. This book duly addresses the tension and interplay between, on the one hand, the structural constraints imposed on refugees by displacement, refugee camps, international agencies, and host countries, and, on the other, refugees' individual and collective agency in crafting daily lives that transformed these structures and spaces. Refugees transformed these imposed and bureaucratized spaces for the displaced into meaningful places, ones that people were willing to die for. In an animated and sometimes violent interplay, Palestinian refugees have been constituted by history and have been active in shaping it. This process also occasioned radical changes in Palestinian social relations of gender, class, generation, and region. Within this dynamic interplay, identities and their public expressions articulated with explicit shifts in spatial boundaries, local power arrangements, and levels of external violence.

Background to Disaster

With the collapse of four hundred years of Ottoman rule at the end of World War I, Palestine came under a British Mandate. In the 1917 Balfour Declaration, the British promised a national home for the Jews in

Palestine, while referring to the indigenous population in the nega-tive—as the non-Jewish community, promising them civil and religious rather than national or political rights. In 1947, Britain turned over to the United Nations the increasingly vexing issue of a Zionist claim to Palestine. Not unsurprisingly, the 1947 UN plan to partition Palestine into Arab and Jewish states was met with opposition by the Palestinians and warmly welcomed by a majority of the Jewish community in Pales-tine. The 29 November 1947 vote in favor of partition, backed by the United States and the Soviet Union while Britain abstained, ignited the war for Palestine. With the subsequent defeat of the Palestinian and Arab forces and the expulsion or flight of between 714,150 and 780,000 Palestinians (W. Khalidi 1992: 582), a Jewish state was declared on 14 May 1948 that eventually encompassed the area allotted to the Jews in the Partition Plan as well as large portions allotted to the Palestinians. This signaled a renewed colonial impulse in the region, a politically and emotionally charged issue in light of decolonization and national inde-pendence in other areas.

Al-nakbah, the disaster or calamity of 1948 and the beginning of *al-ghurbah* (exile) resonant deeply in the Palestinian lexicon. *Al-nakbah* imposed a stunningly sharp chasm between past and present. A new world of violently crafted and maintained borders became a defining feature of daily life—borders that both locked Palestinians in and kept them out. Space was splintered as was time. This rupture has been a watershed event in the formation of Palestinian identity and relations to place and time.

Around 700,000 Palestinians sought refuge in neighboring countries; the rest (about 150,000) remained and became Israeli citizens (W. Khal-idi 1992: 581). In 1949, UN General Assembly Resolution 194, which has been invoked as the international legal framework for a solution to the Palestinian refugee problem, called for repatriation or compensation for Palestinian losses.[1] The core issue is not the conditions under which the displaced departed, a combination of expulsion and flight from con-flict, but the consistent denial of an internationally recognized right of return. The right of return and the demand for its recognition or imple-mentation have framed Palestinian exile politics for five decades.

Prepartition Identity and Place

The notion of Palestine as an entity whose boundaries were defined by the sacred (central to the three monotheistic religions), with Jerusalem at its heart, is the geohistorical basis for a specifically Palestinian identity related to a particular space (R. Khalidi 1997; Scholch 1993). The sacred space was isomorphic with subsequent Mandatory Palestine and the space Palestinians have defined as Palestine. The exterior and the threats it presents have long been prominent in shaping Palestinian identity; the Crusades (*al-hamalat al-salibiyyah*) are often deployed metaphorically to refer to the contemporary colonial-national project in Palestine.

Prepartition Palestinian identities were multiply referenced and imbricated, as was common in the religiously and ethnically complex Ottoman Empire, encompassing elements of kinship, religion, region, city, class, empire, and Arabism. Palestinian identity, in the "incipient sense of community-as-nation," can be traced to the late nineteenth century (R. Khalidi 1997). As the Ottoman Empire collapsed, coinciding with the spread of secularism, the space of Palestine itself became increasingly pivotal in local identities. During the British Mandate (1921–48), Khalidi argues, the foci of identity shifted. With an expanding secular educational system and press, an intensified Zionist project, and nationalist sentiment on the rise in other parts of the Arab region, a distinctly modern form of Palestinian national identity was emerging among large segments of the population, particularly the elite.

In situations of competing claims to space, to assert that all histories are constructed can be problematic, implying equity in claims and tacitly suggesting that the political status quo is acceptable. What needs to be pointed out in acknowledging the constructedness of historical claims is that some are deeply embedded in conscious, objectified national and historical projects premised upon an emphatic denial of others' history and claims, and the power to enact them, while some are not. One strategy to respond to assertions of a distinct Palestinian national identity and rights to place has been to frame it as a byproduct of Zionism. Palestinians, it was claimed, lacked a singular, reified, historically deep and rooted identity critical to the modern nationalist project.[2] Thus the legitimacy of an indigenous claim based on continuous habitation was trumped by Zionist formulations of a national identity and an elaboration of myths and historic religiously endowed narratives of a Jewish right to the space of Palestine.[3]

The presence of an other certainly influenced the intensity and militant dimensions of Palestinian nationalism. In formation for several decades before the gravity of Zionist intentions was realized, Palestinian national identity cannot be referenced primarily to Zionism.[4] Understanding the significance of Zionism should neither distort nor displace the historical depth and contemporary currency of a specifically Palestinian identity and its relation to a particular space. Palestinians claim rights to place by virtue of continuous inhabitation—by being, or having been, there and nowhere else—and a modernist national identity. Palestinian poet Mahmud Darwish eloquently captured the difference between Zionist and Palestinian relations to the land:

The true homeland is not that which is known or proved. The land that emerges as if from a chemical equation or an institute of theory is not a homeland. Your insistent need to demonstrate the history of stones and your ability to invent proofs does not give you prior membership over him who knows the time of the rain from the smell of the stone. That stone for you is an intellectual effort. For its owner it is a roof and walls. (quoted in Parmenter 1994: 1)

The difference is between indigeneity and a settler-colonial project of self-remaking through national construction. The geographer Tuan proposes "a difference between 'knowing' and 'knowing about,'" the former a consequence of "familiarity" through long residence, the latter "a result of conscious effort" in which a sense of time is "abridged rather than extended" (1980: 8). Without suggesting a primordial basis for Palestinian nationalism, Darwish acerbically juxtaposes indigeneity to the constructed link between Jews and the space of Palestine.

Paradoxically, exile generates "knowing about" in a way that resembles the Zionist project of "knowing about" Palestine. There are now Palestinian institutes and oral history projects devoted to producing knowledge about Palestine. The recuperation and collection of material culture and the publication of what are often called memorial books point to a national project to inventory and narrate, and thus claim place and an "authentic" past in it (see Slyomovics 1993, 1998). Dislocation launched the Palestinians on an objectifying pursuit of place; it became explicitly conscious and the subject of political, social, and cultural contestation. Thus they have a sense of rootedness and an objective sense of place simultaneously.

Palestinians always considered themselves part of the Arab world, bound by shared history, language, religion, and the contours of culture. In exile, Arabness became ambiguous and contradictory. With the crushing defeat of the Arab armies in the 1967 Arab-Israeli war, expectations that they would solve the Palestine problem were dashed. It was clear that Palestinians were on their own. The need for autonomy in political organizing was made clear in the course of Jordanian and Lebanese restrictions on Palestinian political activity and expressions.

Thus after 1948 a new set of places, borders, and power relations came into play to set the parameters within which identity formation would unfold. A collective consciousness of shared experiences of statelessness and the trauma of dislocation underwrote this. In spite of living in different states, a particularly inflected Palestinian transnational identity was evident.

Palestinian Refugees in Lebanon

Well over half (4,055,758) of the nearly eight million Palestinians are registered refugees. In the early 1950s, many of the nearly 100,000 refugees in Lebanon gradually moved into the fifteen camps set up by UNRWA; those with some capital or relatives settled in towns and cities. Established by United Nations General Assembly Resolution 302, the United Nations Relief and Works Agency (UNRWA) was established to provide relief and employment in large-scale regional labor projects for the refugees.[5] Lebanon leased land to the UN, or it was rented or purchased by them from landowners to build camps. Along with UNRWA, the Lebanese state formed the apparatus of governance. The number of registered refugees has grown to 390,498 (UNRWA 2003);[6] of these, 220,052 reside in twelve camps.

Few countries willingly host masses of noncitizens. Certainly this has been the case in Lebanon, where refugee-host tensions have been at times murderous. The initial financial burden can be onerous, and a mass refugee presence can generate momentous political and social realignments and upheavals, thus challenging state sovereignty. Multiple factors affect the receptivity to and hostility towards refugees: job competition between refugees and locals, the ability of a host country to provide social services to its own residents, and the ethnic, sectarian, and political composition of the refugee population.[7] Lebanon is a fragile multiconfessional state where political representation and the distribution of resources are apportioned by sect. The main sects are Maronite Christian, Sunni Muslim, Shiʻa Muslim, Greek Orthodox, and Druze. In spite of their dwindling numbers, Maronite Christians long held the reins of economic and political power. Fearful of the sectarian imbalance created by an overwhelmingly Sunni Muslim refugee population, and concerned with the implications of a large pool of low-wage labor, Lebanon has had an ambiguous and contradictory attitude toward the refugees, alternately sympathetic and supportive and hostile and violent. Over a fifty-year period, host-refugee interactions have shifted dramatically.

Although the refugees were initially impoverished, dispirited, and unable to muster a political leadership, this state of affairs changed radically in 1969, following a series of clashes between the emerging Palestinian resistance movement and the Lebanese army. Previously, the Lebanese government had repressed Palestinian political activity, fearing Israeli reprisals and a radicalization of its own Sunni Muslim population.

In November 1969, the Lebanese government accepted an open, armed Palestinian presence in an agreement known as the Cairo

Figure 1. Refugee camp in northern Lebanon, early 1950s. Photographer unknown. Archives of American Near East Refugee Aid (ANERA), Washington, D.C.

Accords, which redefined the regulations governing the refugees. The Palestinian resistance movement was a new political and ideological force that burst onto the regional scene in the wake of the disastrous defeat of the Arab states in the June 1967 war. The Cairo Accords granted Palestinians the right to employment, to form municipal-like committees in the camps, and to engage in armed struggle from bases in Lebanon. From 1968 to 1982, the resistance controlled the camps, assuming their daily management, providing security as well as an array of health and social services. Palestinian military control over and autonomy in substantial parts of Lebanon led to accusations of "a state within a state" and provoked resentment from some sectors of the Lebanese polity.

By the early 1970s, the camps were coming under increasing fire from

Figure 2. Shatila camp, early 1950s. Photographer unknown. ANERA Archives.

the Lebanese army, right-wing Christian militias (the Phalangists and the Chamounists), and Israeli incursions. This gave way to a fifteen-year period of civil war (1975–90), which initially pitted the Christian right against an array of progressive, and largely but not solely Muslim forces known as the Lebanese National Movement (LNM). The state disintegrated, and Lebanon was plunged into anarchy and chaos as competing militias battled for control and territory exchanged hands in a dizzying and murderous fashion. Lebanon's sectarian system, and its intersection with class interests and regional identity were the internal issues propelling conflict.

As political allies of the LNM and targets of right-wing militias, the Palestinians were drawn into the war. Israeli air and land attacks on the camps had proceeded apace since the early 1970s. Rightist attacks further exacerbated the situation and drew the resistance forces into a war to defend their existence and the quasi-autonomy granted them under the Cairo Accords. During the civil war, assaults on the camps resulted in a heavy death toll and substantial physical destruction. The civil war was punctuated by two Israeli invasions; in 1978, they occupied the border area of the south, withdrawing in 2000 after more than twenty years.

The second occurred in 1982, when Israel invaded Lebanon and besieged and eventually entered Beirut. In the ensuing massacre at Sabra-Shatila camps, hundreds of Palestinian and Lebanese civilians were murdered by Israeli-supported and armed right-wing Christian militias. Palestinian autonomy and institution-building came to an abrupt and dramatic end. As a result of negotiations to end the war, in August 1982 the PLO withdrew its forces and personnel from Lebanon, leaving the camps bereft of protection. The refugee community was targeted for reconfinement in the camps and economic and political containment. An image of the future in the past was echoed in the hopeless and bitter comments of a young man made in the immediate aftermath of 1982—"Well, it's back to the fifties. We'll live as we did then."

In the mid-1980s, the camps in Beirut and the south were the sites of a deadly series of battles with the Shi'a 'Amal militia,[8] known as the "war of the camps." Nearly three years of sieges and assaults wrought massive destruction and an untold number of dead.[9] Burj al-Barajneh and Shatila camps in the southern suburbs of Beirut sustained high casualties and severe structural damage. The Syrian-supported 'Amal war on the Palestinians was intended to bring about a dispersal of the refugees, the destruction of the camps, and such a diminishment of their numbers that they would never regain political power or autonomy in Lebanon, minimizing opposition to Syrian control over Lebanon, and removing any obstacle to their seeking peace with Israel. At a minimum, the goal was to return the Palestinians to their preresistance existence: unarmed, politically unorganized, and under the watchful eyes of Lebanese Intelligence. Once the war was over, the refugees were vulnerable to assault, harassment, and widespread discrimination.

These sustained Lebanese assaults on the Palestinian community were intended to reduce it to scale and confine refugees to their camps, to make place, social life, and identity isomorphic. While playing out in Lebanon, the plan had the active support and encouragement of Syria and Israel, as a diminished PLO suited their geopolitical interests. Locally, with the Palestinians isolated, the space of Lebanon would be rendered nationally pure and the haunting specter of *towteen* (settlement) managed. Thus the reincarceration of the refugees proceeded through a succession of military assaults from 1975 to the Israeli invasion of 1982 and the camp wars of the mid-1980s, each punctuated by massacres and sieges. The period from 1975 to 1990 can be divided into more precise categories; for example, the 1975–76 early civil war period, the 1982 invasion, which formally marked the end of Palestinian autonomy, and the post-invasion period until 1985, when the camp wars began. The postwar period in Lebanon can be dated to 1990 when the civil war

Figure 3. Boys posing in front of posters of martyrs, Burj al-Barajneh camp.
Julie Peteet.

came to what is now considered its official end. Overall, this period (1975–90) unleashed a series of events which resulted in reconfinement, disempowerment, and the infliction of particular forms of violence against Palestinians communally and individually. Space was remapped and rebounded and a national and sectarian sorting out occurred. In the end, the refugee camps served most importantly as sites of incarceration and new techniques of boundary maintenance and control. The public space open to Palestinians shrank violently as resistance facilities and offices closed, and their mobility was highly circumscribed due to fear of arrest, disappearance, or assault.

The civil war and its aftermath were battles over the identity of Lebanon and its political-sectarian system and landscape, both of which had been radically destabilized by the militant Palestinian presence. Early in the civil war, largely Christian East Beirut was violently cleansed of both Muslims and Palestinians. In 1976, the three camps in East Beirut (Dbiyyeh, Tel al-Zaʿter, and Jisr al-Basha) were besieged, overrun, and eventually destroyed by right-wing Christian militias. Plans were put forth to transform the now razed space of Tel al-Zaʿter, often regarded as an eyesore, into a shopping mall or luxury apartments. After being subjected to intensive military assault and sieges, Shatila's borders were recrafted to conform to those of the early 1950s.

Shatila Camp and the Postwar Period

Shatila camp was my primary research site although fieldwork was also conducted in Beirut's Burj al-Barajneh camp and ʿAyn al-Hilweh camp near Saida. Located on the southern outskirts of Beirut, Shatila was established in 1949 by the International Committee of the Red Cross, and houses 12,116 people (UNRWA 2003). When I returned to Lebanon in the winter of 1992 after a hiatus of nearly ten years, I had no plans to conduct research. That changed quickly. When I left in late 1982, years of war had ravaged the camps and internal autonomy had become a thing of the past. When I returned, I was stunned by the latest destruction and the thoroughly shattered lives of those who survived. Not only did this tragedy need to be documented, anthropological theory on place and identity needed to be confronted with the potential implications of their disaggregation.

In the early 1990s, masses of rubble and huge tangled piles of cement and steel cables marked the perimeter of Shatila. Checkpoints and armed guards were posted at entrance ways. Camp residents lived as virtual prisoners—allowed to come and go only at the mercy of the Syrian guards. I was led into the camp by an acquaintance. We agreed that I would not speak until we were well inside and if we were spoken to by

Figure 4. Street scene, Shatila camp. Reconstruction is evident in the building on the left. Julie Peteet.

soldiers, he would do the talking. I acted as though it was perfectly natural for me to be there. Indeed, I maintained that posture through several summers of fieldwork in the 1990s when I had to pass through Syrian checkpoints. My strategy was to act as if I knew exactly where I was going. On the few occasions when I was asked where I was going, I simply replied "to the clinic" or "to the kindergarten."

We made our way to Um Khalid's[10] house through a perimeter of rubble, at places passable only by crawling over the collapsed stone buildings. In the late 1970s and early 1980s, when I conducted fieldwork on women and the resistance movement, Um Khalid had been my host and friend in Shatila. We had not seen one another for nearly ten years, although we had managed to keep abreast of each other's news via mutual friends. I knew that her life had been disrupted in manifold ways. In Shatila, once busy and noisy alleys were now deafeningly silent. The bleating of goats and a scratchy and barely discernible rendition of Vivaldi's *Four Seasons*, blaring from a battered ice cream truck that had somehow made its way into the camp in spite of a ban on the entry of vehicles, were the only sounds. At first sight, the camp seemed ruralized. In the midst of a vibrant postwar urban center, this little pocket, with about 500 inhabitants, was physically isolated within its newly carved out boundaries. Donkeys pulled carts through what remained of the few narrow roads once used by cars and trucks. Chickens roamed the alleys and pecked aimlessly in the dirt. Bombed and burned out buildings in a state of perpetual suspension gave the impression that any forceful movement could bring the whole pile tumbling down.

Um Khalid and her family's happiness at seeing me was tempered by concern for how I had entered the camps and whether the Syrians knew I was inside. Generous hospitality was combined with instructions as to how to enter and exit the camp. She feared trouble if it was known that she had received a foreign visitor without permission from the military personnel at the Syrian-manned checkpoint. When I inquired about the situation inside the camps, she replied, "Thank goodness, we now sleep at night. We are still afraid, but we no longer fear people breaking in at night to kill us or take away the men and boys." At the checkpoints, men faced beatings, theft of personal belongings, arrest, or disappearance.

After years of war, basic amenities were sorely lacking. Without full-time electricity, people depended on generators funded by resident subscriptions and run by the Popular Committees, camp-based municipal committees of representatives from each political faction. Electricity was provided a few hours a day and supplemented by small individual generators that might power a television and light a room. Potable water was unavailable. When I first carried out fieldwork in the camp, it had a vibrant infrastructure of social services and facilities such as clinics, vocational training centers, workshops, childcare facilities, clubs, and resistance offices. Shatila in 1992 was a virtual wasteland. Yet by the end of the decade the population had expanded to nearly 12,000; some Lebanese families had moved in, seeking cheap housing. A small number of NGOs were operating to provide a modicum of services.

The end of both the Lebanese civil war and the war of the camps resulted in reconfinement and marginalization of the refugees economically, politically, and spatially. They were convinced the Lebanese government was implementing a plan to compel them to leave by making life miserable. "They are strangling us!" shouted Abu Khalid when I asked him about the situation in postwar Lebanon. "All these restrictions on jobs and rebuilding the camps—they think we will leave if our lives become unbearable." In the aftermath of war, the future of the refugees was hanging in the air.

Marginalization took multiple forms. It was spatial—confinement through the ever-present threat of violence in tightly bounded and surrounded camps; institutional—the exclusion from the public institutions of social life; and economic—extremely restrictive employment regulations. In the public eye, Palestinians were troublemakers and the prime cause of Lebanon's woes, and thus a presence to be managed, quarantined, and moved at will. Four factors left the camps facing extreme poverty and a dire social service situation: severe restrictions on employment, travel, and residency; a decline in remittances from workers in the oil-producing states as a result of the Gulf War; the destruction of the PLO's institutional infrastructure in the social welfare arena and its inability to honor its financial commitments to families of those who died in war; and UNRWA's diminished health and education services.

Early on, Lebanon implemented laws to restrict Palestinian employment. In 1962, legislation placed them on a par with foreigners so that employment required a work permit. While Palestinians circumvented this requirement for nearly two decades, its was vigorously implemented and new restrictions were decreed in the post-1982 period. For example, Decision no. 289/1, issued by the Ministry of Labor and Social Affairs on 18 December 1982, set out the categories of employment closed to foreigners, which ranged from banking to barbering. The ministry also issued a circular detailing the categories of employment open to foreigners with work permits as

construction workers and workers in ancillary tasks, excluding electrical installations, sanitation facilities and glass mounting; agricultural workmen; tanning and leather workers; excavation workers; textile and carpet workmen; smelters; sanitation workers; nannies, nurses; servants and cooks; car wash and lubrication workers. (Natour 1993: 41)

In other words, Palestinians were forbidden to work in all but the most menial positions.

In the pre-1982 era, the boundaries of the camps, particularly urban Shatila and Burj al-Barajneh, blended easily with surrounding Lebanese slum areas. Living in close proximity, everyday social interactions between Lebanese and Palestinians were common. With the 'Amal-Palestinian war and the reimposition of Lebanese governmental author-ity over the camps in the 1990s, their borders, violently reforged and visibly distinct, were marked by Syrian and Lebanese checkpoints at entry sites. Unlike the situation in the pre-1982 period, camp residents infrequently ventured outside for extended periods of time and few had Lebanese friends or acquaintances.

Surveillance by Lebanese and Syrian military forces was intimidating; checkpoints controlled and monitored movement and rumors of informers spread fear and mistrust. Outside the camps, refugees antici-pated harassment, insult, and physical violence. They were denied the right to organize politically and culturally; the Lebanese authorities wanted to contain challenges to the recently established and still fragile sovereignty of the state. Travel restrictions posed a further obstacle to normalcy. Those traveling abroad on Palestinian travel documents were not always guaranteed reentry.[11]

Plans for the postwar reconstruction of Beirut did not bode well for the refugees. With the two remaining Beirut camps (Shatila and Burj al-Barajneh) strategically located near the airport road and in areas likely to be targeted for economic development, rumors flew that they would be razed to make way for a new airport access road, shopping malls, and the expansion of Sports City (a large stadium adjacent to Shatila camp). These plans kept refugees in a perpetual state of uncertainty. Rebuild-ing in the camps was strictly controlled and legally regulated. In the early 1990s some new housing units were constructed on the perimeter of Shatila to house "displaced refugees" from Tel al-Zaʿter, destroyed early in the civil war (1976), and Nabatiyyeh camp, destroyed by the Israelis in 1973, who were living in squatter settlements in and around Beirut.

The PLO withdrawal and Syrian/Lebanese policies and tactics to severely circumscribe Palestinian political activity resulted in a marked void in the local leadership. Once run by the PLO and UNRWA, in the postwar period the camps were run by an ambiguous, amorphous, and highly localized leadership. Compounding the withdrawal of the leader-ship in 1982 was the Syrian policy of creating dissension and division in the ranks of Palestinians by openly supporting non-Arafat, non-Fateh factions[12] and recruiting informers, through a combination of coercion and financial enticement. A coalition of ten resistance groups (non-

Fateh components of the PLO) opposed to Arafat and the Oslo peace process and ostensibly aligned with Syria, were the public face of the resistance although they did not garner widespread trust or support among Palestinians. The Arafatists still had an open presence in Rashidiyyah camp in South Lebanon. The PLO representative in Beirut had limited capacities to intervene with the Lebanese or Syrian authorities. Small-scale local leaderships emerged in each camp in response to local needs and power arrangements. Some were part of the ten remaining political organizations, and others were simply Fateh cadres who still had influence and were appealed to by people in need.

If a tangible and semi-institutionalized leadership had to be identified and localized, one could point to a set of offices in Mar Elias camp where some of the leaders of the ten maintained offices. This camp also housed the offices of the Local Council (*al majlis al markazi*), a loose coalition of representatives of the ten. Often, this is where people with problems concerning residency permits or extreme financial crises went to appeal for assistance. Official Lebanese governmental contact with Palestinians proceeded through these offices and their personnel. Although with vastly reduced resources and power, the Popular Committees, an innovation of the years of autonomy under the resistance movement, continued in the role of a municipality with responsibility for services such as garbage collection, sewage, the provision of electricity and running water, and solving minor conflicts. They also served as liaison between the Lebanese authorities and the camp population, particularly for small-scale matters that did not run the risk of escalating into major crises. Visiting foreign delegations were guided through the camps by the Popular Committees, often in conjunction with UNRWA officials or NGO workers.

Communications between camps were strained for much of the 1980s, as each was subjected to siege-like conditions by various Lebanese militias. Although this had eased by the mid-1990s, social isolation of Palestinians from Lebanese remained pronounced. Ironically, CNN, MTV, and a host of foreign broadcasts were picked up on camp TVs. Although physically and socially isolated in a delimited territory and lacking the accouterments of modern urban life such as reliable electricity and running water, telephones or any other communications apparatus, the global media were a daily presence. Variable positioning—Massey's (1993: 61) "power-geometry"—in a globalizing world was woefully evident. Some easily traversed borders; others were locked in against their express will. "Globalization" seemed pervaded by lines of exclusion. Scores of men had not moved beyond the camps' imposed borders in several years. With high levels of unemployment, the refugees were not participants in the new consumerism spreading over postwar Lebanon.

In effect, they were visibly cut off from developments around them, their confinement a consequence of local, regional, and global events.

The refugees played a distinct role in the postwar process of mending the Lebanese polity and identity fragmented by the violence of regional, sectarian, class, and political loyalties and affiliations. During the civil war, the largely Muslim progressive movement's alliance with the Palestinians was a major factor signaling Lebanon's political fragmentation. Concomitantly, in the postwar period, a Palestinian presence promoted Lebanese national cohesion. With few exceptions, Lebanese of various political and sectarian factions agreed on the need to strictly monitor the Palestinians and on their unwillingness to resettle them. The refugee camps occupied a highly ambiguous place in the Lebanese political order and national imagination. Lebanon was intent on containing and controlling Palestinians in tightly bounded camps until their fate could be determined.

Fieldwork and Methods

Fieldwork for this project took place in a locale where I had previously worked (1979–82), so I had the benefit of prior knowledge and connections (see Peteet 1991) as well as the distinct advantage of working in these camps in a radically different historical period. Once they were heavily armed autonomous zones, sites of embryonic statebuilding. A host of institutions developed and run by refugees and the PLO endowed the camps with a hopeful spirit and buttressed women's demands for equal rights of political participation. The contrast between then and now was so overwhelming that I felt compelled to undertake an ethnography of place to recount this dramatic transformation.

In 1992, Beirut was just emerging from fifteen years of civil war, and the once populous foreign community was nearly nonexistent. Beirut had been off limits to Americans for almost a decade because of kidnappings. I took one of the first planes into the newly reopened airport. We were no more than ten passengers on a jumbo jet. On the streets, in taxis, and in shops, foreigners were something of a novelty. Although graciously welcomed, I was very aware of being in a city just emerging from a reign of anarchy in which foreigners had been targets of kidnappings. To complicate matters further, Palestinians were objects of derision and scorn, if not outright hatred. To reach the camps, I would ask the *service* (shared taxi) driver to drop me a few blocks away. To reach Shatila, I walked through its surrounding and densely populated Shi'a area. Taxis and private cars tried to squeeze their way through the crowded unpaved streets teeming with pushcarts, jostling shoppers, and a colorful array of produce stands. Shi'a symbols were prominently displayed—larger than life pictures of Imam Khomeini and Imam Musa Sadr, prominent Shi'a political and religious leaders, were plastered on the walls. Posters for Shi'a political parties vied for visibility with those of their martyrs. Green flags bearing white Qur'anic verses waved triumphantly in the air.

Why an ethnography of place? Place is critical to those excised from particular places; it is central to their subjectivity and sense of location in the world. In the stark and jumbled ruins of a highly contested little piece of land where Palestinians were willing to fight to the death, an ethnography of place and its relation to identity and subjectivity seemed a way to approach the problematic of structure and agency and thus avoid a simple recounting of the process of victimization.

An ethnography of place runs into the methodological problem that place and the way people experience it can be difficult to elicit. In this project, I pursued what Gusterson calls a "polymorphous engagement" with my topic (1997), which cut across sites and communities and deployed methods beyond participant-observation. I examined archives, plumbed the Internet, mapped terrain, and perused newspapers as well as using the standard anthropological tools of interviewing and participant-observation. I began by doing lengthy semistructured interviews with Um Khalid and her family, focused on their experience of the camp wars and their perceptions of how things had changed since the era of the resistance. Using the snowball method prevalent in ethnographic research, I interviewed her friends and extended family in both Shatila and 'Ayn al-Hilweh. Interviews were conducted with men and women, young and old. The older generation were able to draw vivid comparisons among widely differing eras. Quite a few had been multiply displaced. Sadly, the generation that remembers leaving Palestine and settling in the camps was dwindling. For the youth, with lives scarred by violence and discrimination, the present and future were marked by despair, with only an occasional glimmer of hope. In addition, I conducted interviews with NGO workers, former political activists, and UNRWA employees and teachers, among others. Much time was spent just being there to pick up on the subtleties of place and its meaning in every life and conversation. I noted how people referred to place—how they gave directions in the camps and what they called particular places, which revealed a mix of old and new spatial markers, a palimpsest of violently crafted historical layers. Research on identity was marked by similar challenges. Identity emerged in references to self, to generation, in descriptions of past and present, and in motivations to action. The anthropologist's craft is to elicit and observe, to lie in wait, so to speak, for that revelation, for that casual yet illuminating remark or action, that with deeper probing and observation, indicates a pattern of behavior that might otherwise have been ignored.

Research in a conflict zone poses certain constraints on the ethnographer. Mapping and photography took on a dangerous air, for me and my hosts. Each involves a certain level of visibility that can draw the attention of security forces and informers. With Um Khalid accompanying me, I tried to map the perimeter of Shatila to gauge the changes since 1982. She was casually walking ahead of me and at one point, fairly close to a checkpoint, she became nervous and signaled me to stop. Something set off an alarm bell for her; she wouldn't tell me what. Perhaps she had seen someone she suspected of being an informer. Eliciting mapping from camp residents entailed its own set of problems. Younger people took to it easily; for the elderly, who are often illiterate, transferring embodied spatial knowledge to paper was nearly impossible.

This ethnography of place and identity is set in the context of unabated violence. Kleinman and Kleinman (1997) argue that suffering is "routinely appropriated" and that the globalization of suffering, manifest in its commodification, is deeply troubling. Its appropriation can be a positive, mobilizing force, but I would note, doing so involves hierarchies. Some cultural representations of suffering have been endowed with recognition while others have not. Is such selectivity in itself a form of violence?

Delinkages

A series of delinkages—temporal, spatial, legal, administrative, and policy—have been pivotal in constructing Palestinian refugees as objects of intervention and analysis and have guided political negotiations among Israel, the Palestinians, and the U.S. In some respects, Palestinians have been an exception in the international refugee aid machinery and scholarship. Administered to by UNRWA, international refugee laws, such as the 1951 International Convention on the Status Relating to Refugees and the 1967 Protocol do not apply to them, thus depriving them of international mechanisms of protection. Effectively delinked from international refugee discourse and law, one can ask whether this resulted in excluding Palestinians from scholarly discourses and debates on refugee situations and their solutions. Given their demographic weight and the length of time they have been refugees, their absence in the academic literature on refugees is remarkable.[13]

The media, policy forums, and international diplomacy and dialogue often contain and isolate the contemporary from past places, histories, and events. The past is the basis on which Palestinians demand a just solution. In the 1990s, Israeli and U.S. political negotiators earmarked 1967, the beginning of the Israeli occupation of the West Bank and Gaza Strip, as a point in time and a reference to space from which negotiations should start. This spatiotemporal line in the sand, so to speak, occluded time before 1967. In the wake of Israel's crushing of the Palestinian Authority in 2000, the continual swelling of settlements, the construction of an intricate network of bypass roads and a wall, the point of departure has moved forward, to the present rather than the past, stranding Palestinians in a temporal zone, the present, that is perpetually its own beginning and spaces that are continually shrinking.

Where ruptures have been violently imposed, refugees discern continuity rather than irrevocable chasm. Palestinians vividly link past, present, and future in memory and the political imagination. These refugees narrate their daily existence and plight within a broad sweep of history, with 1948 as the watershed date. For instance, refugees in Lebanon contextualize local events in a protracted and interwoven series of plans and events in a concerted project to make them disappear whether from Palestine or Lebanon.[14] The Palestinian national narrative also insisted on a spatiotemporal linkage and a constancy of place. Written during the first *intifada* (the Palestinian uprising of 1987–93), the graffito "1948 + 1967 = All Palestine"

signaled a historical consciousness of critical moments in time and place and an attempt to recover a historical and geopolitical and social continuity denied or marginalized. Such a graffito also laid out the association among place, time, and identity. These two defining moments—1948 and 1967—are metonyms for the loss and subsequent transformation of Palestine and the fragmentation of its people. These dates are spatiotemporal reference points that in the present bind Palestinians, wherever they are, in the struggle to unite what was fragmented. (Peteet 1996a: 149–50)

"These wars . . . it's like 1948 continued," was how Hanan, a young woman who lived in the Tarshiha quarter in Burj al-Barajneh camp, summed up the camp wars, asserting a continuity of action through time and across space. She had dropped by to see friends I was visiting in the camp. Eager to participate in the conversation, she continued: "The civil war, the 1982 invasion and siege of Beirut, are now making life so miserable that we leave Lebanon—these are all part of an attempt to remove Palestinians from the areas surrounding Israel and to crush our national movement." An account at once individual and collective, it echoed the hallmarks of a standard historical narrative common among these refugees.

Temporal markers such as 1948 and 1967 are apocalyptic, indicating the violently imposed beginning of exile or occupation. Refugees from

1948 will often identify themselves to other Palestinians as "We are from 1948" to assert relative location. 1967 refers to the occupation of the West Bank and Gaza Strip and the defeat of the Arab armies. These "signposts on time's road" (Aveni 1989: 121) are deeply embedded in political events, or, as Allen Feldman points out, events are more than "what happens. The event is that which can be narrated" (1991: 14). This underscores why the right to narrate and be heard resonates so provocatively to Palestinians. Feldman's remarks are more meaningful if amended to take account of situations where the event is endowed with reality according to *who* narrates it and his or her ability to maintain control over that narration. Obviously a Palestinian narrative connecting various times and places by extension creates continuity between past and present. That is why Hanan could easily make the comment about the present as a "continuation of 1948." Contemporary circumstances are "a continuation of 1948" in new guises. Israeli Prime Minister Ariel Sharon certainly confirmed Palestinian understandings of their predicament when he declared the "present war against the Palestinians as 'the second half' of 1948," in reference to the Israeli assault on the West Bank and Gaza that opened the new century (Reinhart 2002: 10).

The relentless focus on the immediate present effectively denies Palestinians the right to a past that has an effect on the future. In toying with renouncing the right of return in negotiations (a right guaranteed by international law, not something that can be bartered away), the Palestinian leadership signaled its willingness to engage in historical amnesia and accept monumental concessions. Readiness to cede the right of return implied that collective memory of the past and the exile community could be silenced. Giving up the right of return means disassembling a past and reinventing themselves anew. It assumes the possibility of making memories irrelevant, yet it privileges the claims of memory by some and makes their enactment a matter of political power. Palestinian narratives which locate displacement in a neocolonial impulse to exclude have been systematically marginalized, and Israeli negotiating platforms offer little, if any, recognition of underlying historical context or issues of justice. This has tended to shift the burden of blame and solutions to host countries and the refugees themselves rather than the originating country as a primary partner in seeking equitable and just solutions.

Western media representations of Palestinian refugees cast them less as having suffered an injustice of historic magnitude and more as deserving of their status as a consequence of their audacity in opposing colonization. Israeli policy has consistently held that Palestinians and the Arab states bear responsibility for their displacement and refugee status. Of the three standard solutions to refugee situations, integration, resettlement in a third country, or repatriation, the latter is the solution now promoted by the international community in most cases. Then UN High Commissioner for Refugees, Sadako Ogata, declared the 1990s the "decade of repatriation" (Ruiz 1993: 20). The emerging consensus that repatriation was the best solution (whether realistic and safe or not) coincided with the growing unwillingness of host countries to integrate refugees. In part, it relieves the international community of the burden of resettlement, because it implies that countries of origin are responsible for the refugees they generated. Increasingly, refugees are considered a destabilizing presence, threatening to state sovereignty and security. Moreover, the majority of refugees are neither white nor Europeans fleeing Communist regimes; they are more destitute, less educated and skilled, nonwhite people fleeing poor and conflict-torn third world countries.

More than fifty years after their displacement, Lebanon appears more resistant than ever to the permanent settlement of the refugees. Palestinians recognize that to accept resettlement would imply ceding rights to their homeland. Current international repatriation policies and initiatives appear selective; fifty years of delinkage from international organizations, policy, and scholarship may offer an explanation. Why doesn't the policy of repatriation apply to the Palestinians? Does an ethos of uniqueness and a status as unworthy victims, along with intense and sustained opposition by Israel and the U.S., serve to exclude them from serious policy consideration?

Theorizing Displacement

Scholarship on refugees is part of a larger body of work on forced migration, displacement, and diaspora studies. It is no coincidence that the 1990s ushered in scholarship on the new scope of human mobility and globalization at the same time. "The satanic geographies of globalization" (N. Smith 1997: 174) are marked by financial deregulations and the diminution of state control over capital, new trade agreements, innovations in technology and their rapid diffusion, new forms and scope of transnational governance (for example, the World Bank and the IMF), an acceleration of human mobility, and the rapid reframing of cultural artifacts rather than cultural homogenization (see Harvey 2000: 60–67). What is new with globalization is not the movement of capital, technologies, goods, ideas, and people across borders but the dizzying speed with which this takes place, as well as the spatial and cultural scope and meaning of this speed. The recent scholarly turn to space and spatiality (see Bird et al. 1993; Feld and Basso 1996; Giddens 1979; Harvey 1989; Keith and Pile 1993; Lefebvre 1991; Massey 1992, 1993, 1994; Soja

1989; and Yaeger 1996, among others) is occurring at a historic moment when space is shrinking by the relentless march of late capitalist globalization. In spite of a diminution of space by time, the significance of place and locality for the formation of identity is hardly irrelevant. This means conceptualizing the local as a site of intersection, constantly in motion, between the local and the global. Indeed, this project contains an implicit critique of the global as the locus of cultural and political production. It suggests that global forces and structures are filtered through local prisms. In other words, human agency intersects with global forces to shape the local. Unproblematic usage of the terms globalization and transnationalism has implications for the conceptualization and meaning of place, the role of human agency in the constitution of place and identities, and the way rights to place are understood. A key issue is the nature of particular mobilities. Few people control their location in a globalizing world, nor is there equal access to the forms of capital and technologies that propel and give definition to the process of globalization.

The refugee illuminates the limitations and possibilities contained in the call for the state to be conceptualized as diminishing under the onslaught of globalization, a notion of some currency in the early 1990s. Twentieth-century social sciences flourished in an era when the nation-state was assumed to be the physical embodiment of social life and to constitute the boundaries of the political process. Assumptions that the state is somehow diminished in the production of everyday social life are certainly tenuous. Brenner favors an approach that posits the national and the global as "relational and co-constitutive" (1997: 13; see also Sassen 1991). In the modern world, space remains pointedly partitioned into nation-states which regulate the flow of people and goods, generate nationalist sentiments, and apportion the accouterments of national belonging and affiliation. States remain heavily implicated in the production of mass displacement and are productive of categories of belonging for citizens and refugees alike. As the group excised from the state, refugees highlight its categories of belonging and their territorial range. This applies to both sending and receiving countries. Palestinian refugees stand as a haunting diagnostic of the exclusionary nature of the Israeli state as well as clarifying Lebanese parameters of national belonging.

Refugees, immigrants, guest workers, and many professionals, intellectuals, students, and financiers traverse state borders and as such are solidly situated within a nation-state frame. With their various requirements for entry, residency, labor, and citizenship, states remain a significant and determining point of departure, enabling, obstructing, and controlling movement. Policies and mechanisms of border control remain entrenched in state legal systems and means of enforcement.

In the last decade of the millennium, displacement and mobility emerged as major concerns in anthropology, constituting an influential zone of theory (Anzaldúa 1987; Appadurai 1993, 1996; Bammer 1994; Clifford 1992, 1994; Daniel and Knudsen 1996; Gilroy 1993; Hall 1994; Joseph 1999; Malkki 1992, 1995a, b, 1996; Rouse 1991; Shami 1996, 2000; van der Veer 1995) and ethnography (Burns 1993; Donnelly 1994; Feld and Basso 1996; Long 1993; Malkki 1995a; Menjivar 2000; Mortland 1998; Paerregaard 1997; Small 1997; Smith-Hefner 1999, among others).[15] A number of theoretical currents and intersections underlie this interest in refugees: questions on the nature of the nation-state, belonging, and new conceptions of citizenship (Appadurai 1993; Joseph 1999), explorations in deterritorializing culture and identity (Gupta and Fergusen 1992), a reconfigured relationship of identity to place in an increasingly mobile world, and a critique of the concept of culture (L. Abu-Lughod 1991; Hannerz 1993; Rosaldo 1989). In other words, scholarship on the displaced is embedded in a set of concerns focused on the interplay of structure/agency, nation-states, mobility, placemaking, culture and identity formation, and a concern with ethnographic methods.

Contemporary celebrations of mobility can be tempered by a concern with different types of travel and the violence implicated in them. Some movements are forced; others are a product of socioeconomic position and the privilege of a passport. These are vastly different sorts of movement. In short, a critical, disaggregated politics of mobility is called for. If refugees are just another sort of traveler, they can begin to disappear as a focus of analysis in a process Shami refered to as "erasure through inclusion" (1996: 8). Refugees, for example, can be distinguished conceptually and analytically from migrants. The former are usually propelled by large scale, organized violence perpetrated by the state or paramilitary forces; migrant flows are often attributed to the structural violence of poverty and discrimination, or the seeking of new opportunities for enhancing income, education, and standard of living. Both migrants and refugees elucidate a global-local intersection that heavily implicates nation-states. Migrants, seeking employment, stability, and a better future, suggest weak economies and states unable to ensure basic necessities and opportunities. By definition, refugees have been excluded from the state and can no longer avail themselves of its protection. Refugee status is conferred by the UNHCR and has international legal standing. Unlike migrants, refugees are an object of intervention and discursivity by international aid institutions that administer to them as an aggregate with basic human needs. They are simultaneously inside and outside the national. Migrants usually retain their citizenship until, and unless, they apply for naturalization in another country, and are not recipients of international aid.

Refugee and migrant studies, however, do share certain theoretical and methodological terrain. Both raise issues of displacement, cultural bricolage, and identities shaped by multiple geosocial sites. When communications technologies were rudimentary and assimilationist ideology was at its height,[16] migration theory assumed that migrants "move between distinct, spatially demarcated communities" and were "capable of maintaining an involvement in only one of them" (Rouse 1991: 12). Rouse's notion of "transnational migratory circuits" (1991; see also Small 1997) carried migration studies in a new direction. Migration theory was reformulated to account for simultaneous engagement and disengagement with multiple places. Migrants, and refugees, I would add, construct and participate in the local while remaining connected to and participating in other distant locales via communicative technologies, economic networks of exchange, and travel.

However, theoretical advancements in migration theory should not be transferred uncritically to the study of refugees. The circuits Rouse's Mexican immigrants were enmeshed in appear unevenly among refugees. Homes can be sites of conflict from which refugees are cut off for the foreseeable future or may be occupied by others. For example, the Israeli-Lebanese border could not be crossed for decades, and there were few linkages or avenues of communication between those remaining in Palestine and the refugees in Lebanon. Nor were Palestinian refugees linked by a flow of remittances to family left behind. Yet the simultaneity of place was clearly evident in collective and individual memory, in the reconstruction, however partial, of place and social relations in exile, identities referenced to place in Palestine, and the insistence upon return. Palestinian refugees are unlike most migrants in that their relations to the geographical space of the homeland have been violently short-circuited.

Both migrants and refugees constitute quintessential border communities, simultaneously constituted in and by the intersection of local, regional, national and global zones and processes. Borderlands are defined not simply by regional or geopolitical designations, but equally by the social practices and cultural forms of everyday life and identities that unfold in and (re)produce them. Thus refugees and migrants who construct places, homes, and identities in an elsewhere may, on certain points, be meshed epistemologically and located in the analytical category of the displaced. Identities for both are profoundly shaped by and referenced to places of origin and residence, multiple boundaries, and routes of travel between them.

The displaced challenged anthropology's once uncritical assumption of a mutually reinforcing relationship among culture, territory, and identity. Refugees and migrants put into relief both the fragility and the strength of ties between people and territory, and also how these complex links can encompass and travel through multiple time-space zones. In other words, identity is spatialized and place remains critical, but in ways that can incorporate high levels of mobility, attachments to points of departure, and multiple meanings of place. Anthropology's critical rethinking of the concept of culture in the mid-1980s and 1990s emerged concurrently with new levels of mobility, the end of the Cold War, murderous ethnic conflict, and the late capitalist globalization of finance, markets, and consumption. If culture was becoming unhinged from place and territory, nowhere should this be more apparent than among the displaced. Yet, if one moves beyond the romanticization of modern nomadism, a deep and abiding attachment to place and an insistence on identities that are place-based remain evident. Identities may be in motion but remain anchored to particular places that themselves may be in motion and invested with profound meaning. However much we live in a world on the move, "it is still the case that no one lives in the world in general" (Geertz 1996: 262).

The displaced also raise methodological issues. The anthropological construction of the native as placed posed provocative questions about the incarceration of peoples and cultures in discrete places (Appadurai 1992: 35). Ethnographic research in small-scale, geographically de-marcated sites, which went hand-in-hand with a conflation of cultural difference with spatial distance and confinement, has given way to a perspective where communities, identities, and culture are increasingly deterritorializing, mobile, and reterritorializing.

Palestinians in Lebanon can conceive of alternative forms of citizen-ship and thus modernities that extend well beyond a nationalism tightly bound up with particular territories. Their identities are not affixed to *singular* places but are embedded in trajectories of exile which have a point of origin in Palestine. Their notion of citizenship is postnational in the sense that national boundaries need no longer contain the citizenry. They can conceptualize a Palestinian state, with citizenship but with residency elsewhere, thus linking a state with its transnational communities. With rumors circulating that a number of Palestinian refugees in Lebanon would be naturalized in the mid-1990s, I asked Samia, a middle-aged friend of Um Khalid's, if she would take Lebanese citizen-ship were it offered. She paused for a few seconds to ponder and then said in a very precise way, her words carefully chosen: "If it were offered, I would take it, but only if I didn't have to give up being a Palestinian and the future possibility of Palestinian citizenship." She was making a clear distinction between nationality and citizenship. For others, the relationship between territory, nationality, and citizenship is more convergent. Refugees from the Galilee do not feel drawn to the West Bank and the Gaza Strip as they do to their places of origin, although they certainly do conceive of these areas as Palestine and the possible sites of a Palestinian state. They say: "It's not our land ('*ardna*). We want our land," referring to homes and places of origin (Peteet 1996b: 30). They can also conceptualize the transformation of Israel from a state of Jewish citizens to a state of its citizens, regardless of ethnicity and religion.

Place and Identity

Space, place, and landscape haunt the Palestinian imagination. Their identities are inseparable from their places of origin, desired places, and the contemporary landscape in which they reside. Place is of paramount significance, a product of a history of contestation in which they are on the losing end.

Until the recent turn to space and place (Carter, Donald, and Squires 1993; Feld and Basso 1996; Harvey 1989; Low and Lawrence 1990; Massey 1992, 1993; and Rodman 1992, among others), place was often unmarked, an analytically unexplored backdrop to culture. Ethnographies of place and identity are few (some noteworthy exceptions include Berdhal 1999; Ghannam 2002; Hirsch and O'Hanlon 1995; Myers 1991; Paerregaard 1997; Stewart 1996).

Anthropological interest in place and in identity converged in the 1990s. Cultural studies focused on the construction, elaboration, and transformation of identity, particularly at the interstices of gender, class, race, ethnicity, and nation among populations on the move, decentering received notions of the relationship between place and identity (see for example Keith and Pile 1993; Yaeger 1996). With displacement reaching record levels, diaspora, refugee, and border studies took off. Displacement became a route through which anthropology could begin to problematize place and subject it to analysis.

Place is socially constructed by a dynamic confluence of external forces, structural constraints, and human agency. Places are "not inert containers" but are "politicized, culturally relative, historically specific, local and multiple constructions" (Rodman 1992: 641). Western commonsense and scholarship have often assumed the primary of space over place (Casey 1996). I avoid a space/place binary in which place is the realm of dwelling, emotion, and attachment and space is abstract, appealing to the human desire for freedom and mobility (Tuan 1977). If place is crafted through the imposition of human meaning and daily practices, space is, and perhaps can only be, defined and take shape through being exterior to place. Thus from an anthropological perspective, with its focus on meaning, practice, and agency, place and space are mutually interactive and constitutive.

Located on the margins of bounded national spaces and local places, refugee camps make transparent the conceptual limitations and possibilities of both. This book looks at the way space and place are in constant motion, slipping and sliding into and out of one another, magnified in the context of prolonged, violent conflict where the control of territory shifts dizzyingly and violently between contending forces. Place is conceptualized as constructed by state policies of exclusion and cultural practices and discourse coalescing in a framework of power that is simultaneously resisted and accommodated. In Palestinian camps in Lebanon, place was a crucial and constitutive component in formations and expressions of identity, while identity acted to shape place. In other words, Palestinian refugees produced place and place shaped their identities, a process of mutual construction constrained and enabled by power.

Reformulating the relationship between place, identity, and culture raises political and ethical questions. It is ethically and intellectually problematic to push for a politically unreflective disaggregation of place and identity. On the one hand, disaggregation can obscure predatory projects and justify dispossession. Israeli rhetoric long claimed that Palestinians had only tenuous attachments to the land, thus legitimizing the denial of their rights to it. Elsewhere I have argued that "a focus that highlights the progressive politics" of such linkages may be a way to avoid the potential political pitfalls associated with connecting culture and identity to a particular place (1995a: 173). It may also be a way to avoid the equally dangerous problem of romanticizing exile and the nomadic subject. The 1948 war, its precipitating events, and its disastrous consequences figure centrally in contemporary Palestinian identity, and place continues to occupy a central position in formulations of that identity. Uncritical disaggregation, as has been imposed on the Palestinians, occludes intimate and long-term relations and rights to place and can unwittingly play into powerful political agendas by obscuring why some insist on such an isomorphism, particularly in progressive anticolonial movements. For nearly a century, Zionist ideology and rhetoric have cast doubts on a Palestinian presence in and right to place. The contemporary celebration of the "nomadic subject" (see Appadurai 1993; Clifford 1994 ; Gupta and Ferguson 1992; Malkki 1992) indeed may, in certain circumstances, lend itself to the needs of global capital as well as neocolonial projects. Still, all experience must be placed in one way or another. In spite of a world on the move, places remain paramount, orienting the self toward the world and others, and as sites of desires and dreams, as the stuff of nostalgia, and as a source of the willingness to kill and die. While the space of Palestine may no longer contain identity for Palestinians, it is always relevant and resonant, standing as a point of departure. Identities are indeed not bound by place, but the extent, complexity, and politics of such disassembling have not always been seriously explored.

Refugee Camps

Refugee camps are a cornerstone of humanitarian and host state responses to an influx of the displaced. Designed to provide shelter, sustenance, and protection, they embody multiple functions and meanings. For aid agencies, they confine in one locale the population to be administered and governed. For host states, they ostensibly cordon off challenges to sovereignty. Camps contain and manage and yet can be sites of opposition. Although spatially bounded units of governance, they are not necessarily spaces of passivity in which refugees wait hopelessly. Refugees inevitably stamp their own imprint on camps, rendering them multiply inflected and often contradictory places. As dynamic and frequently contested places where everyday life unfolds, they are both "foreground" and "background" (Hirsh quoted in Feld and Basso 1996: 6).

Basso contends that "relationships with places are lived whenever a place becomes the object of awareness" (1996: 54). At those moments of awareness, people become "sharply aware of the complex attachments that link them to features of the physical world." The simple act of dwelling in a refugee camp is occasion for such an awareness. Yet in these confining places, Palestinians have fashioned meaningful places in which they live in exile and plan for the future.

Ethnographic research on refugee camps is indebted to Foucault's notion of disciplinary spaces and practices (Long 1993; Malkki 1995a). Malkki writes in reference to Hutu camps, "The precisely planned ordering of space in Mishamo—and, indeed, in any refugee camp—was an intriguing issue, not only in terms of the rationalization of that ordering, but in terms of the sociopolitical *effects* that different kinds of spatial regimes might be expected to produce" (1995a: 137). In some instances, refugee camps have been conceptualized as "total institutions" where bodies are disciplined and control is an integral and defining component of the structure of the institution and its daily routines.[17]

The possibility of modular refugee camps is tempered by examples that do not conform to such a spatialization and its effects. The bulk of Palestinian camps are not organized on a grid but resemble a medieval maze. In Lebanon, Palestinian camps were not consistently sites of confinement or the normalizing effects of a disciplinary regime; quite the

Figure 5. Interior alleyway, Burj al-Barajneh camp. Julie Peteet.

contrary, for a lengthy period, they were controlled and administered by an armed resistance movement. Spatially, they were organized to reproduce the spaces Palestinians left behind and to which they were organizing to return. This suggests the need for comparative ethnographic and historical work on refugee camps, their spatial and administrative regimes, and refugee identities and practices, particularly political mobilizing and militancy. Afghan camps in Pakistan (Centlivres and Centlivres-Demont 1988) and Palestinian refugee camps, particularly those in Lebanon and more recently in the West Bank and Gaza, have been places from which militant opposition to displacement or occupation have been launched. Each has experienced significant levels of internal control and management in tandem, however uneasily, with an international relief regime.

Conceptualizing camps as multiply inflected, contradictory spaces articulates with anthropology's abiding interest in the intersection of structural and institutional constraints and human creativity. As Asad reminds us, "People are never only active agents and subjects in their own history. The interesting question in each case is: In what degree, and in what way, are they agents or patients?" (1993: 4) If histories and social analyses of the displaced are to convey their experiences adequately, illuminating this interplay between spatial modes of containment and the creative placemaking capacity of refugees, in which spatial and administrative regimes were simultaneously subverted, accommodated, and appropriated by refugees for their own purposes, is critical.

This book explores how Palestinian refugees imprinted the camps with a landscape of hope for the future. They crafted meaningful places which in turn shaped refugee identity and subjectivity. This has occurred within and against the constraints imposed by displacing state impulses, host state interests, and international institutions. These relationships and their expression in everyday life were a product of ongoing historical, political, and cultural processes unfolding within a context of oscillating power relations between the interior of the camps and the exterior world.

The Symbolic Capacities of Place: Multiple and Conflicting Meanings

In the politics of place, material, representational and symbolic dimensions serve as organizing frames (Harvey 1993: 23–24). The shifting power scale between camps and host spaces indicates that spatialization can be conceptualized as a hierarchical organization of power. Space, place, and landscape are sites of multiple and conflicting meanings and representations. Representations, often circulated as authoritative, are hardly inert; they can and do inform actions, endowing them with legitimacy and justification. Shifts in representations of Palestinians and their camps provide an index to the refugee experience in Lebanon, tracking its vicissitudes and its power.

In Lebanon, the camps were places of rich and indeed highly conflicting sets of imagery, representations, and rhetorical magnification, ranging from the heroic and authentic to the despicable, violent, and dangerous. In a context of highly asymmetrical power relations and exclusivist forms of nationalism, with their lines of difference and inclusion, conflicting meanings and representations can become significant components in rhetorical violence and deadly conflict. During political conflict, essentialist notions of place and community are often asserted. Thus attempts to reify space through the raw material of representations and rhetoric were hardly uncommon. Once translated into practice, reifications of place provided justification and legitimacy for the infliction of violence. For these Palestinians bound together by experiences of assault and trauma in the enclosed spaces of the camps, collective reifications posited them simultaneously as heroic spaces and spaces of terror. Thus representations and the violent actions of external forces were integral to placemaking, not only in the sense that they had the capacity to effect place, but that responses to these assaults shaped placemaking from the interior as well. As real and imaginary places, camps were constituted at the confluence of external and internal practices and rhetorical configurations.

In examining representations and imaginings, my concern is with a politics of representation that highlights their effects on the fashioning of place and their consequences for daily life. Harvey argues that representations have "material consequences in so far as fantasies, desires, fears, and longings are expressed in actual behavior" (1993: 22). Lebanese, Israelis, and Palestinians represented and imagined the camps as specific types of places and undertook actions consistent with these imaginings. In other words, representations were not inert but were part and parcel of the discursive category of "the Palestinian," with tangible effects. With no visible lines of differences between Palestinians and Lebanese, a discursive concept of the Palestinian, legible in rhetoric and representations, guided and legitimized violence. Representations shaped the parameters of acceptable actions and thus played a productive role in producing spatiality. Israel, Lebanon, and those Palestinians residing outside the camps constituted the exterior around which the specificity of a camp, and the community of camps, was articulated. As Massey argues (1993: 68), specificity arises from the "accumulated history of a place, with that history itself conceptualized as the product of layer upon layer of different sets of linkages both local and to the wider world."

For the Israelis, the refugee camps loomed as the living embodiment of precisely what cast doubts on their exclusivist claims to Palestine.[18] Rather than integrating into neighboring states, the Palestinians were highly visible in these spatial enclaves, internationally administered and on the agendas of international bodies. The camps contradicted the assertion of Israelis such as Golda Meir that "There is no such thing as a Palestinian."

Prior to becoming sites of political organizing, the camps were targets of attack. Israeli cross-border attacks on camps in Gaza and the West Bank were not infrequent in the 1950s and early 1960s. With the emergence of the resistance movement, they were deemed places of terror and consequently sustained armed incursions, sieges, aerial bombardments, and massacres. The concept of "colonial mirroring" (Taussig 1987), in which the colonizers impute to the natives the kinds of barbarity they themselves are inflicting in pursuit of absolute dominance, takes us beyond the media-imposed framework of attack and response (a tit-for-tat logic) by seemingly balanced military forces.

Nabatiyyeh camp in South Lebanon illustrates the practice of excision and dismembering. Designed in the late 1950s as a model camp, it was built on a terraced hillside owned by the Maronite Church. The long barracks, with housing units designed to accommodate families of varying sizes, were arrayed along the contours of the terraces. One former inhabitant described it as having

a clinic, a cafeteria, rations' storage depots, distribution areas, a mosque, and a two-building elementary school. There was one narrow dirt road that cut the camp in half along one terrace, from one end of the camp to the other, and then joined the street leading to the town of Nabatiyyeh. The majority of the people were Ghawarneh from Na'meh and Khalsah but there were also a few families from 'Ayn Zeytoun and Salhah and a few other villages in the upper Galilee. Nabatiyyeh was a "tidy" camp. The other "tidy" camp was Dbiyyeh in the Christian areas.

By 1974, it had been completely destroyed by Israeli air raids and its inhabitants dispersed northward.[19] Like Tel al-Za'ter, it became a space of memory. In the Palestinian narrative, Israel's relentless assaults were part of a long-term pattern of population removal and a permanent state of violence in the border area. In the wake of such assaults, camps residents often said: "This is a continuation of 1948." In Israeli media reports, civilian sites were indistinguishable from military sites and thus the camps were positioned as legitimate targets.

Chapter Two
Prelude to Displacement: Producing and Enacting Knowledge

1948 + 1967 = All Palestine

—graffito, West Bank, 1990

Indeed each new form of state, each new form of political power, introduces its own particular way of partitioning space, its own particular administrative classification of discourses about space, and about things and people in space. Each such form commands space, as it were, to serve its purposes; and the fact that space should thus become *classificatory* makes it possible for a certain type of non-critical thought simply to register the resultant "reality" and accept it at face value.

—Lefebvre (1991: 281)

Nations may well be imagined communities but they are also spatialized. Lefebvre argues of the state, "without the concepts of space and its production, the framework of power (whether as reality or concept) simply cannot achieve concreteness" (1991: 281). Fashioning knowledge about space and its circulation is integral to producing and claiming it. My interest is to connect these spatializing strategies of the state to the production of a refugee population, a population in space.

This chapter broaches the Zionist production of knowledge about the space and population of Palestine and the indigenous relation to place. Such knowledge was pivotal in realizing a colonial-national project in Palestine. The translation of knowledge into power and the operationalization of discourse to produce and maintain a constellation of effects are the focus here. These effects produced an ethnoreligious state predicated on the exclusion of the bulk of the indigenous inhabitants.

In this chapter, the term Zionist refers to support for the colonization of Palestine by Jews, a law of return that gave all Jews the right to settle in Palestine/Israel, and the active pursuit of Jewish nationalism and its statebuilding project. Substantial ideological work went into the discursive marginalization and erasure of the indigenous population. The spatial strategy of the Zionist project was to reduce the indigenous population by installing them elsewhere. Spatial strategies are concrete practices accompanied by ideological ones implicated in the construction of heterotopias, what Deshpande, drawing on Foucault, refers to as real places that "can be pointed to on a map, lived in, visited, or empirically experienced in an obvious way." "Heterotopias enable . . . people to see themselves reflected in some utopia" (1998: 250). An Israeli state in Palestine replaced a culturally, linguistically, and religiously diverse space with an *ostensibly* undifferentiated and utopian world.

This chapter and the next speak to the question of consciousness and intent. Can we cast the Zionist project, aid bureaucracies, and host states in an interlocking, mutually constitutive network of power when they are spatially separate, completely distinct institutional entities, wielding vastly different forms of power, with quite different mandates? In other words, I want to map an interlocking domain of power through time and space by examining its effects. This domain encompasses multiple sites from which power could be deployed—the Zionist movement and the Israeli state, the refugee relief regime, most notably UNRWA, and the various host states and their internal power dynamics. Both the Zionist movement and the refugee relief regime had underlying epistemologies of the native and the refugee: they could be reconstituted as national subjects in another place. The effect of their practices has, however, not always been in tune with that intended by either regime. Underlying both the Zionist and post-1948 administrative projects was the assumption that new spatialities, identities, and a sense of belonging could be crafted for the Palestinians.

My concern here is with how discourse articulated with the practices it naturalized and legitimized. An examination of Zionist discourse and the production of knowledge actually lends a certain credibility to the accounts of the refugees, which correspond closely to pre-1948 Zionist plans for the diminution of the Palestinian population. Ironically, after 1948, the very same plans once articulated by Zionists were denounced as fictions devised by the Arabs.

The Zionist movement engaged in an elaborate discursive construction of the indigenous population through categories of time, space, belonging, and rights, as well as notions of relation to and power over place. The central issue in the construction of a Zionist self was relation to place, the practice of producing it, and nativizing the European Jew. Labor and land were essential components of the project to redeem the

Jew. To constitute a Jewish state in Palestine, a Palestinian majority was an obstacle, for indeed a land heavily populated by another people undermined the notion of Jewish claims to ownership, of a "return" to a place imagined and historically mythologizied as home. The Palestinians would have to be denativized.

Israeli archaeology's crafting of a predominantly Jewish past in Palestine points to the complicated relationship between knowledge, materiality, and the social practices that produce living landscapes and images. Abu el-Haj illustrates how the Israeli "imaginary has been produced very much through the concrete" (1998: 197), a compelling argument for reasserting the centrality of practice and materiality into the study of how knowledge becomes power (see also Abu-el-Haj 2001). Noting the venerated role of archaeology in the Israeli imagination in the 1950s and 1960s,[1] Zerubavel (1995) examines the commemorative narratives of Masada, asserting that reinterpretation moved it from the margins of Jewish history to the center. This "innovation . . . helped weave the end of Antiquity into the beginning of the modern national revival to construct a symbolic continuity between the two periods and underscored their great divide in relation to Exile" (1995: 35–36).[2]

Representations, discourses, and imagery of natives are neither inert or innocuous, nor do they produce an effect on their own. Discourse achieves "its full power because of its historical activation in the institutional context of colonial rule" (Dirks 1992: 176). The issue here is how Zionist discourses, representations, imagery, and forms of knowledge articulated with sociopolitical practices and institutions to structure communal relationships. To the institutional context must be appended the field of power in which discourse, practice, and institutions operated. The British Mandate was the ruling power under whose auspices an increasingly well-armed and financed, and tightly organized settler-colonial society engaged in a statebuilding project. A Palestinian elite, politically fragmented, self-serving and unable to act effectively, in conjunction with a peasantry defeated and fragmented by the 1936–39 war, set the stage for the consolidation of the Zionist state building project in the 1940s.

Although not always neatly orchestrated, a synchronization between forms of knowledge and practice is identifiable where the organization of power is such that those producing knowledge of a subject are in a position to *enact* as well as sustain and reproduce it. Discourses embody elements of predictability. Carefully calibrated wars of words often precede actual military conflict, portending action.

Rupture: Colonial Spaces and Discourses

In a landscape where all the signs of picturesque nature lead to politics, politics leads to silence. (Bermingham 1994: 77)

The rupture of native peoples' relation to place has an extensive history in colonial schemes (Gasteyer and Flora 2000). Such endeavors tended to locate the natives in an alternative temporal zone, itself located within a developmentally hierarchized spatiotemporal scheme. Comparatively speaking, Zionism was hardly unique in this instance.[3] Once an Arab landscape was erased, a Jewish landscape could take shape and Jewish settlers could become natives.

A spatialized classificatory order was central to the Zionist imagination. The Zionist project was neither a civilizing mission nor one of drawing the natives into their orbit of ideological influence. It was intended to colonize the land of Palestine, not to refashion native subjectivities.[4] Unlike colonial endeavors where labor extraction is a defining principle, native time was not appropriated and fashioned according to a colonial production schedule. Zionism was a project in nationalism and self-renewal contingent upon achieving demographic and political hegemony.

Time Zones

Time, Fabian argues, is "a carrier of significance," giving form and expression to relations of inequality (1983: iv). In a broader sense, time is an artifact of power.[5] Rutz argues that "representations of time become ideologies that legitimize the exercise of power" (1992: 8). Zionist thinking about time suggested an evolutionary blueprint. European Jews represented modernity and progress; Palestine was frozen in time. Time was envisioned and represented as static in order to claim space, define place, and bolster the legitimacy of the nationalist endeavor.[6] Zionist representations of Palestine served as rhetorical devices iterating past time as present time, as time recovered. Zionism encoded and eventually carried out a project in "spatialized Time," a discursive and practical device to effect difference. Echoing nineteenth-century social evolutionism, the Zionist construction of difference and hierarchy was both spatialized and temporalized; coevalness was rejected in favor of spatial and temporal distancing.[7] Rather than recognizing that these were "different societies facing each other at the same time," Zionist rhetoric relegated Palestinians to what Fabian referred to as the "allochronic" (1983: 32). Building on modern European notions of linear time and progress, their time was dynamic and forward moving while Palestinians were seemingly immobilized in the past.

If Palestinian time were erased, their contemporary presence could be as well. Between a Jewish presence in the Biblical era and modern Zionism, Palestine was conceptualized as a wasteland. Benvenisti writes, "every Arabic name, even if no ancient Hebrew name had preceded it," was erased from the map, an act equated with a "declaration of war" on Palestinian heritage which he attributed to the Zionist "desire to make direct contact with their own ancient heritage" (2000: 47). Noting the centrality of naming to nationalist territorial claims, Benvenisti comments on his father's leading role in devising a "new Hebrew map of the land, a renewed title deed" (2).

Primers to educate Jewish youth provide an example of Zionist discourse on Palestine, the Yishuv, the Arabs, and the new Jew. Benvenisti, whose father authored a popular primer, claims they were a "mechanism of indoctrination by means of which Zionist ideology was implanted in the heart of the Jewish child" (2000: 57) The introduction to a prominent primer states that "No preparation for Jewish living can be complete without a thorough understanding of Palestine . . . and that every Jewish home should have a copy within easy reach" (Edidin 1944: vii, viii). In Edidin's primer, European Jewish immigrants to Palestine would push the clock forward to anther temporal zone by dint of their labor and their industrial and agricultural technology, in short—their modernity. Arriving in Palestine, they would confront a "standstill."

Palestine's immediate neighbors are . . . among the most backward. . . . While the peoples of Europe and American were discovering new continents, writing great books, inventing machines, discovering steam and electricity, the Arabs in these countries were at a standstill. Today most of the inhabitants of these lands live very much like their ancestors hundreds of years ago. . . . Fifty years ago no one would have called Palestine a land of milk and honey, it was so barren and desert-like. (1944: 62, 66)

The logic of this temporal scheme and its racial coding was part of a larger picture that fostered attitudes legitimizing Palestinian displacement. To regenerate the space of Palestine for Jewish redemption, time had to be set free to move forward, yet connect to other distant times. These encompassed both the past when it was "a land flowing with milk and honey" and the Zionist future that would reconnect it with a time of fertility (Edidin 1994: 66–67). With technology and commitment, the European Jewish settlers would bring Palestine into contemporary time, toward modernity and the cultural, moral and technical space of Europe.[8] The primer described the Arabs as "farming just as their ancestors had farmed for centuries, with the same wooden plows, the same primitive flails, the same inefficient methods. . . . The starved sick soil had to be brought to health before it could become fruitful once more" (132–33). The land would become healthy and productive once more through Jewish settlement, which would also redeem the new Jew.

Maps are both visual renditions of space and geopolitical artifacts. The contemporary mapping of the Palestinian-Israeli conflict that accompanies news media or articles will sometimes assemble a series of maps of Israel dated to 925 B.C. to mark the Kingdom of David and Solomon. A second map, detailing the Partition Plan of 1947–48, is followed by a map depicting Israel and the occupied territories in the present. Strikingly missing are the 3,000 years in which this space was populated by a complex variety of peoples and passed through multiple and complex historical eras, the Roman, Byzantine, and Islamic, among others.[9] Spatiohistorical telescoping was intended to visually support and reproduce a geographic construction of Palestine as nearly unpopulated until the advent of twentieth-century Jewish settlement. To do so, selected eras and histories were endowed with value. On Israeli excavations in Jerusalem, the term "recent periods" includes "everything from early Islamic through Ottoman times—approximately 1,300 years in the city's history . . . bulldozers . . . were used repeatedly to remove more recent remains before the supposedly real work of excavating was begun" (Abu el-Haj 1998: 172).

Zionist ideology imposed ruptures in Jewish history as well. Through commemorative narratives and education, Zionist-inspired scholars attempted to forge a connection between "antiquity" and the present, downplaying and occluding Jewish Exile. Secular Zionists were "reshaping the past" in order to mold the future and facilitate the emergence and consolidation of a distinctive Hebrew identity and subjectivity in the space of Palestine/Israel. In doing so they developed a counter memory toward Exilic Jewish memory and history (Zerubavel 1995: 15). The Zionist periodization of Jewish history, divided into Antiquity and Exile, and the commemorative narrative that developed in the Yishuv, both emphasized the national. The "appearance of seamless continuity" between the past and present meant the "commemorative time created by the Zionist master commemorative narrative thus differs from historical time considerably" (33).

Zionist renditions of Palestine were part of a larger European colonial imagination. An analysis of *National Geographic* photographs and essays on Palestine in the early twentieth century lays bare not merely the representation of Palestine as the Holy Land but the conflation of the Palestinians with a long ago past (Moors 1996). Moors argues that the photographic essays were intended "to correct common-sense Western notions about biblical events" (1996: 283). Time was hierarchized and Palestinians were a "living Museum," as one subtitle indicates (282). Whereas previously Palestine was depicted as slumbering along with a biblical era technology and way of life, by the 1930s and 1940s, Palestine was peopled by European Jewish immigrants who set in motion the path to modernity.

Landscape: Simultaneous Visions

Landscape tropes are significant in colonial projects.[10] Art historian W. J. T. Mitchell contends that "landscape is already artifice in the moment of its beholding, long before it becomes the subject of pictorial representation" (1994: 14). Ways of visualizing and representing landscape are spatial strategies of inclusion and exclusion inscribed with power. Although well populated, in Zionist ideology the landscape of Palestine was in a liminal state. Redemption of the land would occur through the application of European Jewish technology, knowhow, and love of the land.

Mitchell writes that "Landscape is a natural scene mediated by culture" (1994: 5). So, how does a highly populated and cultivated landscape come to appear empty? If the native inhabitants were not seen, or in a line of vision, how were they then construed as radically different and out of place? How does one see and yet not see simultaneously? When early Zionist leaders referred to Palestine as barely populated, they did not literally mean the land was empty of people. Arabs communities were "white patches—terra incognita" in the mental map of Jews (Benvenisti 2000: 56). He goes on to acknowledge that the settlers were aware of the Arab presence but that it "had no place in the Jew's perception of the homeland's landscape. They were just a formless, random collection . . . viewed through an impenetrable glass wall" and had meaning only "as the objects of their perceptions and political concerns, but not as subjects in their own right" (56). The indigenous inhabitants were likened to "the rocks of Judea, as obstacles that had to be cleared on a difficult path" (quoted in Flapan, 1979: 56). As rocks, they were part of the landscape but removable. In an "empty" landscape, the natives were akin to inanimate objects, topographic features that could be rearranged for the land to be cultivated and inhabited by another. In an inversion of the demographic order, the natives were to become foreigners and the colonizers were to become natives through a process of self remaking achieved through a conquest of the land.

With historical amnesia and a mapping that sought Jewish continuity between past and present, the landscape could be imagined as it might have been in centuries past, erasing time in-between now and then. The Arab population was part of the land's liminality as it awaited Jewish redemption. In this ostensibly barren landscape, Palestinians were hardly in sight. A chapter entitled "What of the Arabs?" appears near the end of Edidin's primer. Its location in the text and the question in the title connote an afterthought (1944: 213–30). The chapter begins: "Thoughtful Zionists do not dismiss the question of the Arabs lightly. For it is a fact that the Arabs constitute two-thirds of the Palestine population" (213). The simultaneity of seeing and not seeing is striking. The Palestinian landscape was "foreign" to young Jews who lived separate from and rarely interacted with Palestinians. In the primer, natives are classified according to place and mode of living, such as Bedouin, *fella-heen* (peasants), and city Arabs. Palestinian place is defined negatively, marking its stagnation and underdevelopment.

The nineteenth-century colonial question of native competence and who should own the land is intimately linked to this context of seeing and not seeing. Given that Palestinians were not deserving of the land because they were incapable of developing it, they begin to disappear from *sight.* Differing, hierarchized competencies were a function of technological disparities between Europe and Palestine as well as of cultural differences. Historian and literary critic Yosef Klausner (1874–1958) echoed this: "Indeed our hope that one day we shall be masters of the country is not based on the sword or on the fist but on our cultural advantage over the Arabs and the Turks, which will gradually increase our influence" (quoted in Gorny 1987: 49). Then a significant advance over the concept of race in accounting for difference, the concept of culture can replicate its effects by seeming to be nearly as immutable as race once was for human classification and the assignment of rights and competencies. A ranking of rights and emotions, dependent on location in a cultural evolutionary scheme, endowed the Zionist project with the moral high ground. This sentiment finds rhetorical expression in Lord Balfour's statement that Zionist settlement in Palestine "was rooted in age-long traditions, in present needs, in future hopes, of far profounder import than the desires and prejudices of the 700,000 Arabs who now inhabit that ancient land" (quoted in Finklestein 1995: 33).

It was apparent that Arabs would have to be forced or enticed to move to clear the way for the redemptive project and the awakening of land after a long, deep sleep. Theodor Herzl, founder of political Zionism, suggested that Jewish settlers "try to spirit the penniless population across the border by procuring employment for it in the transit countries, while denying it any employment in our own country. Both the process of expropriation and the removal of the poor must be carried out discreetly and circumspectly" (1960: 343). Jewish renewal was to occur through redemption of the land and for that it had to be depopulated to correspond to its imaginary and discursive emptiness. Through techniques of depopulation pursued during the 1948 war, when Palestinians either fled or were expelled and subsequently denied return, reality was aligned with the imagination. In a futuristic vision of a human landscape where Jews would be unhampered in pursuing redemption, hundreds of years of indigenous presence and history were obliterated from the local imagination.

Objectifying Place and Identity

To construct the new Jew, a relationship to the land was essential—learning about it, settling it, and working it with Hebrew labor were critical. Concomitantly, Zionist schooling and extracurricular activities emphasized first-hand, intimate knowledge of the land. Thus walking tours, hikes, and camping trips for youths were vital experiences, instilling knowledge and love of the land. Akin to "an intellectual effort" (Darwish 1978, quoted in Parmenter 1994: 1), they aimed to nativize settlers through the acquisition of knowledge about and familiarity with place.

Naming of place is a form of symbolic intervention that operates in a field of power. Contests over names point to a cultural politics of landscape and competing nationalisms. In this instance, naming place facilitated claiming it and endowing it with a particular history articulated to statebuilding and nationalist images of historical depth. Names can evoke or commemorate certain historical, religious or political events, or eras. Thus the currency of place names can be an indication of power arrangements and is heavily implicated in the politics of landscape.[11] With statehood, the "Israel Place-Names Committee," preceded by a geography naming committee, was charged with changing place names to either biblical or national/Zionist ones. Renaming was intended to further the "recreation of a biblical ancient homeland" and the severing of "any bonds with the Diaspora" (Cohen and Kliot 1992: 659, 660). Linguistic kinship between Hebrew and Arabic meant this was often easily accomplished. For example, al-Bassa became Betzet, Saffuriyyah became Tzippori, and Beisan became Beit Shean.[12]

Making the reality of landscape match its imagined quality of emptiness drew upon assertions of hierarchically and morally ranked cultural difference. V. Jabotinsky, writer, Zionist activist, and founder of the revisionist movement as well as the Irgun and Stern groups, said "We Jews, thank God, have nothing to do with the East. . . . The Islamic soul must be broomed out of Eretz-Israel" (Shavit, quoted in Masalha 1992: 29). A view of the Arabs as backward and a source of contamination, and the Jews "on the other hand, [as] predominantly European in character, [who] were dynamic, educated and modern" underpinned the segregationist impulse (Gabbay 1959: 24). The imposition of a boundary, at once moral, cultural, and national, was essential to constructing a new Jewish identity. Chaim Weizmann, leader of the Zionist delegation at the Paris Peace Conference, called for a Palestine "as Jewish as England is English." National, political and cultural homogeneity was assumed among both Jews and Arabs (Masalha 1992: 13; Weizmann 1983: 79: 256–57).

In the Zionist imagination, Palestinians were nomadic and could live elsewhere in what was perceived as a vast Arab homeland.[13] Nomadism and the availability of a vast elsewhere meant they could be removed without raising thorny issues of moral accountability or actual resettlement. Most significantly, if they were nomadic, Palestinian nationalism could not be on a par with Jewish nationalism. The nation implies contiguous territory and a relationship between people, culture, and territory. The imagery of the native as devoid of deep attachments to place facilitated the eventual expropriation of Palestinian lands and a continuing abdication of responsibility, and a denial of national rights to sovereignty and identity.[14]

Violent Natures

The notion of "epistemic violence" refers to the process by which colonial thought shaped colonial subjects as inherently different (Spivak 1994: 76). Palestinians were discursively constructed as violent, underpinning and legitimizing their displacement. In a broader context, representations of the colonized often fell into a binary opposition between "inherently violent or innately peaceful" (Nagengast 1994: 112). The paradox between an imputed lack of attachment to place and yet the apparent willingness to fight for it was resolved by classifying Palestinian violence as irrational, without just cause. For example, Zionist discourse referred to the 1936–39 revolt as "a series of riots" and those involved as "a gang of robbers, murderers, and bandits" (Swedenburg 1995: 13), thus obstructing an understanding of manifestations of Palestinian nationalism and their discontent with colonization.

Coupled with a violent nature, the Palestinians were classified zoomorphically. Stern, founder of the Stern Gang or Lehi, precursor to the Likud, said, "The Arabs are not a nation but a mole that grew in the wilderness of the eternal desert. They are nothing but murderers" (quoted in Masalha 1992: 30).[15] This classification has a contemporary resonance. In the wake of Israel's 1982 invasion of Lebanon, then Israeli Chief of Staff Rafael Eitan said the Palestinians in the occupied territories would be like "drugged cockroaches in a bottle." In reference to the *intifada*, former Prime Minister Yitzhak Shamir likened Palestinians to "grasshoppers." More recently, Labor Party leader Ehud Barak told a *New York Times* correspondent, "You know, we are still living in a jungle," which he characterizes as "the dark and backward old Middle East." He explained the difference between the two major political parties in Israel, the Labor and the Likud, "We're both trying to kill the mosquito. . . . But at the same time we're trying to drain the swamp, while Likud is saying the swamp is ours and we'll never give it up. We believe the only way to overcome terrorism is to solve the source of the problem." The path chosen is to "kill the mosquito" by draining the swamp.[16] The term "terrorist" is often applied to any act of resistance and tends to implicate the whole population; otherwise there is no rationale for collective punishment. It is powerful, in part, because it locates the "terrorist" as beyond the pale of civilized society and the reaches of international diplomacy. As such, extrajudicial measures to quell legitimate acts of resistance can be deployed with impunity.

Effecting Transfer

Foucault's notion of biopower concerns the power exercised over life rather than death: the "ancient right to *take* life or *let* live was replaced by a power to *foster* life or *disallow* it to the point of death. . . . Now it is over life, throughout its unfolding, that power establishes its domination" (1980: 138). Removal is extreme—the power to make someone effectively disappear. Foucault contended that biopower has two poles, "the body as a machine" and the "species body, the body imbued with the mechanics of life and serving as the basis of the biological processes" (139). Modern state interventions and controls over the body were effected through a "biopolitics of the population." Arabs who stayed in Palestine after 1948 and became nominal citizens of Israel were subject to the techniques of biopower more in line with the original meaning (see Jiryis 1976; Zureik 1979). However, spatialized techniques of biopower were instrumental in mass displacement.

Both European colonial history and the twentieth-century breakup of empire and ensuing nationalisms provide precedents for mass removal and annihilation. As an example of the former, the German annihilation of the Herero was the "prototype" of settler violence in colonial southern Africa; in the New World, the prototype was the Native Americans, forcibly removed from their lands and relocated (Mamdani 2001: 10). Colonial regimes developed terminologies and practices appropriate to the specificities of place and time. With an underlying notion of an "elsewhere" and a weak native attachment to place, the Zionist idea of transfer intersected with colonial and nationalist discourses from other areas. When the writer Israel Zangwill (1920: 103) penned that the way to create a Jewish state free of non-Jews was "race redistribution" to be effected through a "trek like that of the Boers from Cape Colony," he echoed colonial South Africa and the removal of Native Americans (Finklestein 1995).[17]

The institutional and practical expressions of transfer were the Transfer Committee and the military plans and operations that effected it. According to W. Khalidi (1961), the historical record documents a fairly detailed plan of transfer. Despite the wide diversity of political thought within the Zionist movement, the need to dilute the Arab presence in Palestine met little effective opposition. How does one reconcile the official Israeli stance "they left of their own will" with "they must be transferred"? Post-1948 official Israeli public policy may be an instance of collective forgetting that was productive of state building. Battaglia's concern with "how forgetting gives rise to society" and "forgetting as productive social action" (1993: 430, 440) provides an analytic framework.

How is the production and circulation of knowledge related to realities on the ground? The discursive construction of the Arabs as mobile, weakly attached to place, and unworthy of the land legitimized and made palatable dispossession and the denial of their rights. The events leading to mass displacement are well detailed in other works (W. Khalidi 1961; Masalha 1992; Morris 1987; Nazzal 1978; Sayigh 1979; and Shoufani 1972, among others). By 1947, on the eve of *al-nakbah,* Palestinian Arabs numbered about 67 percent of the population (Center for Policy Analysis 1992: 7). The 1947 UN Partition Plan allocated 55 percent of Palestine to the Jews at a time when the Palestinians accounted for 67 percent of the population and Jews 33 percent. Jewish land ownership amounted to about 6–7 percent of the total land area. With the end of the Mandate in 1948 and the outbreak of armed conflict between Arabs and Jews, some of the civilian population sought shelter in neighboring states while others were forcibly expelled. By the end of the war, most Palestinians were refugees in neighboring countries and their lands were being expropriated and resettled. According to W. Khalidi (1992), 418 villages were depopulated and subsequently razed or resettled. After the 1948–49 Arab-Israeli war, only about 150,000 Palestinian Arabs remained inside the new state of Israel; the rest, around 780,000, were displaced.

A fairly consistent argument widely circulated in international diplomatic circles, and until recently in Israeli and Zionist scholarship, was that the Palestinians left of their own will. The entry of Arab forces into the war of 1948 has been understood to mean that the Arab states were responsible for the refugee situation. The flight versus expulsion debate no longer carries much weight. Extensive research has illuminated a complicated process of both flight and expulsion. However, the heart of the issue is not how they left but the denial of their right of return, guaranteed under international law.[18]

Conclusion

The Israelis were able to construct a geopolitical, demographic, and cultural border of separation as well as an interior landscape nearly free of the native population. The bulk of Palestinians, now refugees, were soon launched on a process of reconstruction. Although international agencies and host countries set the parameters of this process, Palestinian intervened actively to set the course of their daily lives and chart a future.

The political logic of the modern state indicates a striving for symmetry among sovereignty, territory, and citizenship. To establish a Zionist political entity mandated keeping others at bay physically, beyond the borders of the state, or under control through a regime of military rule, as governed the Palestinians in Israel until 1966. In the modern order of nation-states, the refugee perpetually calls into question the nature of the state and society.

Chapter Three
Aid and the Construction of the Refugee

> historically we have been regarded as a population that is essentially disposable.
>
> —Edward Said (1986: 130)

The constitution of the Palestinian refugee has transpired in a multiplicity of places and historical periods and has been shaped by imbricated forms of power, knowledge, institutions and administrative-bureaucratic practices. Both conscious and serendipitous, these processes were historically situated and thus fluid. In other words, the best laid plans can always be waylaid by unexpected and unintended consequences. This chapter explores the centrality of an aid regime in the project of refashioning and managing Palestinians, collectively and individually, and the forms of knowledge on which the project was based and generated. As spatialized strategies for governance and reconstruction, the relief apparatus and refugee camps were productive of the refugee subject. This chapter examines the intersection of governance, bureaucracy, and subjection—how refugees were categorized, administered, and thus rendered governable, and yet responded in ways that affected the contours of governance and their own daily routines. I examine the administrative apparatus of UNRWA as it developed outside Lebanon, due to the fact that the UNRWA archives were closed in the mid-1990s, preventing access to a fuller picture. However, ethnographic materials demonstrate how Palestinians responded to and made sense of UN interventions and how these affected their subjectivity.

The focus is less on aid interventions and bureaucracy as forms of control (Herzfeld 1992) and more on the productive capacity of such bureaucracies to shape subjectivity and community. Much of the theoretically formative literature on modernity and the fashioning of subjects and subjectivity is concerned with colonial or bureaucratic projects embedded in state structures (Biolsi 1995; T. Mitchell 1988; Rabinow 1989). At issue here is the intersection of disciplinary structures, practices, and space that regulated everyday life for refugees, defining and structuring what was possible, and refugees agency that equally shaped the social field.

A pivotal concept in refugee administration, rehabilitation assumed a "psychological disorder" or pathology (Malkki 1995b: 510). By learning new skills and becoming gainfully employed, the refugee could be "rehabilitated" and thus take on a new lifestyle and persona. Acceptance of displacement and renationalization was assumed to follow. The rehabilitation project was modern, refashioning the collectivity and the individual, their identities and subjectivities. The year 1948 marked an irrevocable rupture with the past, placing Palestinians in a temporarily suspended state until the project to remake them would position them on the spatial and temporal side of modernity. A before-and-after and here-and-there schema underlay aid schemes. Through interventions such as vocational training and resettlement, the refugee would enter the modern world, leaving behind traditional time and space. "Works" (the W in UNRWA) projects were central to rehabilitation; through work, refugees would acquire a new sense of self and come to terms with permanent displacement. To the refugees, "rehabilitation" was a euphemism for resettlement and renationalization. They simultaneously rejected and accommodated these interventionist projects.

In Palestinian narratives, there was a correspondence between dispossession and later subject reconstitution through aid interventions. The life course is "a collectively shared image" which "may, through metaphor, provide people with images and motivations that guide their lives as members of society and as individuals" (Becker 1997: 7). For refugees, the life course was unpredictable and fraught with danger. Narratives facilitated forging continuity between past and future. They made sense of the chaos and disruption war imposed by endowing the life course with continuity, coherence, and logic. As a teenager, Um Muhammad walked across the border to Lebanon to escape the fighting in her village. Now in her seventies, she has lived in ʿAyn al-Hilweh camp ever since, and that is where I interviewed her in 1998. Like other refugees of her generation, she experienced *al-nakbah*, the early years of waiting for return, the rise of the resistance, and the long years of war that began in 1975. A widow, she is also the mother of a martyr—one of her five sons and a granddaughter were killed during the war.[1] Her other sons work abroad and send her remittances to supplement her rations. She resides in the al-Bassa quarter (a village near ʿAkka) with the same people she lived with in Palestine and their descendants. When I asked her how she arrived in 'Ayn al-Hilweh, she began as follows: "It was all planned, you see. When we arrived in the camp, UNRWA was set up and ready to receive us. We had been staying in a village near Bint Jbeil when our *mukhtar* [village headman] sent a message to all al-Bassa people to come to this camp. So we came. And not much has changed. They are still trying to drive us away from the south."

It is fruitful to conceptualize aid as simultaneously constraining and productive, as sites of contests for control over strategic resources. The items at stake were international aid resources, such as health, education, employment opportunities, and rations. Relief and rehabilitation launched new identities and subjectivities in new places. In the 1950s, U.S. Secretary of State John Foster Dulles stated that in a generation the Palestinians would forget Palestine. UNRWA was both an instrument of power in daily refugee lives and an institution that enabled a Palestinian identity and social cohesion. Moreover, it endowed the refugees with a legal identity in the international arena.

Refugee aid regimes emerged in the context of twentieth-century modern warfare, which spawned the displacement of unprecedented numbers of civilians. Regionally, the mass displacement of the Ottoman Greeks and Armenians in the first decades of the twentieth century was a template for both future involuntary movements and the organization of relief. Indeed, some of the same figures and institutions (the Kerr and Dodge families and the Near East Foundation) organized large-scale, modern, international relief for both Armenians and Palestinians.

Figure 6. Refugee camp, 1951. Georges Derzi. ANERA Archives.

After World War II, the notion of "rehabilitation" was firmly ensconced in the institutions and modernist discourse of refugee relief. As the primary institution charged with responsibility for the Palestinian refugees, UNRWA's task was to ensure the survival of the refugees, providing education, rations, shelter, and medical care, and to oversee their rehabilitation until a settlement could be reached. UNRWA's other major task was to transform the refugees into productive citizens of other Arab states, a project that generated formidable tensions.

At some level, many Palestinians thought that multiple regimes of power—Israel, the U.S., the Arab states, the UN—worked in tandem, however loosely and seemingly at odds, to thwart their national aspirations. In other words, they conceptualized a single analytical field. Their intentions and effects were similar in some instances but vastly different in others. While one can convincingly argue that aid regimes foster dependency, they can and do enable refugees to survive and, through education, to thrive. For Palestinians, the UN has been the object simultaneously of scorn and of a grudging recognition of the pivotally productive role it has played in Palestinian social development, particularly education and health, and in preventing further fragmentation of exile communities. The refugee/bureaucracy divide was complicated as UNRWA became a major employer of refugee labor. Thus its role in producing Palestinian subjectivity has been ambiguous and contradictory.

Constituting Refugees

Evoking Mohanty's (1991: 55–56) well-known and oft quoted argument, the refugee, like woman, is not an already constituted category. Refugees are constituted through violent displacement and denativization and the subsequent institutional and legal practices and discursivity of administrative bureaucracies. In 1921, the League of Nations opened an office to administer aid to those fleeing the Russian revolution. To deal with increasing numbers of displaced, over the next three decades an international refugee regime took shape which constituted the refugee as an "object of knowledge, assistance, and management" (Malkki 1996: 377). Since World War II there has emerged a "substantially standardized way of talking about and handling 'refugee problems'" (385–86). Malkki argues that the effect "was to depoliticize the refugee category and to construct in that depoliticized space an ahistorical, universal humanitarian subject" (378). Accordingly, Palestinian insistence that they were primarily a political rather than humanitarian issue is directly related to the depoliticization of the category of "refugee."

The 1951 Convention Relating to the Status of the Refugee explicitly sets out refugee access to protection and resources, however paltry. Refugees are a category of persons in international law, whose status is conferred by the UNHCR. For Palestinians, UNRWA confers that status.[2] Paradoxically, the term refugee suggests the very institutions and personnel that constitute them as objects of intervention. As an object of intervention, the refugee subject is constituted by an interlocking international and local network of power. Aid regimes simultaneously constituted, regulated, and legitimized the refugee subject. Aid discourses implicitly classified refugees as spatially and culturally liminal, as deterritorialized people in need of humanitarian intervention. A description of a project run by an American aid worker in South Lebanon during the 1950s is illustrative: "They have penetrated the 'twilight world' of the Palestinian refugee and shown how people who are in danger of losing human attributes of thought, work, and basic independence can be pulled back from the precipice."[3] "Twilight world" invokes liminality, being between the light of humanity and culture and the darkness of the precipice on which these refugees were poised. The aid worker, Mrs. Alma Kerr, had the capacity for human emotions such as compassion, while the refugees were reduced to physical and emotional states of shivering and shock, seemingly bereft of all but the most basic of human attributions.

In refashioning the composite refugee into an object of intervention, visual representations are telling. In a 1950 American Friends Service Committee (AFSC) newsletter, a photo display dramatically visualized the process of refashioning. One photo featured a Gazan refugee nuclear family, dirty, with unkempt hair and bare feet, clad in tattered clothing. In a before and after arrangement, the photo next to it depicts the same refugee family, now clean, shod, and well-groomed, in new clothing provided by aid. A photo series by the Musa Alami Foundation depicted refugee boys at work in agriculture and industry, as well as studying.[4] They never look at the camera, evincing little evidence of individual personality or character. The diligent performance of labor and study subtly suggests rehabilitation.

Reading the records and accounts of early relief efforts provided an enlightening glimpse at the other side of the issue.[5] I had approached relief efforts from the perspective of Palestinians in the 1970s, then highly critical of aid as creating charitable dependency on international bodies intent on resettlement and the depoliticization of the refugee issue. Many aid workers were motivated by deep religious convictions and humanitarian concern; some, like many of the Friends, were politically quite astute. They were acutely aware of the expulsions, the violent events precipitating flight, and the impending denial of the refugees' right of return. The granddaughter of a family of missionaries and educators explained that others, particularly "old Middle East hands," were "motivated by a sense of civic duty, and guilt" toward the victims of a displacing project supported by the U.S. They were often long-time foreign residents of the region with a past history of charitable, educational, and relief endeavors, often members of prominent missionary families such as the Dodges and the Kerrs.

Attitudes toward aid fluctuated with the refugees' political and economic empowerment. During my early years of fieldwork in the camps (late 1970s, and early 1980s), the resistance movement wielded considerable power and was fairly autonomous. They built a network of Palestinian social institutions and community development projects in health, education, recreation, and vocational training. Nonresistance sources of aid were easily denigrated, evoking a past dependency that the resistance (as well as a regional economic upturn) had made almost unnecessary. Unless working in tandem with the resistance movement, outside sources of aid were often considered politically suspicious, part of a conspiracy to resettle or spy on Palestinians, or generally apolitical or charitable, which in those highly charged times carried with it retrograde implications.

Palestinian social and welfare institutions commingled with UNRWA in such a way as to blur the boundaries of the mission and role of UNRWA (see Schiff 1995). Questions of areas of operational authority and the political status of aid employees effectively undercut the possibility of stable categories of aid and refugee. It was not uncommon for UNRWA personnel to be members of resistance organizations. For example, UNRWA teachers, usually refugees, taught a Palestinian version of history not condoned by UNRWA or host governments. The instability of the boundaries between the two organizations reached a heightened level during the 1982 Israeli invasion of Lebanon, when Israel accused the agency of allowing their facilities to be used to store weapons and train guerrillas. Resistance services nearly superseded those of UNRWA in all but education.

Abu Salim, a middle-aged man living in Shatila camp, and I were comparing life in the camps in the 1990s with the 1950s when he commented with irony, "Now, fifty years later, we Palestinians are living as real refugees. UNRWA was like a buffer between us and the realities of being refugees. It provided us with the means to live. As UNRWA services decline and the Lebanese state strangles us, we are now facing what could have faced us fifty years ago." Following the PLO's 1982 withdrawal from Lebanon and the demise of its social safety net, UNRWA was perceived in a different light. Only a few foreign NGOs, such as the Norwegian People's Aid, stayed. In the 1990s, local NGOs in the camps were looked on favorably, as willing to help those desperately in need despite government restrictions and the unpopularity of the Palestinian cause. In some cases, NGOs absorbed political activists who in the post-1982 period had few legitimate ways of pursuing political activism. NGO work broadened the conception of what constituted political work. Where formerly the "social" was denigrated if not under the aegis of the resistance, in the 1990s it was a much welcomed lifeline.

Region and Century: The Context of Aid

If the twentieth century was the century of refugees, the Middle East was certainly an active participant. In 1922, hundreds of thousands of Anatolian Greeks were pushed out of Turkey and into Greece. Driven by an ethnic-nationalist agenda, the Turkish government massacred and deported the Armenians of Anatolia, generating one of the first regional relief organizations. The Near East Relief (NER) was formed in 1915, as a successor to the American Committee for Relief in the Near East, to provide assistance to the Armenian refugees.[6] Like the Palestinians a quarter-century later, the Armenian disaster was an exercise in large-scale dispossession and deportation. NER provided direct relief, medical care, feeding stations, and desert rescue convoys to pick up refugees and save them from starvation or death from exposure. They also provided for the resettlement and long-term care of Armenian refugees through the establishment of orphanages, schools, vocational training workshops, income-generating projects, and medical facilities in Lebanon and Syria. In 1930, the NER became the Near East Foundation, dedicated less to relief, given the end of the Armenian crisis, and more to philanthropy.

The feeding, medical care, education, and resettlement of masses of displaced involved interventionist techniques of biopower—"the subjugation of the body and the control of population" (Foucault 1980: 140)—to manage those violently and rapidly stripped of homes, national belonging and protection, and facing disease, exposure, and death. A knowledge of numbers and categories was paramount and transformative. Techniques of classification and distribution of aid linked the individual refugee with an aggregate population. The sheer number of displaced Armenians and Palestinians reached the level of aggregate populations. Thus relief was life-sustaining in the sense of power over life in both the biopolitics of population management and the disciplinary procedures over individuals (139). The intent was to "normalize" as far as possible the abnormal—the person out of the national order and at risk.

With its focus on the body as a project of intervention, refugee aid can be construed as an undertaking of modernity and the reformation of subjectivities. In the most immediate and visceral sense, becoming a refugee is an embodied experience. Deprived of sustenance and protection, the body is in a heightened state of distress. Becker notes that in the wake of crisis, when the body is "altered profoundly," it becomes "an unknown terrain that must be relearned; flawed and distorted, it becomes the focus of identity, a shaky ground on which a new order . . . must be built" (1997: 81). With aid and its institutions embedded in daily life, new bodies were conceptualized and enacted. The immediate life-sustaining period had ended by the time UNRWA came into existence in May 1950; indeed, UNRWA's main task was supposed to be rehabilitation.

The productive aspects of international relief were lauded by U.S. President Coolidge—"Not only have lives been saved, but economic, social, intellectual and moral forces have been released. New methods in child welfare, in public health and practical education have been introduced" (quoted in Dodge 1973: xiii). NER claims to have trained 1,500 relief workers in various capacities while providing relief to Armenian refugees (Barton 1944: 13). By 1948, there was a discernible international and modular regime of knowledge and techniques of relief. For new states such as Israel, the refugees it produced were managed and normalized by a new international aid regime.

Early relief projects in the Middle East were pivotal for the future planning and administering of aid (Barton 1944: 8). For example, in 1943 the Russell Sage Foundation published a booklet entitled "Administration of Relief Abroad," using excerpts from Barton's 1930 *Story of Near East Relief.* It provided a range of relevant material for the provisioning of relief. In summarizing the accomplishments of NER, the report noted

a series of more than thirty studies . . . notable blue prints in post-war planning covering a wide range of practical subjects such as Public Health, The Rehabilitation of War Injured, Reclothing the Greek people, Agricultural Reconstruction, and Personnel Training for Reconstructive Services in the Near East. These have been commended and received most favorable consideration by the United States government and have been made part of the body of information gathered for the use of UNRRA. (19)

In the spring and summer of 1948, Palestinian refugees streamed across the borders to Jordan, Lebanon, and Syria, and into the Gaza Strip and the West Bank, in a cacaphony of buses, taxis, boats, and by foot. Means of departure depended on location, financial resources, and the scale of fighting in a particular area. Relief was localized and chaotic. Those who had relatives in neighboring states often sought refuge with them. Others camped under trees and slept in caves for months until relief arrived, using their meager savings to feed themselves. In December 1948, International Red Cross workers classified the refugees by age: 12 percent children under two years of age, 18 percent children from three to five, 36 percent children from six to eighteen, and 8 percent old people. Missing from this classificatory scheme were the ablebodied. Classification was derived from assumptions about need, particularly nutritional. Workers found that 25 percent were housed with relatives, 25 percent in the open air, and 50 percent in huts and tents.[7] It often took multiple moves before a family settled into a camp.

Local relief efforts were forthcoming from host state governments, charitable, religious, and voluntary organizations, and individuals. Each host country presented different opportunities, rights, resources, and regulatory measures. For example, in Lebanon, refugees often had friends or relatives and received assistance from churches, the Red Cross, and the government. In Jordan, refugees were received by the government and the Red Crescent. The right to work was a critical indicator of host country ability and willingness to accommodate refugees. Unlike Lebanon which classified the refugees as foreigners, Jordan offered citizenship, and Syria gave refugees the right to work. In Gaza, the refugees overwhelmed a small strip of land with scant resources and almost no local sources of aid.

According to St. Aubin, local governments provided "direct donations, transport, warehousing, post facilities, and other costs in connection with the storing and distribution of supplies" (1949: 253).[8] Syria and Lebanon, for example, both provided cash and food:

In Syria a government grant of 60 piastres per day was given to registered refugees over ten years of age and of 40 piastres to children under ten. Such medical services and other local assistance as could be provided were given without charge. In Lebanon a monthly grant of 10 kilos of flour or bread and 3 Lebanese pounds was authorized for each refugee. . . . It is estimated that with other costs included, Lebanon's expenditure on the refugees equalled 20 per cent of its national budget. (253)

In addition, according to International Red Cross reports, the government "directed the work of refugee relief" by the Lebanese Red Cross and other organizations and "allotted sites for the camps."[9] Local volunteer committees formed to organize the collection and distribution of food, clothing, and blankets.

Harder to calculate was local, often individualized, aid. Refugee narratives are rich in details of how they were received. Some families were allowed to sleep on Lebanese village lands; village schools and guest houses were often converted into temporary shelters. Provisioning food and water placed a heavy burden on Lebanese villagers. It was not uncommon for refugees coming into Lebanon to find shelter and food with kin or friends. A history of cross-border trade and marriage had forged a complex array of social ties between southern Lebanese and northern Palestinians. Norms of hospitality were activated in receiving refugees. Some refugees had very positive, heartwarming experiences that reaffirmed their faith in humanity, while others suffered insults and a denial of hospitality.

Compassion fatigue set in within a year or two and was directly related to the length of stay and the impact on the host economy, society, and environment. Local reactions were highly variable. In Gaza, the locals were simply overwhelmed by the crushing numbers of refugees relative to the local population—around 200,000 refugees to 80,000 locals in a rather small and arid part of Palestine (about 225 square miles). Access to the critical resources of water and fuel caused problems between locals and refugees. In the quest for fuel to cook dry rations, refugees quickly stripped Gaza of vegetation, causing severe environmental degradation.[10]

Local Red Crescent or Red Cross societies distributed aid received from foreign Red Cross societies, usually consisting of blankets, medical supplies, food, clothing, and the seconding of workers. Church groups and the YMCA also responded. By August 1948, UN Mediator Count Folke Bernadotte realized that the "resources, experience and proper organization were all inadequate" to deal with the growing number of refugees (St. Aubin 1949: 254).[11] To face the growing crisis, an international organization of relief was vital, and under his leadership, a sixty-day UN Disaster Relief Project (UNDRP) was established to coordinate aid from various sources (Schiff 1995: 14). Even though relief was forthcoming, Bernadotte realized that a better system was needed. A proposal he submitted to the United Nations prompted the General Assembly call on member states to establish a Special Fund for Palestinian refugees and provide $32 million until 31 August 1949. The fund was to be administered by the Director of United Nations Relief for Palestine Refugees (UNRPR).

Following Bernadotte's assassination in 1948, Ralph Bunche was appointed Acting Mediator and soon warned that the situation was perilous. In response to Bernadotte's July 1948 report and Bunche's supplemental report of 18 October, the UN General Assembly in November 1948 established the United Nations Relief for Palestine Refugees (UNRPR), precursor to UNRWA. The resolution made explicit reference to Bernadotte's recommendation that "action must be taken to determine the necessary measures (of relief) and to provide for their implementation" because "the choice is between saving the lives of many thousands of people now or permitting them to die."[12] UNRPR director Stanton Griffis, U.S. ambassador to Egypt, was assigned the task of coordinating and expanding the relief efforts of local agencies, international organizations, and voluntary efforts for a nine-month period from 1 December 1948 to 31 August 1949 (Buehrig 1971: 5–6). A variety of UN agencies came on board early in the crisis to provide expertise and relief in specific areas. For example, the UN International Children's Emergency Fund (UNICEF) provided supplementary food for children, pregnant women, and the sick. The World Health Organization (WHO) conducted a medical survey and established the basis of a medical relief system. The Food and Agricultural Organization (FAO) estimated caloric needs and costs (St. Aubin 1949: 256). Once the UNRPR project was under way (January 1949) and a system of regularizing rations was in place, refugees were assured of a minimum daily caloric intake. "On New Year's Day 1949 the first shipment of supplies under UNRPR procurement arrived in Beirut—hardly more than six months after disaster had struck" (Buehrig 1971: 29).[13]

Host Arab states faced difficulties coping with refugees. Buerhig notes that there was an "absence of an infrastructure in the countries of refuge equal to the situation" and that these states "lacked not only material resources but also administrative organization and personnel" (29). At this stage, the scope of the disaster and its long-term nature were not yet completely apparent.

The UNRPR coordinated with three agencies operating in the three sectors where refugees had congregated. Relief was then distributed outward from the UN to these agencies and thence to the refugees. In Syria, Lebanon, and Transjordan, the League of Red Cross Societies was the main agency responsible for distributing UN aid; in the West Bank, the International Committee of the Red Cross was the coordinating agency; and in the Gaza Strip, the UN coordinated with the American Friends Service Committee (AFSC).

"Like a Flea on a Hot Griddle": The Friends in Gaza

Before further delving into UNRWA, I turn to the AFSC's work in Gaza, which served as an administrative precursor to UNRWA. The first team of AFSC relief workers arrived in Gaza on 24 December 1948. In an agreement with the UNRPR, the AFSC was given responsibility for the organization and distribution of UN, Egyptian, and Red Crescent relief supplies in Gaza.[14] A brief overview of the aid situation in Gaza illuminates some of the problems during this chaotic period and gives insight into the role of the relief worker. In one of his first reports to the Friends Philadelphia headquarters, Field Director Delbert Replogle described setting up the initial infrastructure and his role in it as being "like a flea on a hot griddle."[15] The Friends wrote detailed accounts of their work and their own feelings and sentiments. The local population was over-whelmed by the arrival of about 200,000 refugees and there was severe pressure on existing resources. Gaza's geographical isolation further compounded matters; AFSC's headquarters for this relief mission was in Cairo, a thirty-four-hour train ride across the Sinai. Communications were relayed by couriers. In short, an infrastructure of relief had to be constructed from the bottom up.

In the meantime, refugees had immediate needs for food, medical care, clothing, and shelter. The head of the mission, Emmett Gulley, said "only basic needs could be supplied and most of that had to brought in through Egypt with their consent and assistance" (1973: 6). The logistics were daunting, as supplies were delivered by train from dis-tant Port Said. One has to ask: how did they do it and do it so well? "With our inexperience, all we knew was how to get the work done" and "the basic spirit of genuine service" was how Gulley explained it. As an exam-ple, he described an incident from the summer of 1949:

The U.N. Conciliation Commission . . . wanted to know how many men there were, how many women and children, ages of everyone, place of birth and home prior to flight, occupation of employable, education, number in family, etc. [At] a conference in Beirut . . . the chairman called on the representative of the League of Red Cross societies. . . . This representative informed the group that it would require a considerable time . . . help and financial aid. Next the chair-man called on the representative of the International Red Cross. . . . That gentle-man was more specific. He said that his organization would need eighty statisticians . . . and three months. . . . He next asked for my opinion as regards the Quakers. I stated that I saw no necessity, or possibility of hiring so many statisticians, nor any need for extra help, or time, or funds. I reminded them that they had requested this statistical information about a month before and we had gone ahead and secured it and had it ready to turn over to them. The silence which ensued was intense. You could have heard a pin drop. Then every-body wanted to know how we did it. It was really very simple. We simply placed a native worker in each distribution line. As the refugees passed down the line, this worker filled out a form giving the needed information. No extra time or money was required. (17)

Alwin Holtz, among the first Friends to go to Gaza, echoed the theme of simplicity in designing solutions to ostensibly overwhelming problems:

Nobody realizes how much we did in a short time in this tiny space. For example, I was with the first seven who came in the middle of January . . . The whole business of timing is expanded in my mind. . . . I mean, in the first six months, really it was only two or three months. . . . Sixteen months was all we were there. . . . A funny thing . . . is that we did so much and we did it so well because we were too naive to tell them we couldn't do it. We did things we couldn't do, but we didn't know we couldn't do them.[16]

They had to set up camps, build latrines, establish hospitals and schools, and organize a system of rations and the enumeration of the refugees. They identified the census and the organization of transportation as their first major problems. The logistical task of establishing a system for transportation, warehousing, and distribution of relief were daunting. Gaza was under Egyptian military administration, so the Friends were obliged to deal with them on a daily basis. Holtz comments on their by and large congenial relations:

We were determined from the beginning that we would do our own thing. There's the famous "Nineteen Points."[17] Colin Bell really invented them and got it put through . . . with the Egyptian authorities. . . . the Egyptians didn't know what they were doing either. . . .

Any time I had a problem with anybody who looked at me crooked, I whipped out the "Nineteen Points" and said "We're running this, that's it. Here's your government's approval" and that always gave them pause. (15, 16)

Some camps were established in former army barracks whose large structures could be easily turned into distribution centers. Others were hastily erected temporary facilities. Initially, distribution in large camps tended to be organized by village. Statistical accounting of rations was made by village and for the Bedu, by tribe.[18] Since the camps were spatially and socially organized on a village basis, each village, or set of once proximate villages, formed a block represented by a leader. Ration cards and rations were distributed according to village. Whole villages were called to assemble, a name would be called, and a male would step forward to receive his card which included his wife and children. Villages or village blocks were assigned specific days to receive rations or use laundry facilities, thus lending continuity and cohesion to village social organization and identities.

In physical structures surrounded by barbed wire, rations distribution was carried out with bureaucratic precision. The following account by a relief worker at Nuseriat camp, formerly a British prison camp, in the Gaza Strip in early 1949 underscored cultural difference and hinted at the role of humor in coping with a daunting task:

Quaker distribution takes place in a Quonset hut. . . . It is divided down the center by a neat stone wall about three feet high. Stocks are stored on one side. An office occupies one corner. One end has a wide door easily reached by truck. The other end has one wide door. On either side, near that end, is a smaller door. At this end of the hut two distribution tables are set up, with scales and measures. People come in through the big door, pass the tables, collect their rations and go out either of the smaller side doors. About the middle of the hut are two more side doors. Distribution tables have been set up by these. People come and receive rations and go out through the same door. Thus four lines of distribution operate at one time. The whole camp can be served in three days

. . . Distribution is usually made by village of origin. Announcement is usually made by a colorful character—a refugee with lungs of iron. He is as effective as a loud speaker and much more interesting to look at. He is swarthy, merry, of medium height, stocky and wears a gorgeous costume of purple (lightly faded cotton) trousers cut in the baggy, Turkish style which give a theatrical, masquerade effect, and a dark green jacket—G.I. equipment dyed green. On his head is a tight cap often worn around here. He carries a stick. And he loves his work. The distribution hut is in the center of a clearing surrounded by barbed wire. Thousands of refugees press all around this. The announcer walks along the barrier, on the inside, flourishes his stick, announces distributions and on occasion generally harangues the crowd, letting everybody know no nonsense will be tolerated.

Generally the crowd is manageable. But the idea of standing in line is completely foreign to the Arabs (apparently) although they seem willing to stand about not in line for hours on end. One day a woman's arm was broken, not especially because the crowd was unruly, but just by the sheer weight of so many human beings pressing as close to the fence as they could. Tall, mustached Abdul Kareem, of the Palestinian Police stands guard. He wears the dark uniform of the local gendarmes, and their wide, high black lambs wool hat, and carries a stick. Kelly Peckham, camp leader here, says he should be in Times Square. Despite the policeman's best efforts, people creep into the enclosure. He clears it out vigorously one minute. Ten minutes later twenty people, tall sheiks, colorful bedouin women in their heavy coins, shy refugee women with the veils held in their teeth, often with a nursing infant under it, old men and frisky little boys, fill the place. They are all smiling, eternally courteous and forever at your elbow.[19]

Soon after setting up services, Palestinian workers outnumbered the Friends by a large margin in an easily discernible division of labor. Foreigners were the professional relief workers, administrators, doctors, and nurses. There were eight or nine hundred "native helpers, interpreters and cooks" (Gulley 1973: 6), as well as warehouse workers, interpreters, drivers, food distribution clerks, and later teachers. Once in operation, UNRWA became the largest employer of Palestinian refugees and trained three generations of administrators, aid workers, and bureaucrats. With few people then trained in managerial skills, Palestinians occupied the lower level clerical and administrative positions as well as doing the bulk of the manual labor, while foreigners occupied the better paying, higher level positions. UNRWA's directors tend to have diplomatic or military backgrounds.

The question of trust is salient in refugee studies (see Daniel and Knudsen 1995). While trust is a two-way street, it is undoubtedly imbued with power in relief situations where the refugee is dependent upon life-sustaining resources from a source over which he or she exercise little, if any, control. In the critical self-assessment of a female relief worker, it was evident that trust was continually up for negotiation:

Each Arab with whom one of the Quakers talked almost inevitably concluded the interview with the warning not to trust someone else with whom we were also dealing. At first it hit some of us pretty hard; later it became accepted as "part of the pattern." But always it invoked "uncertainty." There seemed to be no group or person to whom the Unit could turn with complete confidence. . . . Thus I had the feeling that one has when travelling through a great many countries in a short period of time. Our denominations were constantly changing— according to the last person with whom we talked. And we found ourselves alternately trusting and distrusting the same person. One never really "knew" him. . . . I guess that the worst part is the "not knowing" that makes one ever torn between suspicion and hatred for and disappointment in oneself for this suspicion. . . . The talk and uncertainty appear to be a permanent way of life. . . . The idea that all were treated exactly alike—*makhater* [headmen] included—was a completely new one . . . but once the bulk of the refugee were convinced that we really were trying to make fair and equal distribution, there was a background of understanding, trust and sympathy that made dealings with the individual cases far easier. . . . As one member of the Unit put it, in matters of judgement we were caught between not trusting a mind whose ethic was different from ours and not trusting ourselves because our inexperience [in its world] made us different from it.[20]

A field director's account of cutting ration lists brings to light the instability and negotiation of trust. Two village headmen were told by the Friends they had to cut 200 names from their village list. The relief worker figured they could cut 65 people but gave them 200 as a figure to gain some bargaining space. To his utter surprise, they readily agreed to cut 200. The relief worker added quickly, "Well, we will begin with 200 even though I know you could cut 400 or 500."[21]

Cultural differences were often subsumed under the category of trust. For example, early on, relief workers recognized that the concept of "honesty" was culturally variable. Field Director Charles Read wrote that "there is an entirely different concept of honesty here. . . . It is not thought to be dishonest to try to get a double ration or to list false names . . . if the people who accept them are suckers enough to do so, the responsibility is theirs."[22]

The Friends received no salary, only maintenance. Unlike UN personnel, they were not associated with political involvement in the region that might have aroused suspicions.[23]

Gulley's words intimate how trust was established: "We found the Arab refugees to be highly appreciative of any efforts to help them and generally co-operative. Because of the many unfulfilled promises that had been made to them . . . they at first tended to discount everything we said. We made every effort to scrupulously do everything we promised and it was not long until we had their confidence" (1973: 9).

UNRWA and Aid Agencies

11. *Resolves* that the refugees wishing to return to their homes and live at peace with their neighbours should be permitted to so at the earliest practicable date,

and that compensation should be paid for the property of those choosing not to return and for loss of or damage to property which, under principles of international law or in equity, should be made good by the Governments or authorities responsible. (UN Resolution 194 (III), 11 December 1948)

The UN General Assembly reaffirms this resolution every three years. In spite of an international consensus supporting repatriation or compensation, plans were underway for refugee rehabilitation and resettlement. From this seeming paradox springs much of Palestinians' contradictory sentiments towards UNRWA. Palestinian mistrust of the UN stems in part from the UN Resolution 181 which mandated the 1947 Partition Plan, dividing Palestine into Arab and Jewish states. War ensued, and Israel eventually came into possession of much of the area allotted to the Palestinians. The formation of UNRWA in 1950 ostensibly signaled the end of temporary relief and acknowledged the long-term nature of the refugee situation.

UNRWA was formed out of the UN Conciliation Commission (established by UN General Assembly Resolution 194 (III), 11 December 1948), which aimed at a combined package of repatriation, compensation, social and economic rehabilitation, and resettlement. In August 1949, the Commission established the Economic Survey Mission (ESM), headed by the chairman of the Tennessee Valley Authority (TVA), Gordon Clapp, to facilitate Palestinian resettlement.[24] The Commission grew out of a situation in which Israel refused to implement Resolution 194's call for repatriation or compensation. Israel did not oppose the mission because of its proposed role in resettlement through economic development.

The ESM was charged with developing an economic blueprint to solve an essentially political problem. The first interim report explicitly stated that repatriation, which it was noted the refugees insisted upon, "requires political decisions outside the competence" of the ESM.[25] The report acknowledged that they were well aware of the limits of an economic approach to a political question and the limited capacity in terms of capital, skills, and administrative and managerial experiences of the Arab states to launch large-scale development projects, as well as the refugees' desire for repatriation. It recognized that the agencies were overburdened and that the need for direct relief would continue until men were gainfully employed. The Commission recommended continued relief in conjunction with a public works program geared to regional water projects modeled on the American WPA.[26] Clapp's report noted regional economic underdevelopment and the inability of host states to absorb the refugees. The report suggested that each Arab country initiate development programs in land reclamation, irrigation and drainage schemes, road building, and reforestation to create employment for refugees. Labor intensive projects were projected to reduce reliance on rations and foster local integration (Buehrig 1971: 35).

The Clapp Commission recommendations led to the transformation of UNRPR into UNRWA with an ostensible focus on both jobs and relief. But work projects ended up costing about five times more than direct relief. By November 1950, works programs were on hold because of their prohibitive cost (Stevens 1952: 293), Palestinian noncompliance, and Arab states' inability to develop them due to a lack of resources and skilled managerial and technical personnel. The report also recommended that Arab states take over "responsibility for the maintenance of such refugees as may remain within their territories" by the end of 1950 (ESM Report, 8).

Promoting an economic solution to a political problem can be contextualized in a Cold War foreign policy which considered economic development and integration as a means to prevent refugees falling into the hands of Communism. The Friends were highly critical of Clapp's scheme because of its long-term focus on rehabilitation rather than repatriation. Their apprehensions were fueled as well by the environment of Gaza, the least appropriate place for public works. It was clear that rehabilitation and work meant resettlement. In commenting on the Clapp document, Schiff noted that it avoided "admitting that 'resettlement' had replaced 'repatriation' as the goal" and "never used those words but substituted vaguer concepts such as 'reintegration' and 'rehabilitation'" (1995: 20).

While ESM's proposals for economic development never got off the ground, its suggestion that the successor agency to UNRPR have responsibility for work programs as well as direct relief was adopted by the UN General Assembly in Resolution 302 (IV) on 8 December 1949, which established UNRWA. It was not yet apparent how nearly impossible economic development was as a solution to an inherently political problem (Buehrig 1971). Yet a sense of the long-term contradictions was evident in the report's recommendations for work projects as a way to "halt the demoralizing process of pauperization; outcome of a dole prolonged; the opportunity to work will increase the practical alternatives . . . and thereby encourage a more realistic view of the . . . future. . . . The need for international relief will pass and . . . the refugees will ultimately be rehabilitated" (10).

A press release outlining the contents of the ESM Report stated emphatically that work would not negate the right of return, although this did not appear in the Report itself.[27] UNRWA initially faced two tasks: providing direct relief in the form of rations, shelter, medical aid, and education, and rehabilitating the refugees, taking them from peasants to workers equipped for resettlement. Its second director, John Blandford, was formerly TVA general manager and thus it was not surprising that water projects—irrigation and hydropower schemes—were paramount (35–47).

Until 1956, UNRWA attempted to launch work programs with the goal of integration and reducing the numbers on relief. Refugees resisted these projects both because many necessitated another move and because they were adamant about return. Anything that suggested permanency was suspect in the eyes of the refugees. Apprehensive about resettlement as well, Arab governments obstructed regional development schemes. Prohibitive financial costs also rendered such projects less than feasible. By the early 1950s, it was evident that works projects would not produce the desired results. Work and rehabilitative components were dropped and relief, education, and medical care constituted UNRWA's mission.[28]

With the shift from works to education, UNRWA prepared Palestinians for new forms of employment, although it did not explicitly promote resettlement. The refugee commitment to education was overwhelming and went far toward producing the regional image of the well-educated Palestinian. UNRWA education was often the envy of the Lebanese, whose government schools were of much lower quality. In the past two decades, the quality of UNRWA schools has declined drastically and led to an erosion of academic achievement. Budget restrictions resulting in severe overcrowding, substandard facilities, and a lack of supplies have been compounded by prolonged conflict that has destroyed school buildings and interrupted the academic calendar. In addition, a host of social problems have left children unprepared for learning. UNRWA's superior education and vocational training played a critically enabling role in resistance, and its high standards of English language training facilitated the employment of thousands of Palestinians in the booming Gulf economy in the 1960s and 1970s.

As an institution, UNRWA brought Palestinians together in well-defined spaces where their consciousness of themselves was most certainly heightened. Crosscutting the fragmented spaces where Palestinians resided, it connected refugees with one another through the experience of its institutional forms and practices. In short, it was a shared feature of life. It was theirs and not theirs. Staffed largely by refugees, its agenda was determined at international levels where Palestinians hardly had a voice.

UNRWA possessed identity-affirming capacities. It provided a definition of a Palestinian refugee that was the criterion for determining access to refugee status, rations, and health and education services. The definition states that refugees eligible for aid are "those people or their descendants whose normal residence was Palestine for a minimum of two years preceding the Arab-Israeli conflict in 1948 and who, as a result of that conflict, lost both their homes and their means of livelihood" (Viorst 1984: 13; see also Schiff 1995: 24). The registration card and the Palestinian identity card (issued by the host state) remain documents of vital importance in stating national identity and any rights that may one day devolve to it.

UNRWA has been an absolutely integral aspect of refugee life, with an indelible impact on the everyday life of the group and the individual, yet it has played a most contradictory role. It educated a generation of Palestinians and trained a bureaucracy. It provided a social safety net and forged the early administrative boundary of each camp. As part of an international body that voted in favor of partition, Palestinians tended to see the UN as heavily implicated in their displacement. Financed heavily by U.S. contributions, the very same agency that participated in creating their nightmare was now responsible for their well-being. To add insult to injury, they stood in line to receive bags of flour with "A gift from the people of the United States" stamped on them.

Yet UNRWA was a reminder of the international community's obligation and involvement in the Palestine question. The United States has been the largest UNRWA donor and encoded its assistance as "humanitarian aid," a categorization Palestinians have rejected. They were not a humanitarian cause but a national one, they argued, and to them aid cannot be stripped of a political content.

UNRWA serves as a barometer of larger political plans that involve international consensus and cooperation. In the 1990s it was still perceived by refugees in Lebanon as playing a potential role in resettlement schemes. Frequent budget crises, which resulted in a reduction of services and rations, sent a signal about its possible demise which, to the refugees, foreboded transfer or was read as a form of pressure to compel them to emigrate.[29] Rumors of UNRWA's demise fueled fears of the end of the refugee problem. In the 1990s, camp residents mounted vocal protests, demonstrations, and sit-ins in response to threatened budget cuts.[30]

Local Projects

Local projects to aid the refugees were abundant, but few were sustained over the long term. The Arab Development Society (ADS) is worthy of inquiry for what it reveals about Palestinian sentiments toward the project of remaking the refugee. Initiated by Musa Alami, a Jerusalem notable, the ADS was a nonprofit vocational training center for orphaned refugee boys in Jericho.

The terminology in its printed material was similar to that of Western aid agencies, but occasionally smuggled in a political retort. One fundraising pamphlet is entitled "Miracle in the Holy Land. The Arab Development Society Appeal. 25 Years On." "Miracle" was a loaded term in the Middle East context. It occupied a prominent position in Zionist rhetoric, particularly in the West, where it referred to, among other things, "making the desert bloom." The miracle here refers to the success of ADS in cultivating an area of the Jordan Valley once widely considered unfit for cultivation. It also referred to its ability to continue its work in spite of both initial Arab hostility and later Israeli occupation.

What endowed Alami's project with its miraculous qualities? In 1949, Alami searched for water on a 2,000-acre tract of wasteland near Jericho. Water experts had told him that no water would be found in the area. "Unable to buy or hire drilling equipment, Musa and a small band of helpers set to work digging by hand . . . in August . . . when . . . the temperature was often over 120 degrees Fahrenheit in the shade. Five months later . . . sweet water was found."[31] His project was a success story in crop growing and diversification into poultry and cattle farming at a farm where orphans were boarded and educated in agriculture and academics, as well as vocational training. ADS supporters in the U.S. also deployed the miracle trope in appeals for support. For example, Norman Vincent Peale said, "He has made the desert bloom as the rose."[32]

Reminiscent of NER, the ADS project also had recourse to a medicalized rescue trope. In the introduction to the pamphlet, English historian Arnold Toynbee, a supporter, wrote, "Hopeless adversity breeds despair, and may vent itself in violence. . . . The antidote is hope." Without the advantages of education and training, the boys risked being either "resentful victims" of local political passions or pawns of Communism.[33] Hope was the antidote, achieved through "rescue." A photo next to Toynbee's introduction depicts two young barefoot and ragged boys standing outside a hovel, staring vacantly. The caption reads: "Hundreds like him have been rescued; but thousands more have to be turned away."

Alami's slogan, "Being a refugee is a misfortune—not an occupation. We have to make people again out of the refugees," echoes the conceptualization of refugees as pathological and deculturized. He was intent on ensuring the orphans were skilled and thus employable and on developing areas deemed wasteland. Oddly, he was derided by his fellow Palestinians and Arabs, and during rioting over the Baghdad Pact in 1955, the ADS farm and vocational training center were looted and burned down. His vision fell decidedly within the parameters of Western and international aid agencies where resettlement was on the agenda. During the early 1950s, the concept of training was often locally decoded as signifying resettlement.

Alami's denial of an interest in politics at the time was regarded as peculiar, and his class status as a notable and his possibly pro-Hashemite views were suspect. Financial support from foreign agencies and donors, including most prominently the Ford Foundation, did not augur well for his reputation. Eventually, opposition died down and integration with nationalist objectives was more evident. By the time of the first *intifada*, the ADS reported that "there are a substantial number of commercial outlets for the farm produce. . . . The farm provides basic food requirements for the *intifada*."[34]

"Strike a Blow for Democracy": The Wider Context of Relief

Don't throw away those old clothes! They're urgently needed by one million homeless refugees . . . nearly forgotten by everyone except the Communists. . . . Help to relieve these people, and put Communism out of business. Give clothes to the American Middle East Relief Clothing Drive. (#10)

Help fight Communism. . . . The people of the Middle East are . . . weakened by hunger and homelessness . . . devoid of hope, the perfect prey for Communist promises. It's our job to give them a renewed faith in democratic freedom. . . . Give them your old clothing . . . ! Strike a blow for democracy. (#2)[35]

The larger political climate is vital to understanding the contours of relief, its mobilizing discourses, and the process of subjection. In the Cold War framework of U.S. foreign policy and humanitarian concerns, the Middle East was perceived as a potential target of Soviet manipulation and penetration and the refugees' anger and misery constituted a potent entry point. Aid would mitigate refugee vulnerability to Communism. The bulk of UNRWA's contributions came and continue to come from the U.S. Early in 1950, Assistant Secretary of State George McGhee, in a statement to the House Committee on Foreign Affairs, located the refugees squarely within the domain of U.S. interests in the region and the containment of Soviet influence:

our solicitude for the Palestine refugees, partly based on humanitarian considerations, has additional justification. As long as the refugee problem remains unresolved . . . attainment of a political settlement in Palestine is delayed . . . [and] the refugees . . . will continue to serve as a natural focal point for exploitation by Communist and disruptive elements. . . . The presence of three-quarters of a million idle, destitute people . . . is the greatest threat to the security of the area which now exists. (quoted in Buehring 1971: 37)[36]

The fear of Communism was part and parcel of the impetus to replace direct relief with rehabilitation. The American Middle East Relief

(AMER, an Arab-American group) planned a center in the southern Lebanese town of Marj'oun in the mid-1950s to train refugees and villagers and develop local resources for industrial crafts.[37] With the establishment of small local industries, it was anticipated that private industries would be attracted to the area. The most immediate goal of the project was to "remedy the pitiful condition of the Palestinian refugees . . . who are deteriorating mentally and morally."[38]

The refugees' morale and psychological state were of concern to relief workers and observers. A Friend commented, "Time on their hands and nothing on their minds."[39] Low morale was due not simply to idleness and lack of necessities, but to well-founded concerns. From the standpoint of the refugee, the future was uncertain. In a letter to headquarters in spring 1949, Gulley writes,

the morale . . . is not too good. . . . they want to go home . . . we have had various riots and people have stated that they do not want food or medicines or schools—that they want to go home. . . . continued trouble in No-Man's-Land is a possible source of intense friction, and the thought of going through another summer with former orchards unirrigated, crops unplanted, and buildings damaged, funds frozen in banks within Israel, idleness and nothing to look forward to definitely, all add to the unrest and demoralization of the refugees.[40]

Is there a geography of refugee morale? After a trip to the camps in the West Bank and Jordan, the Friends mentioned that the "morale problem" was more acute in Gaza because the refugees "were so hemmed in and confined" (Bell letter, 3). News articles, briefing papers, government projects, appeals, and relief worker accounts came to the ominous conclusion that the refugees were "demoralized," "desperate," or "apathetic," echoing the refugee as pathological. In the political and ideological conditions after World War II, that made them ripe for Communist recruitment or national reinscription. The contest was over who would reinscribe them and how.

Modernity, Subjection, and Biopower

A prevailing sentiment of modernity is that people can remake themselves, fashioning a new sense of self in new places. When John Foster Dulles made his infamous remark that the refugees would forget Palestine in a generation, the U.S., with its assimilationist impulse, was accepting for resettlement a number of displaced Europeans. The Zionist ideology that Palestinian rights to place and attachment to it were negligible coincided with Jewish settlement in Palestine. Ironically, they set about the project of constructing attachment to a place to which they had metaphysical and mythical-religious connections. In remaking themselves, the assumption was that Palestinians were or should have been just as capable of the same project.

Postwar refugee management regimes assumed that newly deterritorialized refugees were culturally pathological and in need of immediate intervention and rehabilitation. Paradoxically, there was a recognition of the relationship between place, culture, and identity such that when it was ruptured pathology ensued. However, the underlying assumption was that relationships to new places could be crafted through resettlement and bureaucratic intervention and management designed to transform individual and communal subjectivities and identities.

Palestinian refugees were subjected to a series of modern institutions and practices that penetrated their subjectivity—their thoughts, desires, emotions, and sense of location in the world. Yet these practices and institutions had unpredictable and unintended consequences as refugees actively negotiated their effect and meaning. Subjectivity is formed within particular historical and cultural contexts and then has the capacity to act on those very contexts. Intended to constitute knowable and predictable identities, these new disciplinary practices instead produced in the refugees new capacities for action often incongruous with the initial intent. Thus subjectivity, history, and culture are intimately interwoven in a continuously shifting process of internalization, negotiation, accommodation, appropriation, and resistance. The subjectivities that crystalized around displacement and the subsequent management and control by host state and aid agencies then became a source for mobilizing to resist their predicament.

If relationship to property is significant to modern forms of subjectivity, the initial transformation of the Palestinians began when their relations to their land and homes were severed and their lives lost the certainty of a routine. The subsequent spatialization of the refugee population in the institutionally managed domain of the camps indicates techniques of biopower. Disciplining refugees' space and bodies was integral to successfully managing the camp. In 1949, a Friend penned this description:

a camp of 4000 to the north of Ramallah. . . . Each tent was placed on a clay foundation with low clay walls. . . . The CIRC hands out what clothing is available on a work project basis. The refugees work on the paths and roads and camp cleanups and are paid with clothing. The whole camp was policed with Swiss thoroughness. Squads of boys were organized to pick up debris. For any infraction of the rules and regulations rations were taken away for so many days. . . . the refugees seemed to like the order of things quite well. Everything was neat as a pin. If any bits of paper were seen around any tent, M. Courvoisier (of the CIRC) would point them out sternly with his riding crop to the camp director with orders to clean them up immediately. The camp director . . . is himself a refugee. . . . M. Courvoisier waved his riding crop around like a martinet. . . . it was hard to see how this camp could have been any better run. . . . The second camp we visited was an even smaller one south west of Ramallah. . . . M. Courvoisier must be at least 6′4″ in his socks with a long mop of black hair which sticks up almost straight. Truly an imposing figure, stalked through the camp riding whip in hand while we meek little Quakers followed along behind. At the edge of the camp the camp committee, composed of fifteen mukhtaars and others of importance gathered around. Our Swiss friend proceeded to blow them up for failure to clean up the camp properly and then stalked back to the car, saying that he would listen to no requests until the camp was in better shape.[41]

The production of knowledge is a criterion of biopower as well as a technique of discipline and control. Biopower proceeds on the basis of knowledge of an aggregate population, and its operation requires "continuous regulatory and corrective mechanisms" (Foucault 1980: 144). How did an aid regime composed of the AFSC, CIRC, and UNRWA govern and render refugees knowable and manageable? Methods of producing knowledge and techniques of management overlapped in the camps, themselves a spatialized technique of biopower. Specific techniques of management encompassed: classification, enumeration, the census, the rations and medical system that objectified the refugee body and its basic needs, and the educational system, all of which formed the contours of a new set of constraints shaping Palestinian subjectivity. In the AFSC documents, there is almost no mention of any individual, just of "refugees" as an aggregate. Providing aid necessitated a composite refugee requiring a specific caloric intake (determined according to sex and age), shelter, water, and clothing.

Classification and Enumeration

Ascertaining the number of refugees was vexing. How many were legitimate refugees? How many were cheating on the rolls? Since relief only was to be allotted to "real" refugees, how was a "real refugee" to be determined? What enumerative strategies were deployed to render a knowable, serviceable entity? Myriad problems surfaced over how to count the refugees, determine the amount of aid needed, and ascertain the channels of distribution. In the West Bank and the Gaza Strip, for example, the refugees were interspersed with the indigenous Palestinian inhabitants. On one hand, they were internally displaced, but in a legal and administrative sense, they were refugees. The problem of numbers is common to all refugee situations. For aid to be determined and delivered, numbers and population variables, such as sex and age, are critical. By the early summer of 1948, an estimated 250,000 Palestinians were homeless; by mid-July 1949, the number had grown to approximately one million. The events of 1948 severely disrupted economic life in the

West Bank and Gaza. The local populations were in need as well and many tried to gain access to international relief.[42]

UNRWA inherited refugee lists compiled by agencies already in the field (Schiff 1995: 22). The AFSC system of population classification and enumeration was subsequently adopted by UNRWA as a model. Upon arrival in Gaza, they worked with a census prepared by the Egyptian Army and a local refugee committee that estimated 260,000 refugees. They promptly initiated a new census to arrive at a more accurate count. From the beginning, the village as an aggregate unit was the point of departure for organizing and distributing aid. Holtz said, "we did everything by villages. People were from Jaffa or they were from Beersheba or wherever they were from. That was the organization and that's the way we listed our rations, and we knew who the mukhtars were in charge of" (28). The village headmen served as intermediaries with aid organizations, providing lists of village residents and verifying the rolls. On the basis of villages as aggregates, the first rations were calculated and distributed, contributing significantly to continuity in place-based identities.

In a highly gendered fashion, families were defined as an adult male and his dependents. The AFSC allotted each male head of family a ration card that indicated "a man's name, his village of origin, his present camp and the number of members in his family."[43] It was assumed that the *ideal* patrilineal kinship system and its categories were natural occurrences (rather than a particular social practice imbued with power). Allotting ration cards to male heads of household meant that women and children's relationship to the rations system was mediated through kinship with a male. To this day, Palestinian women refugees cannot transmit refugee status to their children, nor do their children have rights of residency in a host country based on their mothers' status. If a Palestinian woman marries a non-Palestinian, or a nonregistered Palestinian, she may retain her refugee identity card, but cannot use UNRWA services (see Cervenak 1994). The consequences of this gendered classificatory system have been significant. Jumping ahead in time, in the aftermath of the war in Lebanon and the lack of resistance social services, refugee women who had married nonregistered Palestinians or foreigners, and then were widowed or abandoned, faced harrowing circumstances in providing their children with education, access to medical care, residency, and rations. In the few remaining resistance offices after 1982, women with complicated stories of dead or disappeared husbands and children without residency or access to services could be seen daily pleading for help.

The AFSC December 1949 Operational Report organized refugees and AFSC operations into two categories.[44] The first category was the population to whom rations were distributed, arranged by age and reproductive status. The former category was divided into age groups: zero to two years, two to fifteen years, pregnant women, and others (the largest category). The second category, also based on those who received rations, was entitled "Population by Villages of Origin and Family Groups of Refugees receiving UNRPR Rations" (16). It was organized into three categories: villagers and townspeople, mixed villagers and Northern Bedu, and Beersheba Bedouins. Every entry was followed by 1946 or 1947 population figures. The category "Palestinian refugee" was thus defined and enacted by relation to place of residence and/or origin and by kin or family groups. Other lists compiled by the Friends classified refugees according to occupation and by camp of residence. Basically refugees were classified according to occupation/way of life (settled or Bedouin) and by place of origin.

In late 1949, the UN compelled AFSC to cut the rolls by 20,000 due to financial constraints. They started by checking the Mandate Government's population lists for towns and villages against the current registration of refugees. This gave a picture of where villages went and whether they stayed together or split. For example, Yassur in the Gaza District registered a 1947 population of 1,450. As refugees, the village was listed as having a population of 646 (16). What social and political dynamics caused this fragmentation? Conversely, the village of Basheet (Ramleh District) had a 1946 population of 1,770 and a post-1948 population of 1,720 in Gaza, indicating that it remained intact (17).

There is a "commonly held belief that refugees are inherently untrustworthy" (Voutira and Harrell-Bond 1995: 219), or what Appadurai referred to in colonial India as the "mendacity that is seen as constitutional to most natives" (1996: 125). Voutira and Harrell-Bond write that the relief enterprise is "fraught with competition, suspicion, and mistrust" (219).[45] Archival records indicate that Palestinian refugees certainly tried to subvert and manipulate the system of classification and counting in order to receive more rations. Tactics included double entering their names in the lists or registering in more than one region or under different names, adding family members, and declining to register deaths or departures. Gulley recalls the "tricks and deceptions" and how the Friends responded:

We sent out people who would go from tent to tent, at appropriate times of the day to get an accurate census. The tents were close together and the children were numerous. We discovered that after the first children in a tent were enumerated, they would slip under the wall of the tent and be counted again in the next tent. It was impossible to get an accurate total until we finally contrived a scheme that did work. We got a large number of callers to go out at 4 a.m., when the children were asleep and count them while they slept. We got a pretty accurate count this way and found that we were responsible for 230 thousand refugees. (1973: 7)

The refugee became a number in a scheme of biopower, and indeed numbers played a prominent role in cultural expressions evocative of the Palestinian disaster. Mahmud Darwish's poem "Write down I am an Arab, my card number is 50,000," resonated profoundly with the experience of being reduced to a number and the subjectivity and practices it foretold.[46] To UNRWA, refugee families resembled military units in their internal structure of authority and its relation to UNRWA. Thus it is not surprising that the registered family was termed *nefar*, an Arabic term referring to units in the military.

Early Palestinian attitudes toward enumeration and classification mimicked their ambivalence toward UNRWA. On the one hand, the census and population figures were empirical evidence that Palestinians existed in the aggregate and as such could claim basic services and an internationally recognized identity. On the other hand, early UNRWA efforts to take a census to clean up the lists given them by the various international agencies were met by riots (Schiff 1995: 23). Today, Palestinians in Lebanon harbor volatile suspicions of any kind of counting or change in the system of classification, regarding them as precursors of resettlement schemes. Registration amounted to proof of a Palestinian identity in the only legal sense available and thus, in the event of a political settlement, a claim to return or compensation.

Enumeration, classification, and labeling had long-term implications for identity. Initial procedures conceptualized villages as aggregates with identifiable leaders; once in the camps, identity cards listed camp residence, adding another place to a multiply imbricated identity. UNRWA operational maps, divided into five sectors (West Bank, Gaza Strip, Lebanon, Jordan and Syria) with the camps of each area marked, made visually apparent and put into practice the counting, classification, and servicing of refugees by host state and then camp. The classificatory impulse integral to aid regimes entered the nationalist imagination. Cognitively, the nation was noncontiguous, so mapping divided it over multiple states and spatialized it by camp. Rhetorically through poetry and jokes and an everyday mapping of the world, Palestinians located and identified themselves according to particular host states. Classifying Palestinians by camp redirected Palestinian identities in a new fashion, as did region of refuge. Palestinians began, and continue, to refer to themselves and other Palestinians by place of refuge, for example, the "Palestinians of Kuwait," "of Lebanon," "of Syria"; the Palestinian census lists the population according to state of current residence.

Enumeration was a condensed form of biopower. For refugees, it was a basis for access to food, shelter, medical care, and education. Indeed, UNRWA had and still has the ability to confer and take away refugee status. Palestinians who acquire citizenship are supposed to lose their refugee status, but in reality few do. Numbers have been used to press the case for additional resources in the areas of education and medical care. Most important, UNRWA statistics stood as an indicator of Palestinian existence in an era when that existence was flippantly denied, which sheds some light on the ambiguity of the refugees' relationship with UNRWA. Fraught with contradictions, UNRWA facilitated survival and social continuity but also was part of an international regime of management and containment which imposed new categories of identity and forms of subjectivity. With the passage of time, national identity became connected to, although certainly not contingent upon, UNRWA registration, which endowed them with an official refugee status and thus a legal identity referenced to Palestine. Rafiq, a fifty-five-year-old man who had grown up in Nabatiyyeh and 'Ayn al-Hilweh camps, told me that

The ration card was a badge of identity while the identity card [*hawiyyeh*] was derided by Palestinians. It was the host state telling you "you don't belong here, you are an alien." The ration card had the opposite meaning. It meant international recognition. It said: "You have lost your land. You have a temporary status until your return." So Palestinians understood the ration card as a national identity card. It meant we had rights somewhere. The UN is giving you a ticket home, a claim to your right to return. If you have it, it means you are a Palestinian. We were not grateful—we knew it was temporary relief—the minimum for survival. We knew we wouldn't be subdued by a kilo of flour! We knew we had more rights than that!

Participation in a set of aid institutions constituted a significant facet of collective daily life that only camp Palestinians experienced. Classification and enumeration reaffirmed lines of difference within Palestinian society, thus delineating complex lines of inclusion and exclusion. On the one hand, it divided Palestinians according to class and access to resources, and it imposed on religious difference another level of meaning. Most Christian Palestinians in Lebanon were naturalized and thus few had recourse to UNRWA services beyond an initial year or two. Those who had some form of movable capital in 1948 usually did not need to register with UNRWA, and non-UNRWA registered Palestinians rarely resided in the camps. On the other hand, use of UNRWA services distinguished camp Palestinians from others, replicating pre-1948 Palestinian class and regional lines of cleavage (urban/rural). Although their financial situation often allowed for private schools for their children, citizenship (largely confined to Palestinian Christians) gave them access to Lebanese government schools. UNRWA schools provided a far superior education which sometimes led to resentment from the local Lebanese population. In addition, UNRWA provided registered refugees with

a social safety net unavailable to poor Lebanese. Both reinforced difference with the local population.

The practice of enumeration and classification also contributed to
forming a Palestinian bureaucracy in exile. Literate refugees, particularly those with some knowledge of English, were often hired by
UNRWA. UNRWA fueled a new Palestinian civil service (under the British Mandate, a nascent Palestinian civil service existed). It was the largest
employer of Palestinian labor among registered refugees. Appadurai
contends that native functionaries were disciplined in the "empiricist
practices of colonial rule . . . and instilled with a whole series of numerical habits" (1996: 124). Palestinian functionaries likewise served as
gatekeepers between their communities and UNRWA services. With
UNRWA employment, new lines of patronage took shape. Families
attached themselves in a client-like relationship with UNRWA employees
living in their midst. Rafiq's family in 'Ayn al-Hilweh had a long-term
relationship with an UNRWA employee, Abu Kamal. Initially, Abu
Kamal taught in an UNRWA elementary school. In that capacity, he
developed friendships with students and their families, often visiting and
taking meals with them. He built a long-lasting and warm relationship
with Rafiq's family. Eventually, he gained employment in the UNRWA
administration. Rafiq said, "He was our *waasta* (connection or middle-
man) in UNRWA. When we needed anything—to register something or
get a document—he would do it for us." They did not pay for these services; Rafiq was adamant that the relationship was based on friendship.
Rafiq's family maintained a visiting relationship with Abu Kamal, often
taking gifts of food or sweets to his house. Later, when his brothers
returned from working or studying abroad loaded with gifts for relatives
and friends, they often brought something to Abu Kamal and made sure
to visit him. Some of these relationships have endured for nearly fifty
years, involving gift-giving and hospitality in return for ease of access to
bureaucratic formalities enacted in the idiom of friendship.

For several states in the region, enumeration has been a critical political issue.[47] The Israelis, U.S., and Lebanese have an abiding interest in
refugee numbers. How many could be permanently resettled in Lebanon? How many could possibly be settled in the West? How many family
reunifications in Israel are feasible? Lebanese government officials and
political leaders have for years deployed often highly inflated numbers
of the refugees as an impending threat to the integrity and identity of
the state. Exaggerated figures are sometimes publicly touted to remind
the international community of Lebanon's heavy burden and to provide
justification for the harsh policies of postwar containment. Thus Pales-

tinian population figures are fraught with meaning and embody a host of political agendas for the various parties to the conflict.

Penetrating the Refugee Body: Rations, Health, and Education

UNRWA interventions (rations, health care, and education) constituted techniques to inscribe on the refugee body their new status and penetrate subjectivity. Rations aimed at the subjective transformation of the displaced from angry, potentially volatile refugees to docile recipients of food aid. The ordering of rations was intended to prevent starvation and to socialize them into a temporary dependency as recipients. How were rations simultaneously accommodated, negotiated, and resisted? How did refugees internalize these practices and their associated discourses? Suddenly a multitude of new items appeared in the Palestinian lexicon: refugees, rations, tents, camps, residency, return, latrines, cafeteria, supplemental feeding, delousings, DDT, cisterns, immunizations, gelatin, cod liver oil, powdered milk, lard, distribution centers, camp administrator, and permits, among others. Shared by everyone in the camps, these new terms overrode regional differences due to proximity and participation in the same set of institutions and practices.

Before refugees are counted and housed, they must be fed. Along with immediate protection from violence, this is the most pressing need, constituting the line between survival and death. Rations meant dependency, reminded of the abnormality of refugee life, and made vividly tangible the rupture in modes of subsistence, household autonomy, and relation to the land. They encoded the power to effect human subsistence and had implications for subjectivity. Fifty years after *al-nakbah*, rations continued to play a role in daily life and in the construction of communal and individual subjectivities. I had animated discussions with elderly camp residents and their now middle-aged children in Shatila and ʿAyn al-Hilweh camps to elicit information about food and diet.

As peasants, Palestinians had produced and processed their own food, using cash to purchase some items such as sugar, tea, coffee etc. Fresh, seasonal vegetables and fruit balanced a diet based on grain and pulses. Home-grown food was considered higher quality, tastier, and more meaningful than market-bought products because one knew its origins. Purchased food was "unknown." "Unless you grow it yourself, you can't be sure where it came from, how old it is—and anyway food from our land simply tasted better," Um Samir, an elderly woman who came to ʿAyn al-Hilweh as a teenager, said emphatically. I was visiting her and her family in the camp and we got on the subject of how things had changed after 1948. Her middle-aged children, who lived close by, chimed in and humorously recounted that to their father, it was inconceivable to eat an egg not produced by his own chickens. "He didn't want to eat eggs from a shop, he wanted his own eggs." Rations were a constant and intimate reminder of the violent separation from the land and the fruits of one's own labor. Consumption was now subject to conscious thought and critique, as exile transformed refugees into consumers in a cash-based economy as well as recipients of international aid. Um Samir described in some detail the kinds of food eaten before 1948 and how the diet had changed:

Before 1948 we ate what we grew. We ate burghal which we grew and prepared rather than rice which could only be purchased with cash. And we did not have cash because of the taxes we had to pay. After 1948, we were on rations and so we had the basics. A refugee man who worked only earned one and half liras a day—a woman—only half a lira a day. What could we buy with this?! Rations provided the basics! To give you an idea of how things changed—you know the small cups for Turkish coffee? We used to send the children to the shops to buy tomato paste and carry it home in the cup! We bought burghal by the kilo. We no longer had our *mooneh* [provisions].

Food, and particularly water were mnemonic devices prominently positioned in the elderly's narratives of 1948 and the early years in Lebanon. They recounted people passing out from thirst on the road to Lebanon. In host-refugee relations, water stood as a profound life-sustaining metaphor of acceptance or hostility. Stories invariably included animated accounts of villagers offering water and bread in spite of their own poverty. Other accounts mentioned terrible thirst met by refusals of water.

In late 1948, the FAO determined that 1,300 calories a day were the minimum necessary for an adult refugee. Accordingly the Gazan refugees were supplied with 1,592 calories a day of flour, pulses, rice, oil, sugar, and occasionally fish or meat.[48] Supplements of powdered milk were distributed to children and pregnant women. Supplying refugees with culturally inappropriate foods can be attributed to more than just relief administrators' lack of knowledge of local dietary traditions. It was assumed that refugees, stripped to a basic living organism requiring a certain quantifiable ingestion of food and stripped of cultural preferences, will eat anything. Stanley Kerr, who worked with NER in 1921–24 aiding Armenians, wrote to AMER,

My experience with feeding refugees was . . . they will not eat food they are not accustomed to! Our orphanage children . . . sat on a "hunger strike" rather than eat cornmeal mush! Nor would they eat bread of cornmeal. Only when we disguised it by mixing it with regular flour would they eat it! Also—oatmeal without liberal quantities of milk tends to accentuate any tendency to rickets. . . . In short, oatmeal causes a loss of calcium and unless this is compensated by the calcium in milk—this is calcium deprivation. I wonder why UNRWA approved the shipment of oatmeal if it is not acceptable to the refugees?[49]

In a letter to the Kerrs about oatmeal and My-T-Fine Pudding, a UN employee in Amman wrote,

Refugees don't have the milk to mix with it. They . . . are not willing to try. How much of the shipment gets into the camps I haven't a guess but what does will mostly be sold to small street vendors, a "refugee food shop" patronized by non-refugees and foreigners, etc. I daresay AMER has thought through . . . the refugees being able to sell a product to get cash to buy a food they like. (Kerr file)

If food is central to cultural identity, refugees were deculturized, expected to consume anything just to stay alive. In one of our many discussions, Rafiq provided an amusing and telling vignette: "I used to think there were two kinds of milk—that from animals such as the cow or goat and UNRWA milk."

Selling culturally inappropriate and impractical foodstuffs is commonplace, evoking the stereotype of the cheating refugee. Selling rations was akin to resource replacement, that is, trading rations for cash to buy culturally appropriate and preferred foods (Long 1993: 76). An economic and gendered logic was at work as well. Usually women and children, or often young boys, picked up rations. For men who were employed, a day spent at the distribution center equaled a day of lost wages as well as the humiliation of accepting relief. Noisy and chaotic sites were full of women and children jockeying to get in line and hold their places, as UNRWA workers struggled to ensure orderly distribution. Donkeys and taxis were hired to transport the heavy bags of flour. Selling rations, especially the large bags of flour, was often done at the distribution site in order to avoid carrying the heavy loads home to sell. For families whose numbers were decreasing or who were receiving remittances from abroad, it made economic sense to sell the flour and use the cash to buy other needed items, especially bakery-produced bread. In addition, it was simply not worth the money to pay to transport the rations when cash could be had on the spot. Women usually sold the rations to other women refugees or Lebanese who had larger families to feed.

Most important, by selling rations, refugees gained some measure of control over the domestic economy of food and consumption. Um Mohsen, a mother of ten who came to Shatila as a teenager, was Um Khalid's close friend. She and Um Khalid used "go for rations" (*rayeh al ʿasheh*) and then sell a portion. When I asked Um Mohsen why she sold two bags of flour to a Lebanese woman at the distribution center, she replied, "My children are nearly all married and have their own homes. I don't

Figure 7. Distribution of UNRWA rations at Shatila camp. Julie Peteet.

want to bake bread for my husband, me and the three children at home. It takes too much time and I would have to get up very early in the morning. I prefer to decide what I prepare at home and what I buy. Why should I bake bread when I can buy it!" The trade in rations was only possible, however, with an enhanced standard of living that resulted from wage labor and later remittances from workers in the oil-producing states and resistance employment.

Although this was deeply troubling to many Quakers in the early days, rations were used to induce compliance with camp rules and forms of order. Two Friends wrote of the distribution of rations in Breij camp in Gaza in 1949 as "undoubtedly the best organized . . . with distribution going on in a rapid and orderly fashion, with a long and apparently firm queue . . . anyone who breaks his or her line has the ration card taken away until they promise contritely never to push ahead again!"[50]

What is the cultural meaning of aid? "A Gift from the People of the United States" is stamped in bold black lettering on the sacks of flour distributed to Palestinians. As a "gift," are rations precious goods in a game of reciprocity in which givers and receivers are differentially empowered (Harrell-Bond, Voutira, and Leopold 1992)? Malinowski conceptualized exchange, a series of gifts and counter-gifts, as fundamental to the continuity and meaning of social relations. Weiner (1992) advanced our understanding of reciprocity through the concept of "keeping-while-giving," which asks what is withheld as well as what is given, shifting the focus to power, gender, and history.

Linking aid, reciprocity, and power brings into focus the issue of subjection and resistance, opening the way to examining aid as constitutive of identity but also as a target of appropriation of meaning by those it purports to serve. In other words, aid's meaning and ownership is contested. Where giving occurs in the cultural context of a highly elaborated system of etiquette that creates social bonds and debts that must eventually be repaid in kind or in political loyalties, many refugees wondered what was expected in return. If the acceptance of aid involved a social debt, what were the Palestinians obliged to give in return? They feared that accepting rations initiated a deal exchanging rations for acquiescence to displacement and denativization. They conceptualized aid as an item of exchange in a lopsided relationship. To resolve this quandary, the refugees rationalized that aid was the least the UN could do, given its past diplomatic involvement in their dislocation. It was recoded less as a gift and more their just due, although certainly not adequate to compensate for their loss.

Once mobilized and activated for distribution, however, rations embodied profound political, symbolic, and cultural meaning. As rations became large-scale, systematized, and internationalized they acquired an intensely political meaning that took the "gift" well beyond the realm of interpersonal relations to the collective level of the national. Rations became a poignant symbol of Palestinian exile, dependency, and powerlessness which included even those who did not receive rations.

As prolonged waiting turned into bitterness, rations became a material sign of compensation by the international community for its inability to achieve a just solution to the Palestinian issue. Since the UN was responsible for their fate, it was also responsible for feeding them. In this case, the question of who owns aid can be extended in a new direction.

Rations distribution has a salient gendered component.[51] Women and children often stood in line to pick up the family's allotment because for a man to do so was humiliating.[52] In the post-civil war period of extreme poverty, a renewed dependency on rations underscored Palestinian defeat. In the absence of the resistance movement, which was a venue in which masculinity could be performed, picking up rations was a further humiliation. In the mid-1990s, I arrived at Um Khalid's house to find she was at the distribution center. I asked her daughters, in their early twenties, where it was located. To my surprise, they had no idea. The camp was a square kilometer where they had lived most of their lives. It was not considered appropriate for young, unmarried women to stand around and pick up rations, even though there were no strange men lurking about. I found the site by asking children in the alleyways. The site was crowded with young boys, middle-aged women, and a few elderly people. Only Um Khalid's ten-year-old son was helping. Her otherwise helpful teenaged sons did not feel compelled to help their mother lug home fifty-kilo sacks of flour in a broken-down, rickety wheelbarrow which she had to upright every twenty meters or so under the weight. On the way home we passed groups of men sitting in small circles, drinking tea, and playing cards while women struggled with their onerous loads.

For fifty years, rations, like camps, have been a trope of refugeeness. A host of meanings and elements of identity were encapsulated in the act of receiving rations: economic marginality, denativization and landlessness, the absence of citizenship, camp residence—in short—refugeeness. It could be argued they were a medium for affirming identities. Being a recipient of rations differentiated them from the host population and indeed from other Palestinians. One of the reasons the PLO extended its services to the local Shi'a community in the 1970s was to downplay the advantages of receiving rations and medical, and educational services unavailable to their poor yet supportive neighbors. In other words, this extension of services was a distance-reducing intervention with the intent of putting into practice a political rhetoric of sameness as victims of dominant economic and political systems. Thus, rations simultaneously produced similarity among recipients while crafting difference with other Palestinians and the local Lebanese population.

The meaning of rations should be seen in a historical light. Grudgingly accepted in the 1950s and 1960s, by the resistance era rations were less resonant as a symbol of exile and dependency. For many families, an enhanced standard of living had reduced their reliance on rations. With remittances from abroad and employment in a local economy dominated by the PLO, incomes rose enough that rations were no longer a necessity. Later, with the demise of the resistance movement and the ensuing poverty, rations were once again precious items. As a symbol of international recognition and commitment, hints of cuts in services have been met with loud protest. Thus, in the refugee imagination, rations were, and still are, indelibly linked to political projects of containment.

Returning to the argument that the aid apparatus constructs a universal humanitarian subject and, in "abstracting their predicaments from specific political, historical, and cultural contexts humanitarian practices tend to silence refugees" (Malkki 1996: 378), the Palestinian case underscores the cross-cultural, historical, and political variability of the meaning and effects of aid. Palestinian voices were disqualified or marginalized less by aid regimes and more by the silencing impulses of U.S. and Israeli diplomatic and scholarly communities. In this particular instance, UNRWA did not silence the refugees; indeed, it endowed them with legal status and representation in the international arena. Palestinian identity documents are issued by the Lebanese Ministry of Interior Office of Palestinian Affairs based on records maintained by UNRWA and are the only official identity documents the refugees possess. Refugees take possession of their identity cards through UNRWA offices. If UNRWA were to cease operations, Lebanon could deny the refugees a legal identity and residency. Moreover, to Palestinians, UNRWA registration is proof on the international stage of their existence and their origins in Palestine.

Between 1948 and the rise of the PLO, UNRWA was practically the only organization keeping alive the refugee issue on the international diplomatic scene. Palestinian leaders were publicly critical of the mid-1990s transfer of UNRWA headquarters from Vienna to the Gaza Strip. Faruq Qaddumi, head of the PLO Political Department and Palestine Foreign Minister, said: "it was a mistake to transfer the agency's headquarters to Gaza. . . . The headquarters is supposed to remain abroad to continue to get international attention."[53] In their eyes, such a move diminished the international visibility of and commitment to the refugee issue.

Refugees often do contest aid regimes while simultaneously partaking of their transformatory projects. Indeed, the refugees themselves incorporated the aid regime into daily camp life, its social structure and relations, and its political configurations, and tried to appropriate it where feasible. Their dependence precluded struggle against aid as a technique of resistance, but they certainly did try to manipulate it to their advantage in small-scale ways such as cheating on the numbers and retaining UNRWA registration even if they held citizenship.

Refugee/aid regime relations were further complicated when the majority of staff were refugees. As the largest employer of refugees in Lebanon, UNRWA generated a patron-refugee system of accessing resources and services. While the higher level positions were held by foreigners, and policy was made elsewhere, the refugee employees were integral components of the quotidian administration and provision of services. Thus to cast this refugee/relief institution relationship into one of categories of imposition and resistance is neither credible nor fruitful. The mass employment of refugees by UNRWA blurred the line between aid workers and refugees, as did the later affiliation of substantial numbers of UNRWA workers with the resistance movement. The situation became even more complex and tenuous when the resistance movement initiated mass mobilization in the camps. As UN staff, refugees were not allowed to join political organizations, nor were UN provisions to be supplied to refugees who belonged to the Palestine Liberation Army. This probably unavoidable commingling of political activists with UNRWA staff aroused the ire of Israel and the U.S. The empowerment and militarization of camps in Lebanon during the late 1960s and 1970s and the PLO UN observer status muted accusations and the consequences of local UNRWA staff involvement in political activism. A modus vivendi was achieved due, in large part, to the PLO's superiority in arms and its recognition and appreciation of the role of UNRWA in daily refugee life, particularly education. The PLO and UNRWA cooperated in numerous areas. The PLO provided security and access to the camps during the civil war in Lebanon. The two cooperated to maintain services in the camps and the PLO lobbied the Arab states for increased contributions (See Schiff 1995: 100–109; Viorst 1984: 24–25).

The giving and receiving of rations fostered a set of paradoxes. Some refugees, especially those classified as "hardship" cases such as widows without means of support, were in the post-1982 period once again precariously dependent on rations to survive, but their potency was as a political symbol. For most, it means continued recognition of their refugee status and the rights that accrue to it and the international community's commitment to them, however ambiguous.

UNRWA also was heavily involved in the health arena. Techniques of biopower encompassing nutritional and hygienic interventions became integral to the school day routine. Rafiq recalled this aspect of school life:

Every day we followed the same routine. The home-room teacher would come and inspect us, just like in the army. They inspected: our hair, to make sure it is well combed, our clothes, to make sure they are tidy and not dirty, not too dirty, at least, because we used to wear our clothes for many, many days before we washed them. We had our heads inspected every morning for scabies. Boys had to shave their heads to prevent lice and scabies from spreading. Those found with either had their heads shaved and painted with a purple or green ultra-violet gelatin. Their heads glittered in the sun! Most importantly, they checked to see if we had our handkerchief and that our nails were trimmed and clean. We had to put out our hands, holding the handkerchief in both hands, with palm downward, so your teacher, who was carrying a wooden stick, could see your fingernails. With fingers outstretched, our hands were inspected for cleanliness. Those found not to have cleaned their hands and nails properly were punished with a slap across the knuckles with a ruler. We always made sure our handkerchief was clean—the fear of being hit with the ruler made us comply with this morning routine.

The teachers also made us swallow a cod liver oil capsule each morning. We hated it because if it broke it tasted absolutely foul. Many of us would try to avoid taking it by throwing it over our shoulders instead of into our mouths.

My first memories of milk are of UNRWA milk. In the morning we had to drink a cup of milk. They served it to us in a tin cup, like army cups. We had to pick up a cup or someone would hand us one and then stand in line. Oddly they distributed the milk next to the restrooms. Why? Because of the water supply. They would dump the milk powder in these big barrels, pour the water from the hose, and stir it. So we would line up, get our cups and drink that milk. My memory of that milk is that it was horrible, so awful! We would try to find ways to get rid of it without having our teachers notice. Naturally the teachers wanted to make sure we drank it because it was good for our health. Anyway, we devised all sorts of ways to avoid drinking it. We would watch to see if the teachers were watching us. If they were not—if they were busy, we would go and pour the milk in the sink, wash our cup quickly and say we drank it. Or you took the first sip and made sure that your lips were all milky as an indication you were drinking, and then you managed to spill it or pour it out somewhere and then wash the cup. But most of the time, guess what?—we had to drink it. Our tricks didn't always work, because you were being watched and maybe you could get away with it once or twice, but most of the time, most of the students ended up drinking that milk.

Driven by the same impulse—to make the camps orderly and hygienic sites for governing and transforming the aggregate displaced body—other techniques included public health campaigns, mass immunizations, supplemental feedings at schools and UNRWA stations, and delousings. Those who attended UNRWA schools in the 1950s and 1960s remembered the UNRWA clinic staff coming to school on appointed days and administering the required childhood vaccinations. Most camps were sprayed with DDT to prevent the spread of malaria. Children's heads were painted with purple gelatin to prevent infection from lice or scabies. Rafiq's friend Hassan, who had resided in Nabatiyyeh camp as a child, vividly remembers when he was painted: "That purple gelatin was painted on my shaved head several times at school. They did it quickly and sloppily so that beads of it ran down my neck, turning a brassy color as it slid further and further down my body. It would take weeks to wear off! We felt like cattle who were painted—this reduced us to a low status, it marked us in a way like an animal. It was humiliating."

Health education occurred at the intersection of transformations of aggregate and individual behavior. Colorful public health posters, a central technique in rendering the camps hygienic spaces, reminded people to take children for checkups and supplemental feedings if necessary. Invariably, refugees recall the UNRWA latrines installed at selected points in the camps. Hassan said emphatically:

We detested them because they were so smelly and full of big black flies that buzzed around you relentlessly. Worst of all, the stalls were open—there were not doors on them. So we had no privacy. We preferred the open fields. It was much cleaner and there was not that horrible smell. They had to have a campaign to get people to use the latrines. I remember a poster about defecation in Nabatiyyeh camp; it read "Defecation in open areas is disgraceful and harmful." I wasn't quite sure what the word "defecation" meant, but I grasped the meaning through the series of sketches encouraging us to make use of the latrines and avoid relieving ourselves in nearby fields.

In short, they were telling us our old way of defecating, in fields where we and our families had worked, was no good. They implied we were dirty. Moreover, these posters used a classical Arabic that we children couldn't easily understand. Our parents, who were uneducated, certainly could not make sense of these posters! I wondered what each word meant. It was a learning experience—like learning a foreign language.

When I would run home to relieve myself—small children often would have a little pot at home they could use—my parents would make fun of me, saying "Why don't you just go where you are playing? Why do you run from the fields just to use a pot?" Eventually we all started using those detested latrines because of the increasing lack of open space around the camps and the overcrowding inside them. There were fewer and fewer private places.

Education and Work

"After years of hopelessness and despair, about 6,000 refugees . . . were given something to live for and skills which restored their self-respect by making them useful and productive members of society."[54] This statement in reference to a vocational training project in the 1950s invoked its transformative properties. The future comes into vision, pathology wanes, and the reconstituted refugee emerges as a productive member of society. Projects to form industrious and self-respecting refugees were the starting point for rehabilitation and resettlement.

Both work and education projects were intended to transform the refugees into mobile workers. Gaza was not targeted for large-scale works projects by UNRWA. Economically marginal and nearly devoid of natural resources, it was deemed a disaster area from which the refugees were to be moved. Indeed, one consultant's report "Stressed the importance of projects not being developed which would tend to identify them [the refugees] permanently with the Gaza area."[55] The Friends did not engage in large-scale work projects, in part, because of ambiguity about the future. As their reports and correspondence indicate, they wondered if there would be a return or a resettlement. In the meantime, the demands for relief were overwhelming. In spite of uncertainty, the Friends set up carpentry and weaving workshops to train people in new skills and provide needed items to the refugees. Even if they did return home, new skills would be needed to cope with landlessness and a new economy.

UNRWA embarked on a long-term project to enable refugees to support themselves and form a mobile regional labor force. They shifted resources away from relief and into rehabilitation and education. They did so through a well-regarded educational system that had strong vocational and academic components. In Lebanon, UNRWA's Siblin Vocational Training Center opened near Saida in the early 1960s and trained a generation of skilled workers, many of whom subsequently worked in the oil producing states. The calamitous events of the summer of 1982 illuminated the way the Palestinian community attempted to make such institutions their own and bend them to their own agenda. After Israel invaded Lebanon in June 1982, "Siblin" was added to the rhetoric of Palestinian space as a domain of terror which, logically, made it a legitimate target of military attack. The Israeli claim that it has been taken over by PLO military forces (see Schiff 1995: 105–9) included accusations that weapons were stored and serviced at the site and young men were forced to undergo military training after vocational classes. In short, it was accused of violating the rule of separation between UN facilities, employment, and political activities. Widely aired in the local and U.S. media, this bolstered the image of Palestinians as ungrateful terrorist-refugees who had duped the UN.

In gendering the rehabilitation project, men and boys were directed to vocational training, while girls and women were encouraged to expand their knowledge and skills in domesticity, particularly childrearing, food preparation, and dietary management. The Family Service Centers (FSC) run by the Near East Ecumenical Committee for Palestine Refugees in Lebanon focused on homemaking practices. In other areas such as the West Bank, Gaza, and Jordan, the FSC integrated health and domesticity. After initially providing direct relief, their stated goal became "rehabilitation" in which education was to be "essential . . . dedicated to the task of helping individuals learn better those behavioral patterns and skills that will enable them to fulfill effectively their roles as family and community members" (Khuri-Otaqui 1971: 1–2).

Domestic competence is foundational to self and collective definitions of Palestinian femininity. The newly emerging domesticity was based on scientific principles of hygiene and nutrition, and FSC courses were part of an integrated approach to community development which would help "improve their lives and their home conditions" (23). An explicit subtext of morality pervaded their projects, which were described as "indirect preventives against juvenile delinquency . . . particularly . . . where the temptations for young girls, especially when poor and needy, are many" (25). Just as significantly, well-maintained and clean refuges were disciplined, managed, and consequently deserving.

Education was profoundly transformative for the refugee community, reconfiguring gender, class, and generational orders. UNRWA established free elementary and middle schools in most camps in the early 1950s, a compelling factor in encouraging many families who were still in temporary living situations in towns and villages to move to the camps. Mass education affected every area of daily life, from gender relations to the organization of domestic routines to subjectivity and identity. In Mandate Palestine, the Arab educational system was under the authority of the British administration (the Jewish Agency administered Jewish education). The British were less concerned with educating the masses and more with the "production of a small elite to man the administrative system" (Abu-Lughod 1973: 103) and thus concentrated educational facilities in urban areas. Secular education for the rural population was still embryonic.[56] As landlessness intensified and Palestine was increasingly drawn into the international economy, demand for secular education intensified.

UNRWA schooling differed markedly from the village religious schools (*kuttab*) where the previous generation of rural men had learned to read and write. A standardized curriculum with examinations to ascertain learning, an array of subject matter and texts, secular rather than sacred knowledge and sources of authority, multiple lay teachers whose abilities established the foundations of respect and authority based on modern secular knowledge, and foreign language instruction introduced students to a new world of knowledge, attitudes, and pedagogical practices. As is often the case, the intended outcome, the educated, mobile Palestinian amenable to assimilation, had unforeseen consequences. Refugees found in secular education the means to transmit a Palestinian national identity, and UNRWA inadvertently prepared a generation of educated youth for secular, militant nationalist activities.

With parents eager for their sons to acquire an education, male attendance was high. For the first time, however, Palestinian girls had equity in access to education and parents fairly quickly seized the opportunity. By the mid-1960s it was common to find young girls attending elementary school. While their enrollments lagged behind the boys, the gap was slowly closing.[57] In families where the grandmother and mother were illiterate, girls have often graduated from high school and some have gone on to university. Enabled by education, they sought employment and joined the ranks of political movements.

Education transformed Palestinian subjectivity in profound ways. The story of Abu Nabil's sister captures the emergence of a modern subjectivity strongly shaped by education. His family had lived in Burj al Barajneh since the early 1950s. His sister Fadia had always been an excellent student. After finishing UNRWA middle school and completing her studies in a private Lebanese high school, she took advantage of a PLO scholarship to attend medical school in Russia. While there, she met and fell in love with a Lebanese Christian student. They decided to marry upon their return to Lebanon. Her five brothers were fairly supportive, although her mother threatened to disown her. Marriages of Muslim women to Christian men were very rare and any intimations were usually met with swift familial intervention. With her father deceased, it fell to her brothers and her mother to handle the situation. Her mother repeatedly pleaded with her sons to intervene actively to stop the marriage, pointing out that it was their duty to act as guardians for their sister. They did not feel compelled to do so. I listened as Abu Nabil explained vehemently to his mother: "We—all of us—agreed to her education, to her pursuing a medical degree. We sent her abroad to study. She is now twenty-seven years old. You think we can suddenly tell her who she can marry!? We can't do that. We made a choice. We can't go back to the traditional way of doing things with her. It's either that way or this way—where she chooses whom to marry." She married and her mother didn't speak to her for several years, although gradually the ice was broken and family relations were mended.

As this story indicates, individuals developed a sense of the possibility of choices in their lives and the fragility of family authority. Refugee life, with its constraints and yet possibilities, effected how people thought about their lives. Abu Nabil's argument drew upon a pronounced contrast between the present and the past. The sister's plan of action enacted a new sense of possibility in individual choice and a rejection of her parents' ways of doing things.

The new educational system enabled another unforeseen and unintended consequence. The construction of masculinity, once referenced to physical strength and the ability to know when to deploy it, the skill of forging alliances, and the attributes of generosity and piety, and their associated patterns of respect and deference, were challenged by secular education and the values and skills it imparted. Secular education introduced a critical awareness often underdeveloped in religious education. Personal attributes and experience remained influential in constructing masculinity and its privileges, but modern forms of knowledge and training and foreign language skills assumed a new saliency.[58] It was possible for secularly educated men to attain the respect formerly accorded older men. They mediated between the family and increasingly complex bureaucracies which required literacy and a knowledge of organizational structures and methods of operation. Their employment prospects and income-generating potential differed vastly from that of their fathers. Secular education prepared the way for the emergence of the resistance movement in the camps.

With mass schooling, particularly of elementary age children, women's daily routine began to revolve around the school schedule. In pre-1948 Palestine, women's time had been organized around agricultural labor and the production of consumable foodstuffs and household management and childrearing. The daily routine followed a pattern set by the seasons, the demands of agriculture, and infant care. Preparing children for school was another chore added to their daily agenda. Older daughters were called on to help in the preparations, which sometimes had the effect of reducing their time for school. Rafiq recalled of the early years of UNWRA schooling: "My eldest sister, she's four years older—was a student in the same school. Because she was a girl, however, and an older girl at that, at least for my younger brothers and me she was in charge of getting us ready. My mother would have been up since 5:00 A.M. to bake bread so my sister had to make sure we put on our clothes, combed our hair properly, and washed our faces. In addition, she would help my mother fix breakfast. Mainly we ate za'ter (thyme) and tea. Sometimes we would eat labneh (strained yoghurt). We ate very quickly and were off to school. Now, my sister would wait until we were all ready and then she would get herself ready." Women's daily routines were now heavily shaped by schooling. In addition, mass education's temporal rhythms reaffirmed and reproduced gendered inequality. Mothers drew upon elder daughters' labor to meet the needs of the younger children for an education.

Tensions over curriculum surfaced in Palestinian-UNRWA relations.

Rather than a Palestinian oriented or designed curriculum, UNRWA schools adopted the curriculum of the host countries. Refugees resented the sidelining of Palestinian history, geography, and social studies. What transpired was a pedagogical process with unintended consequences. Eickleman suggests that "the forms of knowledge shaped and conveyed in educational systems" are "to be considered in relation to the social distribution of power" (1978: 496). With Palestinians unable to determine their own curriculum it became an implicit and explicit site of contestation. At the risk of losing their jobs, Palestinian teachers smuggled in Palestinian history, geography, and a national narrative. Rafiq commented that

> In the curriculum, there was no political education and yet the teachers managed to slip in all sorts of information about our cause, what had happened, how it had happened, what the Israelis did, and what the Arab governments did. So we were always fed this information unofficially; it wasn't part of the curriculum. Yet this was a chance to learn it. There was continuous talk about the "situation." As if it were a class that wasn't in the curriculum but you were getting an education about it. On national occasions, like the Partition of Palestine and the Balfour Declaration Day, the teachers were not supposed to do anything, otherwise they would be suspended. Yet they managed to make sure that the students were aware so that they would do something on their own to commemorate the day.

The Lebanese authorities monitored the political activity of UNRWA teachers. In a sense, UNRWA was the space in which a contest was played out between aspiring political activists and the Lebanese authorities. Many UNRWA teachers were active in underground nationalist organizations and later in PLO groups. Conflict arose when they sought to introduce Palestinian national and political issues in the classroom. Some students recall that their teachers, particularly in the era before the resistance, tried to encourage students to raise national issues in the classroom and to take the initiative in organizing strikes and demonstrations. The Lebanese authorities attempted to recruit or intimidate the teachers to provide information on their colleagues' and students' political ideas and involvement.

Education is the one area where ambiguity in attitudes toward UNRWA was minimal until recently. Palestinians were quick to acknowledge its role in providing a solid, well-respected education to a generation of refugees. Today, parents speak nostalgically of the schools of their youth, with their rigorous educational standards. As the first generation of refugees to excel in school, they lament the current situation in which schools are overcrowded, lack financial resources, and are faced with traumatized and impoverished students.

Conclusion

In the 1990s, graphic media footage of refugees in Bosnia, Rwanda, and Kosovo was viewed on TV in the camps. Expressions of empathy—"Ya haram" (how sad or what a pity), "nas meskeen" (poor people), and "God help them" punctuated the viewing and brought forth poignant reflections on collective memories of *al-nakbah*. UNRWA's name was invoked as having saved them from what others were suffering: hunger, thirst, and trauma. "Without UNRWA—we would have suffered what other refugees suffer. UNRWA helped us survive and educated us," uttered Um Khalid's eldest daughter while watching the news. UNRWA, like the camps, is and is not Palestinian space.

Constructing a newly tooled, modern, and mobile subject was a project of modernity closely aligned with the settler-colonial project in Palestine. Criticism and skepticism of UNRWA circulated easily with a grudging recognition of its accomplishments. On the one hand, there was a ready appreciation of its enabling role in educating a generation that participated actively in the resistance movement and its institution-building sector. On the other hand, conflicted attitudes towards UNRWA were inevitable. The UN partitioned Palestine, granted recognition to Israel, and adopted UN General Assembly Resolution 194 of 11 December 1948, which calls for return or compensation. Thus the UN played a paramount role in both their displacement and survival while also validating their national claims in the international arena. UNRWA regulated their daily lives while providing new forms of knowledge and institutions. Forms of modernity ushered in by aid regimes constructed new subjects in a double sense. As an international body, UNRWA, along with host governments, spatially constrained the refugees and constituted them as international recipients of limited resources, in effect, maintaining them in a liminal national state where they lacked citizenship. Yet aid introduced new forms of knowledge and organization that enabled refugees to organize and participate in a militant national movement. Paradoxically, the purpose of aid in rehabilitating and constructing an object of intervention and transformation was reinscribed locally into practices and ideas of resistance.

In the discourse of aid, the refugee is a silent subject, an object of intervention materially, physically, and psychologically. In historical documents and press reports from the time, the voice of the Palestinian refugee is conspicuously missing. They were "ragged hordes," "susceptible to every agitation," their camps "a reservoir of smoldering antagonisms"—a mass of human suffering, stripped down to those human essences of the need for food and shelter and the emotion of hate (Stevens 1952: 281–82).[59]

Aid institutions transmitted more than relief. They initiated a series of developments—new forms of organizing and new educational institutions, curriculum, and practices that challenged traditional forms of knowledge and their transmission and an aged and gendered authority structure. The refugees were neither rehabilitated nor resettled. Most important, they did not forget.

Palestinians once tended to see foreign aid workers and their projects through a lens of suspicion. However well designed to meet refugee needs, there was a fear they were integral to a larger political agenda of resettlement and denativization. One could convincingly argue that they were not always off the mark. Rehabilitation was geared to resettlement or local integration.

Yet in Lebanon, refugees have inextricably linked their fate with that of UNRWA. A cessation of operations would signal the end of the refugee problem which is at the heart of the Palestinian political cause. Its demise would nullify their rights as refugees, another instance of the kind of linkages their world view is made of.

The next three chapters take up the issue of place, violence, and identity. They elaborate the process, linked to levels and forms of externally imposed violence, by which the refugees made camp spaces their own. They became zones of militancy and nationalist political expression and organizing where new types of identity were forged and enacted.

Chapter Four
Producing Place, Spatializing Identity, 1948–68

Why then should those whom the waves of forgetfulness have cast upon the shores of Beirut be expected to go against nature? Why should so much amnesia be expected of them? And who can construct for them a new memory with no content other than the broken shadow of a distant life in a shack made of sheet metal?
—Mahmud Darwish (1995: 15)

When I returned to Beirut in the early 1990s after a hiatus of nearly ten years, the contrast with Shatila camp in the 1970s and early 1980s was stunning. A once vibrant, jam-packed camp with a fairly decent standard of living was now a debris-encircled, rubble-filled, geosocially isolated, and poverty-stricken patch of land. The historicity of space, as well as its violently contested nature, was tangibly inscribed in the new perimeters and devastated interior. While the relationship between space and society, between spatial forms and power, and the role of history and social institutions in the built environment is theoretically developed, "concrete data are often missing" (Low and Lawrence 1990: 455–56). In the remaining chapters, I illustrate the social production of place, that is, how it is given meaning and definition by the regular, patterned activities and social relationships that unfold in it and the cultural rules governing them. Place must also be juxtaposed to the space surrounding it, the exterior from which it is distinguished by its social landscape, the activities in it, and the meanings they generate. The relationship between place and identity is one of mutual interaction within a field of power, external and internal, that limits as well as shapes possibilities for both. Thus the social activity that produces locality is "not only context-driven but also context-generative" (Appadurai 1996: 186).

Producing Place

Multiple contexts are involved in the production of a refugee camp, and they themselves generate ever mutating contexts in their local, regional, and global environments. As localities, they are produced by and productive of everyday social relations and practices. Yet a qualitative difference distinguishes camps from other places; they are products of violent discursive and spatial practices that accompany displacement and attempts at denationalization.

Previous chapters elaborated how the Palestinian refugee as a category was produced by exclusivist ethnoreligious state formation and the imposition of a bureaucratic-administrative regime. Although repressive, the spatial device of the camp simultaneously engendered transformations in Palestinian community and identity. Displacement is profoundly paradoxical, giving rise to productive permutations but also to terrible mutations. Refugees creatively imposed their own imprint on the space and meaning of the camps in ways which, if not oppositional to the apparatus of control, at least served as obstacles to its full realization. In their stark and bounded physical form, they symbolized colossal loss and defeat, but they also became a potent political field in which to organize and express national identity and sentiment. In the process of crafting places, identity stood as a point of departure and yet itself was transformed. In the national narrative and imagination, these tragic symbols of loss, victimhood, and dependency eventually served as a counter-image epitomized in *al-fidaʾiyyin* (the guerrillas), fondly referred to as "sons of the camps."

A protracted refugee situation allows for a longitudinal perspective and brings into focus refugees' response to the spatial practices that constrain and enable them. A more expansive frame comprises the spatiality of the camps and their bureaucracies, refugee agency, expressed in their spatial practices and their social relations and activities, regional and global arrangements of power, the host government and populace, the institutions and practices of the resistance movement, and representations of the camps and refugees. A multifaceted framework renders a complex portrayal of the constitution of place, the refugee, and community and lays the spatial and material foundations for an elaboration of Palestinian identity.

Palestinians have a conscious and profoundly political sense of place. Through culturally grounded practices of ordinary living, they imposed their social organization and cultural maps on the camps, thus crafting particular, meaningful places at odds with yet accommodating of their original intent. The social activities and relationships enacted in them and the organizing and naming of units of space produced place, attesting to the remarkable human capacity to create new cultural and social forms of daily life in the face of monumental loss. These landscapes of despair are spaces of bereavement for the loss of the homeland over five decades ago. Organizing and naming camp space by village crafted both a memoryscape and a practical spatial enactment of the lost homeland. Designed as transit centers to prepare refugees for local integration, Palestinian camps instead became oppositional spaces appropriated and endowed with alternative meanings. Spatially, few camps were organized in an easily discernible order, characteristic of urban planning and modern camps and conducive to mass management. Instead, like medieval cities, they resembled a maze, a series of winding alleyways and unexpected dead ends, interspersed by occasional nodes. This can be tracked to human settlement patterns, as most camps were settled in fits and starts as families staked a spot and set up their tents. However, there were a few neatly arranged barrack style camps such as Nabatiyyeh in South Lebanon, which was designed for refugees who were then called to come settle in it. In Lebanon, not only were camps not consistently sites of incarceration or the normalizing effects of disciplinary regimes, but for a significant period of time they were controlled, patrolled, and administered by an armed resistance movement.[1] The militant Palestinian identity fomented in them asserted that defeat, loss, and bereavement did not mark the end of a process but rather were a spur to action.

Shifting spatial practices and expressions of identity encode fifty years of refugee history. Rapid and violent rearrangements in camp borders, scale, and control accompanied shifts in the organization and assertion of power between refugees and host. This raises multiple questions of periodization and identity. How do we define the outer limits of a period? How is it articulated to place and identity? Do spatial organization and practices which constitute place also demarcate historical periods?

Local Palestinian periodization articulates with the camps' shifting borders, the kinds of social relations they contained, and the identities that took hold. Rapid rearrangements in scale, whether externally or internally generated, signaled shifts in the empowerment of the refugee community vis-à-vis the host. Thus the invisibility characteristic of the 1950s and 1960s gave way to hypervisibility as Palestinians transformed the camps into autonomous and militant spaces. Eventually they reverted to spaces of reincarceration in the 1980s and 1990s. Refugees narrated and organized their life stories around fairly standard temporal markers. Shared lexical references were indicative of a division of time which articulated with spatiality and identity. The terms *jeel* (generation) and *'ayyam* (days) embody time, place, experience, and identity. Generations were marked by particular temporal events. Experiences imprinted

Figure 8. Interior alleyway, Burj al-Barajneh camp. Julie Peteet.

Figure 9. Woman standing near drinking water tank, Burj al-Barajneh camp.
Julie Peteet.

characteristics and identity on a generation and behavior was often referenced to them. For example, mothers attributed their children's naughty behavior to 'ayyam al-harb (days of war) when domestic and schooling routines were severely disrupted.

The jeel filasteen (generation of Palestine) were those elderly people who remembered 'ayyam filasteen (days of Palestine) and endured the disaster of 1948. The jeel al-nakbah (generation of the disaster) overlaps with the jeel filasteen. The 'ayyam al-UNRWA (days of UNRWA) refers to the 1950s when it became a pervasive feature in everyday life. For some, it evoked years of dependency and humiliation. As Abu Fadi put it sardonically, "Those were the days when they gave us crumbs [rations] to make us forget." Yet it simultaneously connoted the then young generation, the first to have been born and raised as refugees, who were indelibly marked by their UNRWA education.

In 1968–69, the resistance movement ushered in the 'ayyam al-thawra (days of the revolution), setting the stage for the jeel al-thawra (generation of the revolution). From the vantage point of the present, both 'ayyam al-UNRWA and 'ayyam al-thawra are remembered nostalgically. The jeel al-thawra experienced first-hand the exuberant days of the resistance when hope was palpable and a future seemed possible. In the immediate wake of the 1982 invasion and decimation of the social safety net, older women from the jeel al-nakbah were not always sympathetic to younger women and their difficulties coping with the absence of a network of services. Like many older women, Um Khalid's elderly aunts and their friends quickly noted that the jeel al-thawra were unskilled in making do with scarce resources and navigating for meager services; they had honed their skills at this after 1948. The jeel al-harb (generation of war), raised in the post-1982 period, 'ayyam al-harb, have known little aside from sieges, assaults, high levels of poverty, and officially sanctioned discrimination. The days when the camps were autonomous and bustling with politically assertive Palestinians are unknown to them except in the stories they have heard.

The activity of placemaking, carving out definable, identifiable, and meaningful domains, engendered difference with an other, sketching communal identities in spatial form and grounding them in daily materiality. The difference between refugee and host, and the power it entailed, radically fluctuated in kind and intensity, affecting the meaning of camps as particular kinds of places. Gupta and Ferguson's assertion that identities are a "mobile, often unstable relation of difference" is particularly salient among refugees (1997: 13). This "mobility" was heightened and relations of difference were markedly unstable, oscillating dramatically between everyday Lebanese-Palestinian friendships and proclamations of "There are no differences between us!" to murderous assaults in which each attributed to the other almost "species-specific" characteristics. Both engaged in an at times murderous dance of difference as the spatial terrain was mapped and contested and cross-spatial mobility was deemed transgressive.

Identity

In anthropology, the notion of "rooted" or fixed identities has given way to a more elaborate and fluid portrait of identities as embedded in matrixes of mutually constitutive strands. Identity is apt to be conceptualized as an always-in-formation cultural product of sociospatial location and practices within a field of power. The parameters of Palestinian identities can be located in historical frameworks of power that operate in and through the articulation of multiple sites, institutions, discursive formations, and social experiences and practices. These include the legal and military power of host states and international bodies with their capacity to impose internationally recognized and legitimized identities.

Within this conceptualization, there is room for the rather standard approach that pinpoints common origins, a territory, a shared sense of history, and a putative set of cultural attributes. Although not fixed in time or place, identities do have geocultural points of origin from which subsequent reformulations can be launched. Although they are not already constituted categories of analysis or ways of being in the world, neither are they completely detached from a past. For Palestinians, location has been a beginning, not necessarily an end. Palestinian identity was more oriented to constituting a future than to recovering a past; it was a process of becoming rather than simply of being.

Common denominators in denoting contemporary Palestinian identity in Lebanon were origin in and continuing attachment to the space and particular places of Palestine, the collective loss and trauma of exile, a keen sense of injustice, Palestinian nationalism and militancy, and the imagining of a future return. The contours of their interaction with the host Lebanese also endowed Palestinian identity with the specificities of place, otherness, and power as did the collective experience of UNRWA institutions. In the post-1982 period, marginalization and the fear of transfer, along with a sense of abandonment by the Palestinian political body, should be added to the identity equation.

Identities were embedded in three broad sets of phenomena. First, the refugees were from Palestine and nowhere else. Violent displacement followed by the vigorous denial of a Palestinian national identity launched the objectification of their identities. To be a Palestinian was now freighted with insecurity, contingency, and the fear of invisibility.

The second set was constituted by the social and cultural crafting of place in the camps. Third, the militant anticolonial political activities that unfolded in these places were productive of identities.

In the atmosphere of displacement and camp life, the relationship between place and identity was mutually constitutive. Identities and affiliations, belonging to a particular group whether family or village, nuanced the process by which camps became places of attachment and identification. In turn, these identities were profoundly transformed by life in these bounded spaces. Displacement and subsequent confinement generated resistance, which then reshaped both these places and identity. This suggests that local identities should not be seen solely through the lens of derivativeness, contingency, and spatial location. By imposing their own sense of spatiality on the camps, crafting a microcosm of the Galilee, they subverted the denativizing intent of respatialization and a legally imposed refugee identity.

The spatial arena figured prominently in the constitution of identity. The camps were akin to a borderland: "a territory defined by a geopolitical line: two sides arbitrarily separated and policed but also joined by legal and illegal practices of crossing and communication" (Clifford 1994: 304). At these places where two cultures rubbed up against each other, refugees reassembled ideas and practices of self and community. To understand identity formation and (re)formation requires zooming in on the intersections of time and space, of past and present, homeland and exile.

A five-foot high, neon green cement mini-obelisk topped with the Palestinian flag indicated the checkpoint to enter or exit 'Ayn al-Hilweh camp. A wooden map of Palestine, on which was roughly painted the Dome of the Rock, was affixed on its front. These potent national symbols, map, flag, and sacred space asserted the presence of Palestine in exilic space. For refugees, place was a lived experience carried from one site to another. As it traveled, home intersected with these new places, nuancing identity along the way. Palestinian identity remained territorialized in a world on the move, but in complex ways. It remained intimately connected to, but not confined by multiple places. Grounded in specific villages and regions or cities, it was deterritorialized and reterritorialized moving from points of departure through a trajectory of places and times manifested in the terms *jeel* (generation) and *'ayyam* (days). It was akin to Anzaldúa's statement that "in leaving home I did not lose touch with my origins because *lo mexicano* is in my system. I am a turtle, wherever I go I carry 'home' on my back" (1987: 21). Memory and identity were thus multisited, shifting uneasily between the original village and a trajectory of exilic places, expressed in nostalgia for the homeland, both actual and imagined, as well as particular places of exile. Abu and Um Sabri, new friends of Um Khalid's who had moved into a newly constructed building in Shatila for displaced refugees, wistfully reminisced about the "good days" in Tel al-Zaʿter "when the camp was like a big village, not like Shatila with all these strangers. People used to know one another, know where they came from." Those who survived Tel al-Zaʿter were still known, nearly twenty years later, as "Tel al-Zaʿter" people. Their new building was popularly referred to as the "Zaʿter building." Thus identity formation was multisited, mobile, and dialogic. Experiences such as *al-nakbah* or the camp wars imprinted identity on a generation, endowing it with a shared narrative. These multiple geopolitical sites meant that the process of identity formation had important local qualitites. Palestinians refer to the "Palestinians of Syria," or the "Palestinians of Kuwait," categories of place and experience. These mappings, with their sociopolitical and legal ramifications, structured experience and subjectivity. Host country policies towards the refugees were variable. For example, Jordan gave Palestinians citizenship but clamped down violently on political organizing. Syria offered a number of civil rights, such as the right to be employed, but tightly controlled, severely suppressed, and manipulated Palestinian political organizing.

For a refugee, identity had its point of departure in specific places. Villages were contemporary sociospatial referents. A group of ten to twelve boisterous young boys were following me in ʿAyn al-Hilweh while I was taking photographs. To initiate conversation, I asked where they were from and they replied, nearly in unison, "We are from al-Bassa." Turning and pointing to a little boy with a sheepish grin on his face, they laughingly shouted, "He's from Ras al-ʾAhmar." Three or four generations removed from direct experience of the homeland, the children's cognitive map of their location in the world was a transposed Galilean landscape.

Difference and exclusion were critical in the formation of identity. Hall writes: "it is only through the relation to the Other, the relation to what it is not, to precisely what it lacks, to what has been called its *constitutive outside* that the 'positive' meaning of any term—and thus its 'identity'—can be constructed" (1996: 4–5). In other words, identity is positional, strategic, and relational (Hall 1996; Mouffe 1994), implying a relationship with an other. The "constitutive outside" was variously the Israelis, the Lebanese, the Arabs, and other Palestinians. Multiple others' strategic significance has been closely articulated to arrangements of power. For refugees, statelessness imbues everyday life and identity with a sense of absence and vulnerability, an acute lack of protection. In the world of nation states and their accouterments, such as passports, being without, so to speak, draws definite lines of inclusion and exclusion with perilous implications for opportunities and safety. One could reside in Lebanon but not belong to it. Notions of Arabness, or pan-Arab identity and belonging, further complicated the designation and elaboration of the other. Palestinian refugees were simultaneously inside and outside of multiple overlapping boundaries. Stateless, they had few legal rights. Yet pan-Arab ideology served as a form of pressure for their acceptance, however grudgingly.

Palestinian identity was further forged in the process of resisting displacement. It was more than a site of mobilization for social movement; it was itself interventionist in projects of domination and in the process was sustained, reaffirmed, and took on new contours. It was around this identity, whose relationship to place of origin was violently ruptured, that the resistance movement organized and mobilized, launching the reconfiguring of Palestinian identities.

At times, and under "certain circumstances," political but also intellectual, we can "risk essentialism" (Calhoun 1994: 17). Calhoun writes, "where a particular category of identity has been repressed, de-legitimated or devalued in dominant discourses, a vital response may be to claim value for all those labeled by that category, thus implicitly invoking it in an essentialist way" (17). Palestinian essentialism would hardly be surprising. Indeed it is precisely at the intersection between displacement from a homeland claimed exclusively by another and everyday life in refugee camps that contemporary Palestinian identity was taking shape. A continuous state of violence, modern structural, spatial, and disciplinary forms, always accompanied by brute force or the threat of it, and place emerged as defining factors in Palestinian identity. The paradox of exilic nationalism is that it runs the risk of transforming itself from a progressive anticolonial force into a narrowly conceived nationalism. Yet Palestinian nationalism has displayed the capacity for a progressive conception of a polity in its initial calls for a democratic, secular state of its citizens (Muslims, Christians, and Jews) in Palestine.

The next section and the remaining chapters set out the changes in camp spatialization and how refugees defined themselves against a backdrop of resistance and nationalism and vis-à-vis bureaucratic and administrative designations of them as "refugees." There was a distinct correspondence between spatiality, power relations, and identity. Identity was very caught up in spatial boundaries and the way they produced and were reproduced by relations of power and disempowerment.

Displacements

In Lebanon, Palestinian lives have been punctuated by persistent violence, uncertainty, and continuing displacement. After my initial visit to Um Muhammad, Um Khalid's friend who had just come back from a visit to Israel, I returned to her to talk about the places where she had lived. Her memory of a fifty-year trajectory involved the common pattern of repeated violence-driven mobility and an unpredictable future. After crossing the northern border in 1948, a few days were spent near Sour, a southern Lebanese town, and then her family (parents, brothers, sisters, paternal grandparents, and two unmarried paternal aunts) headed to the capital, eventually settling in Maslakh, a slum area near the Beirut port (razed by the Christian rightist forces in 1976).

We have a Lebanese branch in our family and we came to them. We built tin shacks in al-Maslakh and stayed there for around nine years. Then the government came and tore down the shacks. They drove us out! There were many people there—from Syria and other places who came to find work. The government said they were tearing down our houses because there was an outbreak of chicken pox. We were not sick but they said all Palestinians and all the others have to leave. We were forced out; we had no shelter, only the ground beneath us and the sky above us. It was raining hard by this time. We left our houses and went to the Karantina area. They put us in a place called al-Mkallas, in East Beirut. By then UNRWA and the Red Cross had built camps for Palestinians. So we were taken to one by the army. We stayed two months in very ugly conditions. Mud was all over the place. Our mattresses and our straw mats were full of mud. Then they moved us to Tel al-Zaʿter. We had to move into the tents of people who had moved into cement houses. The tents were full of holes, the ground was wet and everything was infested with ants and mosquitos. We could not sleep at night. We tried to clean with kerosene to burn out the bugs. Finally we went to the police station and told them we had no home, that the insects had invaded everything. The police came and checked it out and were surprised that other people had been able to live in these tents. They gave us a new tent. Eventually we built tin walls—the government did not allow us to build with stone—and spread the tent over the top to make a roof. We expanded the tin sheets as the family grew larger. We built a small room where my husband could make bitter coffee {bedouin coffee}. We stayed that way until the *fidaʾiyyin* came. Then we were free to build with stone. We paved the streets, and the camp became a much better place, clean with sewage facilities. It was a good time.

One day [1975] a *fidaʾiyyin* from Jordan was martyred and was being taken to Jordan through Syria. On the way, the funeral procession had to pass through al-Khahhaleh, a Christian town. For no reason, the Phalangists shot at the procession. A fight ensued. During the civil war, Syria joined forces with the Phalangists and besieged us in the camp. They slaughtered us like sheep. They would tie the men by their feet and drag them behind their jeeps, three or four at a time. They brought trucks and loaded us into them. They picked all the men and shot them to death. That is what they did to us—killed all the men.

After Tel al-Zaʿter fell [August 1976], we were taken by the resistance to Damur.[2] Every time a Muslim Lebanese or Palestinian passed through, they used to kill him. The *fidaʾiyyin* and the Lebanese progressive forces had attacked Damur and kicked out the Christians. The Christians took boats to Jounieh.[3] When we got to Damur, we found the houses were burnt and were without windows and doors. We covered them with plastic sheets and stayed there until the Israeli invasion of 1982. During the invasion everyone fled to Beirut. My husband, daughter, and I did not find a house in Ras Beirut so we went to the Horch area near ʿAkka Hospital [on the edge of Shatila]. When the Israelis came there that summer, they tried to be nice to people, talking nicely and giving the kids candy. Then the Phalangists came and started the massacre. They would go into one house and move on to the next and call out "Abu fulan (father of so-and-so), come out." They would ask for the names of his neighbors, kill the family, and move on. We were in Horch so we did not see anything directly, only the flares at night. They said people were being massacred but we would say that can't be. We did not hear much. The next morning, a little boy came to our door and told us all about it. We went to check it out at the hospital. There were foreign ['ajanib] doctors and nurses in 'Akka hospital. Suddenly we heard loudspeakers announcing that people should surrender and they would be safe. We were men, women, and children and we were lined up against a wall. An Israeli soldier came and said "All the Palestinian dogs line up on this side." The Palestinians did so. They separated us into Lebanese and Palestinians. It was Friday noon. They lined the men against the wall. They were all older men—seventy-five to eighty years old. No young men. They said to get into the jeeps. My husband had a kufiyyah on his head. He took it off and threw it in the street. He had a bag that contained his cigarettes. They took us to Bir Hassan. Everybody was marched—200–300 of us—over to a wall and lined up. An old man came and told the Israeli that his wife at home was paralyzed by a stroke and asked if he would let him go. He said "Okay, you can go." He walked away but before he could cross the street, they called him back. So he went back to the line. He told the soldier they had sent him back and the soldier said it was all right for him to go. This happened three or four times. The last time he came back, he stood by the wall away from the others. One soldier came up to him and asked why he was not standing with the others. He tried to explain that he wanted to go take care of his wife. The soldier banged his head against the wall.

They lined us up with the foreigners on a separate wall. Then they marched all of us, Lebanese and Palestinians, to the Sports Stadium. The line was encircled on all sides by soldiers. We walked through the area of the Kuwaiti Embassy. We heard sprays of shooting. I said "They killed all the men." They brought water tanks and offered us some. A young Israeli solider came and I asked him what had happened to the men. He did not understand what I was saying. He went and brought me a bottle of water. I asked a woman next to me to try again. She asked him what happened to the men who had been lined up against the wall. He asked us who had lined them up—the Jews or Haddad's men. She replied that Haddad's army did and he [Haddad] is with the Israelis. He said "We'll see, they just want to investigate them and then bring them back." They did not. They took them and we never saw them again. This is our story.

We have been in Shatila since 1982. I don't know what is going to happen to us. Where are they going to put us, throw us, I should say. God knows.

1948: Reterritorialization and New Landscapes

Um Fadi, Um Khalid's aunt from 'Ayn al-Hilweh, was visiting her family in Shatila. In a room crowded with nieces and nephews and their children, she told me and retold the second and third generations the story of their family's displacement and how they came to Lebanon from 'Akbarah and settled in 'Ayn al-Hilweh.

Israel came upon us in the early hours of dawn around the call to prayer. We were still asleep. It was raining very heavily. We were in your family's land in the upper west side of the village.[4] We had spread a quilt on an olive tree, but it had started leaking. We were sleeping there because we had heard the Jews were coming and we wanted to be able to escape quickly if they started shooting. Somebody said, "Let's go back home." Actually, the Jews were in the area but they had not started firing yet. It was still dark but we went home anyway. We hardly went to sleep when it all started. Bombs were exploding like light bulbs, the bullets were falling like rain! The Jews were very close to us. We left the house and headed to the fields hoping we could move under cover of the wheat. The old man [her husband] was tall and had a turban on his head. The Jews were already there by the road. I started shouting at him to lower his head. Your mother was carrying Samirah, Amira, and Taleb, and you were walking beside us. I was carrying Muhammad. I told Abu Fadi, "Are your going to take him or shall I throw him away!?" I was pregnant and I was afraid to carry him. So he told me "I'll carry him." We kept running and running until we were way outside the village. The Jews went into the village and started destroying the houses. We kept walking until we reached Bint Jbeil [in Lebanon]. By the time we arrived, our feet were swollen. We stayed without food for two or three days. We were starving.

We were planning to go back to our country. Five days later we started our journey back to 'Akbarah, our village. We reached a wilderness area in Lebanon. We stayed there for four or five days. Those who had money were able to buy food and eat. I had no money. The old man left to search for food. Suddenly, he showed up, with three donkeys loaded with food—flour, burghal, honey, milk, and yoghurt. One woman told me that all the women were with their people except me. I said I can't leave because of my son and she said I could leave him with her. So I had to go. I was so hungry and I had no money to buy anything. Your mother had money to buy herself food. So, with another woman who was alone, we followed the men. We called out to them. The old man started shouting obscenities at us, asking us where we were going walking alone in the wilderness. It was not the wilderness of our country, it was a wilderness we did not know. Anyway, we walked all the way from Lebanon back to Palestine. We reached 'Akbarah and the men started sneaking into the village to get food-stuffs—flour, eggs, chickens, vegetables, etc. My husband went back to Lebanon to take food to the son I had left there. His father then started insisting that I go to Lebanon again as well. I said, "I am not going back there! Why should I? Go back to hunger?!" The old man, with his bad temper, insisted I go. But I had been dying of hunger there! I said, "I don't want my son. Let him come here!" They gave me more food to eat. When I finished they put me on a horse. So I went back to Lebanon.

We spent three months in the wilderness. The water was so scarce. We had taken a few goats with us and your mother would take them one at a time to Horfeish to sell and buy food.

One day, your uncles came back and they told us to follow them on their way back in. We started running and running until we reached Sa'adeh. In Sa'adeh, there was a cave in the mountain. We kept walking to Meyron and then to Horch. Since we wanted to go to 'Akbarah, we sent one man ahead to view the village. He came back and said the Jews were in the area. My father said "You are seeing things out of fear. We will stand here and fire our rifles one time in their direction. If there are Jews there, they will return the fire. If not, you are a liar." There was no response to our gunfire so we went in.

There was a man walking by the spring. My father knew him from the village and called out "Are you a traitor?" He called out "No. We are looking for food. All we want is to eat." With him were two old women, one of whom was blind. They could barely walk. They begged us for help. They had no money and begged us not to leave them. My father carried one of them on his back and every few feet he would put her down to rest. We went to our house where we stayed for a few months.

Eventually we left. My sons came with a horse and took me to Damascus. We stayed there around five months. Again we went back to the village and we harvested the wheat, barley, and lentils, and gathered the olives. Suddenly the Jews showed up and poured some kind of yellow fuel on the crops and burned them. So we left. I was nine months pregnant and carrying Muhammad. I took a pile of clothes to use for the new baby in case I gave birth on the way. We walked and walked. We spent the nights in the wilderness. Then one of our relatives came and said the Jews had taken the area. They were stopping people and taking their money. They took six pounds from your father and beat him.

My son wanted to drink water and there wasn't any. Your grandmother had a jug that had a last drop of water in it and we gave it to him. We walked and walked until we reached Hurfeish. There the Israeli tanks were firing in the air. I felt I could not walk anymore but we reached Rmeish.

In Rmeish, people would come after us beating on empty tin cans so that we would go away. So we walked and walked. Your uncle went to get water from a nearby village. Your father said, "I can't walk any more. I will stay here with the things"—we were carrying things like bedding and flour. We went to Bint Jbeil where we bought cans of water for five or ten piastres. Then we walked to Yaroun and buses came and took us to Sour. We stayed there until the Army took us to 'Anjar [in Eastern Lebanon] around seven months later.

They divided up the Sour camp and took people to B'albak and 'Ayn al-Hilweh. The camp in Sour wasn't big enough for all these people. In 'Anjar, it was so cold. We said we will go for seven days and then we will go home to Palestine. Then seven months later we said we'll be back and . . . we never did. A few years later we moved to 'Ayn al-Hilweh to be closer to my family. We were in bad shape and we still are. We are going to die running.

When Palestinians arrived in Lebanon, particular social divisions vigorously asserted themselves, and indeed were magnified. The urban/rural divide was noticeably marked as residents of urban areas and small towns settled in urban Lebanese areas where they could draw upon a network of social and business relations and kinship ties. Movable capital could be used to rent apartments and eventually start businesses. Those who ended up in the camps were overwhelmingly peasants, with few resources and little education. The refugee experience was markedly different for camp residents; Palestinians in urban Lebanese areas, largely lower, middle, and upper class urbanites, were subject to less surveillance and control over movements and avoided the harshest aspects of refugee life.

The location of the camps was related to the logic of Lebanese sectarianism, economic factors, and political strategies (Sayigh 1994: 25). Refugees were scattered in the south, east, north, and around Beirut. The

UN established official camps at sites where large numbers of refugees were gathered, usually because relief of some sort was available there, or in areas where land was available to lease. They incorporated refugees already on site or nearby. Flight from Palestine was highly chaotic. As Um Fadi's story illustrated, family units, rather than whole villages, tended to flee and remain together. Villagers departed at different stages of fighting and sought shelter in nearby villages or across the border. With the exception of camps in East Beirut (Tel al-Zaʿter, Dbiyyeh, Jisr al Basha), most were set up in largely Muslim regions, often near areas with substantial agricultural activity such as Bʿalbak, Tripoli, Saida, Sour, and Nabatiyyeh. Large numbers had sought shelter in the southern town of Sour, leading to the establishment of Rashidiyyah, al-Basas, and Burj al-Shemali camps. "Declaring the border a military zone" and forcibly transporting refugees, like Um Fadi, from the south to the east and north (25) was an attempt to prevent a concentration of refugees on the border. Sayigh refers to an initial contradiction between these state attempts and "the demand of Lebanese industry for cheap labor" (25). Subsequent movements were closely tied to the availability of work, possibilities of reuniting with kin and villagers, and access to camps offering education, medical care, and an efficient and routinized rations distribution. Some movements were less than voluntary, as refugees recounted being forcibly taken to ʿAnjar or Bʿalbak in eastern Lebanon or north to Tripoli. In search of work, some families headed for Beirut. The proverbial village grapevine spread the word that work was available and about the new camp in Burj al-Barajneh. Families heard of kin or fellow villagers settling into Burj al-Barajneh and proceeded to join them, which facilitated its discernible village clusters. Some families ended up in other village areas because space in their own villages was full.

Over fifty years after settling into the camps, the question of how people arrived in them is best asked of the elderly, whose memories are sometimes fading, or their children and grandchildren who have inherited memories of the family saga. How did refugees etch the camps' landscape? How did their social relations and practices shape the physical and social environment, distinguishing it from the exterior, and impose symbolic meaning on place? Memories have faded and the past is narrated from the perspective of the present, where they are "still running," according to Um Fadi. Arrival in the camps was varied. Families and villages did not always end up in a camp immediately after 1948. Hassan, a *fidaʾiyyin* until 1982, remembers as a child being forcibly moved to Baddawi camp in Tripoli.

Nineteen Palestinian families from the villages of Suhmata, al-Jaysh, and Adamuni were living in the Al-Mina section of Tripoli. In 1957, the owner of the land asked the army and the police to clear the area of refugees. Army trucks came and they piled us into the back with a lot of fighting. See these scars on my arms—I was nine years old. I tried to fight with the soldiers. They took us to Baddawi camp where we lived for nearly two years in tents. Then we built cement houses. Unlike other camps, Baddawi had Palestinians from cities like Haifa and 'Akka. Some of them had been living in the Khan al-Askari. In 1956, the Abu 'Ali River flooded, displacing them. So Baddawi was built to house them and then we came in 1957. There were Ghawarneh from Ramel living in the area of Tripoli where the rubbish was dumped.[5] The area was called al-Rubbaysh [Arabization of the English "rubbish"]. They also came to the newly established camp. People from Loubia and Al-Dahriyyeh had taken refuge in the train station. They were also moved to the camp.

Samir, an UNRWA employee and graduate student in sociology, told me how his family came to Nabatiyyeh camp:

It was a planned camp; it did not arise on a spot where refugees had already gathered en masse. In 1956, there were Palestinians living in the city itself and in the villages around it. Others were living near the border. In 1955, the government decided that there were too many smugglers between Palestine and Lebanon and that it could affect the security situation—military operations could be undertaken. So they decided to gather all the Palestinians in the area. They coordinated with UNRWA to build this camp for these stray groups of people near the border area. They attracted them in a number of ways. My father was the *mukhtar* of our village. So they said to him, "We have places for your and your people—you are not obliged to pay rent and there will be a school." So there were certain motivations to accept the camp.

Some camps, such as Nahr al-Bared in Tripoli, were "accidental." Samir explained that the "people who settled there were on their way to Syria. When the Syrian government decided not to accept any more refugees, the border was closed and they were obliged to stay there. Later, UNRWA transformed the site into a camp."

How a camp was set up goes a long way in explaining its spatial layout. Those camps which were previously army barracks (and had once housed Armenian refugees) were laid out in grid formation. Thus Rashidiyyah camp had two main sections. One was based on the old barracks. The other section, which grew over the years as families expanded, was a maze. 'Ayn al-Hilweh, with its narrow and winding alleys branching out from a few main streets that traversed the camp, also resembled a maze. It was built in a location where refugees had gathered immediately after 1948; gradually others came because the village headmen put out a call to their villagers to join them.

Refugees without sufficient resources to settle in urban areas turned to the camps for shelter, rations distribution, education, and medical care. By 1952, one-third of refugees were dwelling in tents or barracks run by UNRWA. In their fourth year of operation, the population of the camps had grown by 10 percent due to natural increase and economic pressures. High unemployment and the exhaustion of personal savings compelled those who had initially managed to live outside the camps to seek their services (Stevens 1952: 288). The appeal of educational facilities cannot be underestimated. As the possibility of immediate return receded, refugees realized that education, a mobile and symbolic form of capital, would enhance survival in an uncertain world.

By 1961, tents, those despised symbols of misery and homelessness, were a relic of the past. The transformation to more solidly built cement houses was gradual. First, a cement block foundation one to two feet in height would be constructed around the perimeter of the tent to keep out rain and prevent drafts. From there it was a matter of building upward, level by level, gradually replacing the tent with a cement structure. Roofs were another story. Forbidden by the government because they conveyed permanency, zinc roofs were a potent symbol in a rich lore about early camp life. Invariably, these narratives make explicit reference to roofs to highlight the repression of the Lebanese government. The elderly avidly related stories of putting up roofs only to be forced to dismantle them. In Burj al-Barajneh camp, Abu Salim, now nearly ninety years old, told me, "I was here from the beginning, when it was tents. Then we added zinc roofs. The *maktab al-thani* [Lebanese Intelligence Services] would pull women from their baths to shout at them about a roof or water running from their small houses! Even the sound of a hammer on a nail was enough to make the police come running." Zinc roofs architecturally encoded the possibility of *towteen* (settlement or implantation).

Lebanese representations of the camps and the refugees were difficult to separate because the camps were sites of governance and residency for the latter. Thus, they were metonyms for one another; the camps were living embodiments of the Palestinian presence in Lebanon. Initially nuanced by sect and class, by the 1980s there was almost unanimous opposition to their presence. Initially, for the Lebanese working class, which cross-cuts sect, refugees were potential competitors for agricultural and industrial employment. The Lebanese elite and upper classes nervously perceived a potential economic challenge from Palestinian capital. With substantial commercial and real estate holdings in West Beirut, by the early 1960s the Palestinian business sector had established a formidable financial and trading empire (Smith 1984: 13).

Lebanese attitudes toward and representations of the camps were shifting and intersected with broader political issues. Initial Lebanese rhetoric in the press and by government officials cast refugee-host relations as those of guest (*dayf*) and host. While Arabs are widely known for their generous offerings of hospitality, which mandates that hosts do not inquire of their guests as to the length of their stay, the underlying assumption of both parties is that the guest will eventually depart. More important, it is incumbent on the guest to respect the host, his home, and resources. Middle-aged refugees recalled that the Lebanese Army dropped leaflets on the camps asking the Palestinians to

> 'Ardihim ma dumta fi 'ardihim
> Darihim ma dumta fi darihim
>
> (Please them as long as you are in their land
> Treat them with care and respect as long as you are in their home)

The context was an attempted coup in Lebanon in 1961 by the Syrian Nationalist Party (a pan-Syrian party). Prior to the emergence of an organized Palestinian political movement, Palestinians were perceived as and often were allies of pan-Syrian or Pan-Arab movements. The rhetoric, an old Arabic adage and play on words, unmistakably stated the behavior expected of guests: they are not to take over their hosts' homes.

Micro-Geography: The Village in the Camps

The intentions underlying camps and their borders were spatial confinement and the administration and management of a displaced population. Repressive spatial tactics and practices were enacted by the state, and in this instance the aid regime, and embedded in everyday routines. The barbed wire fences surrounding some camps and the pass system were boundary-maintaining practices to control and monitor external movement. In the early 1950s, Shatila camp had two points of entrance and exit controlled by the Lebanese. Residents had to put their names on a list when they exited and note the expected time of return. Confinement was a recurring theme in memories and narratives of this period. "We couldn't go here or there," Abu Bassam recalled. In his eighties, stately in his sparkly white *kufiyyah* and neatly pressed but frayed trousers, he sat in front of his house sharing the *'argeelah* (water pipe) with his friend Abu Issam. We were talking about the early days of camp life. Abu Issam explained, "If we wanted to visit family in another camp, we had to take permission from the police, get a pass, and sign in and out." Over time, these institutional constraints on mobility permeated the collective sense of self. Abu Kamal, a friend who frequently joined Abu Issam and Abu Bassam to smoke and drink tea, echoed their comments: "A refugee could not do this or that—life was full of new rules. At the beginning, we had to sign out to leave the camp. If we wanted to travel to the south to visit kin, we had to have a pass. A Palestinian was simply not allowed near the border. They didn't want us to see our homes."[6]

Mobility was monitored in order to obstruct political organizing and keep the border area quiet and free of infiltration. Intent on keeping it clear of refugees, Lebanon declared it a military zone and prevented Palestinians from entering it. Within the camps, surveillance was pervasive. Initially the Lebanese Army and police watched peoples' comings and goings, keeping an ear open for information about political organizing; in 1958, the Lebanese Intelligence took over these tasks. Controlling mobility from the exterior was not very efficient, so the visually apparent controls and surveillance were moved inside as the *maktab al-thani* and Lebanese police recruited informers.

The space of the camps reterritorialized Palestinian villages, but only in partial ways. It is these that are pivotal in exploring the relationship between place, identity, and social relationships. Simply to assert that refugees settled according to villages and that those formations still exist is hardly adequate to convey the complexity of camp spatiality. This fragmented geosocial reconstitution generated a new landscape, enhancing the presence of the past in partial ways while suggesting new possibilities for present and future. It opened spaces for new dynamic social processes, knowledge, and identities to emerge. Initially, the refugees' common experiences were life in Palestine, dispersal, and camp life. Tracking the ways in which villages matter, spatially and socially, can be a means of following and measuring the scale of refugee empowerment.

The inscription of a Galilean landscape in the camps launched the crafting of place out of space and made apparent the simultaneous continuity and transformation of social life. Villages were relocated, newly landscaped, and socially reconfigured, while their original geographic spaces were renamed and occupied by Israeli settlers (see W. Khalidi 1992; Slyomovics 1998; Bauman 1995). Setting up camps where refugees amassed meant that families were already clustered, and the initial autonomy accorded refugees in setting up their tent sites resulted in many families of a village staying together. The act of dwelling may impose the most basic features of placemaking. Setting up patches of private space, however small, imposed encumbrances on space such as social organization, cultural forms including notions of the built environment and domestic space, religious affiliation, gender organization, and cosmological order. Proximity enabled refugees to draw on a past history of support and exchange to cope. For example, Burj al-Barajneh camp was constituted by a spatial array of a number of northern villages in six named areas: Kweikat, Tarshiha, al-Kabri, Sheikh Daoud, al-Ghabisiyya, and al-Chaab. ʿAyn al-Hilweh had named quarters for the villages of Saffuriyya, ʿAmqa, Loubia, and al-Bassa/al-Zeeb, among others. To move around inside many camps, one passed from one named village to another. In daily usage, the term *ahl* (people) referred to people of a particular village, for example " 'ahl 'Amqa," locating people, individually and collectively, in terms of particular places. Named village areas in the camps were actually family or clan units of particular villages that settled together. The larger the village, the more distinct its area.

Smaller villages occupied spaces intermediate to larger, more visible, and marked villages. A sampling of other villages, 'Amqa, al-Bassa and Um al-Faraj among others, were scattered in Burj al-Barajneh. These small clusters, consisting of a few families, were often segments of large village clusters in other camps. Al-Bassa, for example, had a quarter in Rashidiyyeh and shared a quarter in 'Ayn al-Hilweh with al-Zeeb. A few families resided in Burj al-Barajneh but were not enough to form a *hayy* (quarter). Within a *hayy*, smaller sections were sometimes known by the names of prominent or large families. In Burj al-Barajneh, village quarters contained within them smaller areas or streets named after prominent families of the village. Thus village leadership and status were evident in the naming and mapping of space.

On occasion, neighboring villages in Palestine found themselves neighbors in exile. Al-Zeeb and al-Bassa, small neighboring villages near 'Akka, occupied adjacent areas in 'Ayn al-Hilweh referred to as al-Bassa/al-Zeeb, shrinking geographical space and connoting close ties. Social relations of neighborliness, with intensive visiting, intermarriage, and the exchange of goods and services cemented this long-term relationship. Thus, Palestinian settlement by villages, however partial, asserted an intimate claim to now distant, relandscaped and occupied space, forging a connection between time and space which was inherited by successive generations through dwelling in these camp areas and being part of a social world organized, in part, on a village model. In a sense, villages areas have been the physical and symbolic memory, transmitting the space of Palestine to the present, giving the displaced a deep visceral and everyday connection to past time, place, and social relationships.

Some villages did break into smaller units that stemmed from the chaos of war, the refuge-seeking process itself, and variations in social contacts in the wider region. Palestinians often use the term *shataat* (dispersal, scattering, fragmentation) to describe the aftermath of 1948. Bits and pieces of villages are scattered in different camps. For example, al-Bassa has quarters in both 'Ayn al-Hilweh and Rashidiyyeh. Other Bassawis stayed in Palestine; some are living in the U.S. Saffuriyya occupied large sectors in 'Ayn al-Hilweh and Nahr al-Bared camps as well as a quarter in Nazareth, where those who remained in Palestine were relocated after 1948. The village of 'Alma also dispersed between countries. The population went in two directions in 1948: to Lebanon and to Syria because men who fought with Syrian contingents in 1948 sought refuge there. In Burj al-Barajneh, *hayy* Tarshiha and *hayy* Kabri among others are identifiable and named spaces that are subdivided into smaller areas named after particular families. Named village quarters are dotted with individual families from other villages.

Initially, village patterns of social organization and status were viable and relief agencies dealt directly with *al-makhater* as village heads to help compile lists of residents to be registered as refugees. *Al-makhater* send word to the scattered families of their villages to come to the camp they were settling in, further facilitating a village settlement pattern. Um and Abu Taher, who have lived most of their lives in the al-Bassa/al-Zeeb quarter in ʿAyn al-Hilweh, recalled that their parents came because the *mukhtar* of al-Bassa called Bassawis, scattered around the South, to come and settle there. *Al-makhater* distributed rations, and UNRWA appointed them as Camp Services Officers, a liaison position between camp residents and UNRWA. Corruption and patronage eventually led UNRWA to develop the position of Field Officers, chosen more on the basis of wider influence and merit. Eventually they resembled village notables in the emergent status system of the camps (Schiff 1995: 144).

Villages were points of departure in organizing and thus creating place. Small fragments of Palestine were etched onto space, providing cognitive maps and endowing space with everyday practical meaning. The construction and naming of place emanated from these spatial configurations and their centrality. Villages existed not just as geographical traces of Palestine but as social units as well. Large villages were able to impose their demographic presence and weight on smaller ones. Majd al-Krum monopolized power in Shatila camp until its hold lessened as the resistance movement superseded traditional forms of leadership and the exercise of power. In the 1950s and 1960s, Nahr al-Bared camp in the north had a significant number of families from Saffuriyya. Hassan, a charming curly-haired schoolteacher from Saffuriyya, was a distant relative of Abu Khalid who visited him occasionally in Shatila. Upon hearing our conversation about village areas in the camps, he eagerly described the early days of Nahr al-Bared and its social layout.

In the 1950s, 90 percent of the people in the camp were from Saffuriyya. The camp is bisected by a road that divided it into upper and lower levels. The upper level was occupied by the Saffuriyyis and the lower level was a mixture of numerous small villages. They were hesitant to come into our areas. Our men would sit in the alleys and anyone who passed through who was not from Saffuriyya was asked, "Where are you going?" or "Who do you want to see?" They were treated like strangers. This was village behavior. Now the camps are more mixed.

Thus, while villages did break up, or were forcibly separated, and entered different camps, the camps themselves resembled a microcosm of northern Galilee, a landscape reassembled and spatially inscribed in novel formation in Lebanon. However, in reassembling, different units were spatially arranged in new ways with unforeseen consequences. Thus village sociospatial arrangements in the camps map the effects of 1948 on Palestinian space and its partial reconstitution in exile.

Shatila's early history departed somewhat from the standard pattern of settlement in that the role of a single village, Majd al-Krum, was foundational in its establishment. Sayigh (1994) provides a detailed account of its early history. 'Abed Bisher, a Palestinian fighter (*mujahideen*) from Majd al-Krum, acquired some twenty tents and negotiated the lease of a small plot of land (200 by 400 meters) on the outskirts of Beirut owned by the Shatila family. He traveled through Lebanon, gathering fellow villagers for the move to the new camp. In the early 1950s, he worked with the International Red Cross, then the primary relief agency in Lebanon until UNRWA took over, and the Arab Higher Council. He forged contacts with UNRWA and managed to secure their services for the camp—a school, clinic, latrines, and rations. He was the first head, or representative, of the camp to the administrative authorities. With his sociopolitical connections and obvious leadership qualitites, he was able to find jobs for his relatives and fellow villagers. These original inhabitants were quickly joined by a smattering of other Galilee villages. Eventually upward social mobility propelled most Majd al-Krum families from the camp and into urban life as other Palestinian families moved in. The leadership once provided by Abed Bisher, his son, and grandson as Camp Services Officers was superseded by the takeover by the resistance movement in 1968.

Camp spatiality extended well beyond the village. It was accompanied by and overlaid with other sorts of space, institutional and later political, as well as subject to demographic changes. Camps were sites for the elaboration of new forms of social relations generated by spatial shrinking and proximity, the legal status of refugee, and participation in camp-wide social institutions. In the crowded camps, daily interaction between refugees expanded dramatically, creating the conditions for new social networks and friendships. Friendships arose between people living in adjacent areas. The difficulty of maintaining privacy was legendary and made daily routines highly visible to others. Jokes (*nuqat*) that still circulate about the 1950s and 1960s point to humiliating or painful encounters and are deployed as humorous although bitter commentary on the refugee situation. Many spoke bluntly to the issue of privacy. A refugee family lived in barracks where only a blanket separated each family's cubicle. A husband comes home late from an evening at the café with his buddies. Tired, and with little light to guide him, he stumbles into the wrong cubicle and tries to get into bed with a strange woman. The privacy and sanctity of the home are highly loaded cultural complexes. The sudden absence of homes with solid walls, and the shrinking of space between domestic units, attested to the loss of ability to maintain privacy and the social chaos that could ensue.

Institutional signposts dotted the camps' landscape, providing cognitive and pragmatic mappings, indexing refugee status and pointing to the services available to sustain it. Rations had to be picked up, children all attended the same UNRWA schools, and its medical clinics served everyone. When I asked people to describe the camps in the 1950s, they start their mapping with village quarters and then UNRWA distribution sites, offices, schools, feeding centers, and clinics, new types of public space utilized by all refugees. For the younger generation, schooling had an extraordinary impact on refugee lives, expanding the geosocial range of friendships and interactions well beyond the village. It brought together children from a multitude of villages, who in pre-1948 Palestine had little chance of knowing one another, and laid the basis for new social relations that would last well into adulthood. These were a significant departure from the previous village and kin-based social world of most refugees. For example, Hussein had a wide range of friends from numerous villages that he became acquainted with at school. His father had a much smaller network of friends, mostly from his village. A reconfigured political and social leadership, secular, nationalist, and less bound by the ties of village or region, was emerging among the newly educated young men. Educated in a uniform secular curriculum, they eventually formed a sociopolitical movement that effectively cross-cut village and clan loyalties and affiliations.

Women met and made friends in their daily trips to camp bakeries, where they were exposed to different culinary styles and recipes. Foods particular to one village began to circulate through women's visiting networks. Culinary habits mark cultural boundaries, symbolizing group belonging through their particular patterns of consumption. Indeed, food can be a way of tracking social encounters and new relationships. Palestinian villages are known for their regional specializations. These dishes circulated among women now socializing with once distant villagers. Um Khalid was always on the lookout for new dishes, which she would introduce to her family as from such-and-such a village. Much of her culinary repertoire had been acquired through such exchanges, starting as a young girl in the 1950s and later as a bride in the 1960s. She and her friends often discussed dishes from other villages or variations on regional ones, and asked for recipes in order to replicate them. Fish *muhammar* (a sweet red pepper and onion paste) was a specialty of the coastal villages, and Um Khalid learned it from other women in Shatila. The first time she made it, she took small samples to her neighbors and friends so they could taste this new and delectable dish. While serving it to her family, she explained that it came from the villages near the sea. The embryonic emergence of a national cuisine can be seen in these culinary exchanges.

Although village endogamy remained vital in the 1950s and 1960s, it was beginning to weaken. As young people begin to marry exogamously, they reduced social distance and extended affiliation over a broad national and geosocial expanse. For example, in 'Ayn al-Hilweh, the villages of 'Akbarah and Sa'sa' developed close relations, cemented by marriage exchanges. For example, Um Khalid married her cousin but her two sisters married men from Sa'sa'.

Stories from a village circulated easily, and the events of 1948 formed the defining elements of a new national narrative of suffering and injustice. The trauma of one village was not its alone; collectively, the stories were those of all camp residents. Hussein, the *feda'i*, knew the stories of what happened to a host of villages in 1948. *Dawaween*, informal social gatherings, occurred with regularity. These traditional gatherings often took place at nodes in the camps, small, open, places where several alleyways might meet, or in front of homes They were usually composed of men, particularly the elderly, but young boys and girls listened intently to the elders' talk. Most significantly, the *dawaween* brought in people from other villages. As a young boy Hussein listened avidly to others' stories, incorporating them into a coherent narrative of pre-1948 village life, the war period, and *al-nakbah*. He was passionate in his defense of the *dawaween*: "I learned so much just from sitting around with these old men. It was like a geography and history lesson on Palestine. Later when I did mobilization work in the camps and spent a lot of time visiting families and trying to help with their problems and get them to join the resistance, I already had knowledge of their villages and their sufferings." Sharing space, narratives, and experiences set the stage for common interests to foment, take shape, and become recognized as such.

In the close quarters of the camps, regional and village stereotypes enabled Palestinians to locate their new neighbors cognitively. These stereotypes had circulated loosely in Palestine, but with the proximity imposed by the camp, they flourished. At a small gathering of teachers in Burj al-Barajneh we got onto the topic of stereotypes, and this group was more than delighted to spend a considerable time discussing them. I was aware of some of them from previous fieldwork; others were new to me. A standard stereotype among Palestinians in Lebanon concerns Tarshiha people, original residents of Burj al-Barajneh with a named quarter. They were known as highly educated and as a consequence, conceited. 'Amqa natives were known for their 'asabiyyeh (loyalty), which could be seen alternatively as virtuous or reactionary. One teacher described them as "stupid, rough and uncouth—and they marry too early." Al-Kabri people were purportedly hardworking, while in Kweikat, Hateen, and al-Bassa the women were strong and domineering. Ras al-Ahmar natives were stubborn (*aneed*) and opinionated. The Bedu were generous and admired for their adherence to traditional Arab culture, while the Ghawarneh were considered volatile, poor, backward, uneducated, and conservative. Urban Palestinians from Haifa, ʿAkka and Yaffa were educated but overly concerned with appearances. In ʿAyn al-Hilweh, Saffuriyya, long dominant numerically, wielded considerable local influence. Sarcastically referred to as the "capital" of Palestine, its residents were perceived as conceited and full of themselves. Even Saffuriyyis referred to their village as the "capital." What accounts for this collective sense of self? As one of the largest villages in pre-1948 Palestine, it was the site of Roman and Byzantine ruins, attesting to its historical significance and depth. A regional trade center, it played a prominent role in the 1936 revolt against Zionist settlement and the British Mandate (see W. Khalidi 1992: 350–52). In the task of making place, the refugees imprinted and marked personality and character on space; stereotypes were a way of knowing and classifying other refugees and spaces. While these village stereotypes flagged and expressed difference, they also claimed these places within a spatially compressed, heterogeneous national entity.

The camps themselves began to acquire character. Camp location, whether rural or urban, initially structured these images. Shatila, Tel al-Zaʿter, and Burj al-Barajneh quickly took on urban characters. They were originally built on the periphery of Beirut, but the city expanded so rapidly and extensively that by the late 1960s the camps were part of the city's landscape and fabric, particularly its urban labor market. Rashidiyyeh was considered rural, as large sectors of its work force participated in agricultural labor in the surrounding fields and orchards. Tel al-Zaʿter, which provided a workforce for nearby industries, was known to be progressive. Even now in talking about Tel al-Zaʿter, people will parenthetically interject, "they used to drink beer there" to call attention to its urban, liberal character. Wavell camp in the more remote Bʿalbak area of central Lebanon was known to be conservative and traditional about gender relations. An honor crime in Wavell elicited this comment from Um Khalid: "What do you expect? They have always been backward out there."

Just as exile did not gloss over pre-1948 stereotypes, neither did it erode village rivalries and feuds. Indeed, some were reinscribed in the new environment. Rivalrous relations could be reconfigured and integrated into local and later nationalist politics. Two al-Zeeb families, the Nassers and the Tahers, settled in ʿAyn al-Hilweh after 1948. Some of the

Tahers joined the urban middle class and were living in Beirut. Prior to 1948, the two families had a running feud over the killing of a member of one family that occasionally sparked violent encounters in the village. Cramped quarters meant the known enemies now lived closed to one another. On a quotidian level, their animosity was expressed in avoidance, petty quarrels, the occasional fist fight, and women's nasty and boisterous verbal exchanges. In part, as a consequence of urbanity, the Tahers were widely perceived as corrupt. When a prominent member of the Tahers became an informer to the Lebanese Intelligence Services in the early 1960s, this provided further evidence of corruption. As an informer, he gained the enmity of other refugees. The Tahers took advantage of this affiliation to intimidate and harass the Nassers. The informer's reputation and that of the Tahers was irrevocably tarnished. The Nassers had a long history as nationalists, which earned them the moral higher ground. With the arrival of the resistance and the marginalization of the *maktab al-thani* in the camps, the Tahers' sociopolitical standing fell dramatically. The Nassers quickly aligned themselves with this new political and military force, irretrievably tipping the balance of power in their favor. Their moral standing swelled and they reached the pinnacle of their social and political stature when Abu 'Ali 'Ayyad, a widely acclaimed hero of the Palestinian battles with the Jordanian Army during Black September in 1970, paid them a visit. A visit by the revered militant solidified the Nassers' nationalist seal of approval. The Tahers tried to forge connections with resistance cadres but were rebuffed, indelibly tainted by their informer status. Their hasty attempt to portray their informer status as one of "infiltration" rather than collaboration failed. In the early 1970s, two Nassers on a motorcycle, by then members of al-Fateh, assassinated the informer. The Tahers then left the camp en masse. The few who stayed kept a low profile and the feud effectively ended.

Camp spatiality partially transposed a pre-1948 gendering of space and mobility. Comparing the early years in the southern camp of Burj al-Shemali with that in Shatila, Um Faris, a widow living alone, said,

Shelling drove us out of Burj al-Shemali and we came to Shatila because of work opportunities. I had much more freedom there. Here in Shatila I do not go anywhere. There we used to sit all the time and have a lot of fun. We used to live in village quarters. People used to live as if they were in their own villages.

Um Faris explicitly invoked the geospatial proximity and intimacy of village life. In such a setting, in which people were kin or social intimates, women and girls enjoyed more mobility than they did in places such as Shatila, where a village mapping was less pronounced.

Domesticity was the nexus around which daily routines were estab-

lished and thus was pivotal in imprinting place physically and symbolically. The daily temporal rhythm of life began and ended in domestic
space. Palestinian refugees have always received dry rations, and thus
food preparation and consumption were domestic based.[7] Domesticity
set up a spatial boundary between households and was a way of demar-
cating and claiming space as one's own.

Public/domestic spatial issues can be exceedingly complex in Arab-
Islamic societies with their gendered notions of the spatial. Camps present yet another opportunity to complicate notions of private and public
spheres. Camps most certainly contain arenas of public space, such as
clinics, schools, and offices, as well as clearly marked domestic spaces.
Yet domesticity overflowed the confines of homes in the cramped quarters of the camps. Women's food preparation activities, in particular,
often spilled into public space, as front door stoops became spatial
extensions of domestic cooking space, used for cleaning and preparing
vegetables or grains. Women walked though the camp on their way to
and from the bakery, carrying trays of food balanced on their heads.
When doors to homes were open, allowing a line of vision into domestic
space, they became part of a public landscape. The same applied to situations where passersby were welcomed to come in, or people greeted
one another through open doors and windows. Closed doors, usually in
the early morning, late afternoon, or late night hours, signaled a more
private domestic space. Thus space was multivalent, shifting in meaning
and genderedness depending on time of day and usage. Public/private
merged into and out of each other.

To further complicate matters, the camps resembled domestic units
writ large vis-à-vis the exterior Lebanese space. Dress styles were illustrative. Within the camp, clothing styles were informal. In the small alleyways, women entered neighboring homes or ran errands wearing house
clothes, usually a *jelabiyyah* (a long, often embroidered dress) in which
they cooked and cleaned. In larger camps such as ʿAyn al-Hilweh or
Shatila, when they went beyond their immediate neighborhoods, they
often changed into more formal street clothing. To go into urban Lebanese areas required accessories such as a handbag, a freshly washed and
ironed head scarf, and proper shoes rather than plastic sandals. In
smaller, less urban camps such as Rashidiyyeh, women wore house
dresses all over the camp. Girls and women walked more freely within
camp boundaries than they did on the exterior, unknown and dangerous, where one was not known and thus lacked protection. Excursions
outside the boundaries of the camp required supervision, or girls had to
go in groups. Thus there are gradients in the meaning of space. The
camp as a whole, in relation to the exterior, was familiar territory where
girls were fairly free to walk. Small neighborhoods, those quieter sec-

tions away from the main streets, resembled quasi-domestic space as domestic tasks spilled into them. Hussein told me, "I have always felt at home in the camps. When I enter them I feel safe and secure, as if I am with my people and can behave the way I want." These embodied sentiments evoked home and security and they point to an interioriza-tion of the camps as a type of domestic space whose meaning is consti-tuted against an unwelcoming or potentially dangerous exterior. The camps themselves became intimate domains on which were imposed the values and expectations of neighborliness.

The rearrangement of domesticity in the camps gradually stripped away facets of women's previous household autonomy, some of which are encapsulated in transformations in food. At a family gathering in 'Ayn al-Hilweh, several women from al-Bassa were discussing how food, its preparation, and the concept of *mooneh* had changed. Um Samir remembered a specific room in her house in Palestine where provisions were kept and where her mother-in-law would decide what to cook each day and allocate labor in the household. Patting her breast, where elderly women store their small coin purses, she said, "Women used to control the money and men had to ask them for pocket money. That's how it was in al-Bassa. I don't know about the rest of Palestine." Her sister-in-law chimed in, "In the camps, we had to start buying food with cash because rations weren't enough. Rations didn't provide fruits or vegetables." Women no longer transformed agricultural produce into consumables, nor were they able to keep substantial provisions, a critical hedge against lean times. Abruptly brought into a quasi-market and aid economy where they were dependent on wages and rations, there was some loss of female autonomy in household management and food processing. The skills of making do and stretching scarce resources were called into play.

In a sectarian based country, religion became freighted with symbolic and social capital. Exile magnified and respatialized religious differ-ences. Christian Palestinians were offered, and most accepted, Lebanese citizenship, which conferred significant advantages. Beyond access to the Lebanese education and health care system, the protection of a state and residential stability were undeniably valued assets.

Some Palestinian villages in the Galilee had mixed Muslim-Christian populations although Christians were a numerical minority (al-Bassa, Tarshiha, Ijzim, 'Atlit, Dayr al-Qasi, al-Damun, al-Birwa etc.). Though spatially close, residential quarters were distinct by religion; intermar-riage was rare and actively discouraged, but social relations were amiable and respectful. Um Samir of al-Bassa said, "We always visited the Chris-tian houses on their holidays. We baked lots of sweets the night before and took them to their houses. They did the same on our holidays."

After 1948, Christian villagers, as well as some urbanites, settled in largely urban and often suburban Christian areas of Beirut. Maryam, a now middle-aged Palestinian Christian woman, recounted the stories her parents told her about their flight and settlement in the predominantly Christian East Beirut suburb of Jounieh.

My father was a journalist. He was working in his office in Haifa when the Israelis were attempting to take over the city. He locked himself in the office with one of his assistants. Meanwhile my mother was at home. My father's office was on land he owned and we think that today it is the site of an Israeli bus station. My mother was home with three of us kids—my brother, sister, and me. My eldest brother was fighting with the Palestinians. The Israelis came to my father's office and warned him that if he would not leave within 24 hours they were going to blow up his office, with him in it. So he had to leave. He told us of running through the streets of Haifa with fighting all around him. Some of the fighters helped lead him through the streets until he reached our home. Then, he, my mother, and we kids stayed in the house for a few days before going to Lebanon. We were effectively locked in the house until we left. I don't think my parents realized the magnitude of what was happening around them. Sometimes, we went to Lebanon for summer vacation, so we decided to go there. We thought we would come back once things settled down. My mother even packed her sewing machine. She still has it. And so we took off for Lebanon. They also packed our papers, the deed to the house, and the house keys.

At that time, the Israelis were pushing the Arabs of Haifa down to the port and into boats. As my parents tell it, it was mass chaos and a number of people drowned being pushed into overcrowded boats. My parents were able to find a taxi to take them to the border. They went directly to Sour in south Lebanon. We didn't know anyone there. But what they found as soon as they got there was a bunch of Lebanese Christian men looking for Christian refugees. They offered to give them assistance and take them to Jounieh. My parents told us that the Lebanese Christians helped us because they wanted us to increase the number of Christians in Lebanon. So that's how my parents ended up there.

In Jounieh, my father and some of the other Palestinian Christian men tried to determine how many Palestinians were in the area because they wanted to open a school for the children. In conjunction with UNRWA, they opened a school in the Christian camp of Dbiyyeh. That's where the Christian Palestinians who were peasants were settled. It was church land in the Christian area. We were sent to school in Dbiyyeh camp where my father was employed as a teacher. We didn't visit with our classmates since they lived in the camp and we lived in the town. We went to the camp in the morning and back home in the afternoon. So there wasn't much chance to socialize.

We never socialized much with the Lebanese Christians either. They always referred to us as the "Palestinians" and they would comment on how we were "different from those other Palestinians." I never felt like I belonged there. My father should have known better than to settle us there. By the time I was a teenager in the 1960s, I had been to West Beirut and visited and got to know Palestinian relatives and Muslim Palestinians. There, being a Palestinian was not much of an issue. I felt more relaxed and accepted. I was angry with my father. I asked him, "Why would you come and live here? Why did you have to put us in this place?'' I know this tortured my parents—my misery and alienation and blaming them for it.

As Maryam's account illustrates, settlement patterns in exile spatially and socially separated Muslim and Christian peasants. Urban Christians continued their separation from rural Christians in camps like Dbiyyeh, reproducing pre-1948 sociospatial configurations. Urban Christians who settled in East Beirut were spatially distant from urban, Muslim Palestinians. Whereas West Beirut had a highly cosmopolitan Palestinian population of Muslims and Christians who actively socialized, within the camps, the reconstituted villages, formerly inhabited by both Christians and Muslims, in effect became religiously homogeneous. For example, Dbiyyeh in East Beirut and Mar Elias in West Beirut were Christian camps, the latter on land belonging to the Lebanese Greek Orthodox Church. Inhabited by Christians from mixed Galilee villages, Mar Elias was only a couple of kilometers from the overwhelmingly Muslim Shatila and Burj al-Barajneh, yet there was little interaction.

Initially some refugees attempted to maintain long-distance relationships with former villagers in now religiously homogeneous camps. Abu Nidal, whose family was from al-Bassa and still resides in 'Ayn al-Hilweh, remembered as a teenager being dispatched to Dbiyyeh camp with a message announcing the death of a Muslim in 'Ayn al-Hilweh. He was instructed to deliver the message to the villagers of al-Bassa in Dbiyyeh. With the passage of time, and the difficulty and expense of such trips, they eventually dwindled.

Traditional anthropological notions of community which tied it closely to place have been undermined by a recognition that communities are not necessarily confined and defined by place. The increasing rapidity with which time and space are traversed, and the reinscription of social relations and communities in new locales and/or their continuity over long distances have portended a more fluid, mobile, and transnational analytical frame.

It is important to set out the parameters and various levels of refugee community which constituted a critical foundation for identity formation and reformation. These accidental communities became a prolonged way of life and developed a distinct recognition of themselves as communities with loyalties and affiliation to place. A number of questions arise concerning community and camp. What is the role of both shared and fragmented space for community formation and sentiment? How does community articulate with identity? What is the role of suffering and violence in forging community? Communities of suffering attest to the remarkable human capacity to fashion new social worlds and relationships in the face of trauma and violence. At the most elementary level, community is articulated in the invoking of unity and similarity on the one hand and distinction from the exterior on the other. For the refugees in Lebanon, the "we" aspect of their narratives pointed to a collective experience. Community implies some form of proximity and cross-cutting structures that bring people together. Yet exile extended proximity, so that Palestinians in the north or south of Lebanon identified themselves as members of a community of refugees in Lebanon. The most immediate ways they formed community were their displacement, residency in camps, legal status as refugees lacking citizenship and civil rights, collective sentiments of Palestinianism, and a constitutive exterior. As a collectivity, they resided in a space of nonbelonging in the national order.

Immediately after 1948, village-based social ties between camps facilitated the foundations of community. Abu Nabil, a middle-aged man who grew up in south Lebanon, described how refugees communicated within and between camps in the first decade and a half of exile.

In the beginning, in the camps, we used the same way to get and spread news as in the village. In our village we did not have a loudspeaker in the mosque and so announcements were made by the village *muadhin* [reciter of the call to prayer], who usually had a strong voice, or by an individual with a good voice. So in the camps we used the same method. When they made general announcements it was called *deeb al-sawt* [the raising and spreading of the voice]. *Deeb al-sawt* was traditionally a very powerful tool, not just because it spread news but because it had moral or religious overtones. For example, it could be used to announce the loss of a valuable item. If one of the villagers had found that item and not reported it, he would feel obligated to return it. If he didn't, he would feel he had committed an illegal or unreligious act. Once the *al-sawt* announced the loss of an object, it was no longer property to be had by the finder. It had an owner and keeping it would be tantamount to stealing. *Deeb al-sawt* was also used as a cry for help. If a child was lost and the *al-sawt* is called in and announces it, everyone hears it and is obliged to help in the search.

Initially the *deeb al-sawt* was reserved for circumstances that required some kind of action. With the spread of the mosque loudspeakers in the mid- to late 1960s, the mosque started to be used more and more for announcing other news, mainly funerals, but not weddings. For weddings, and sometimes deaths, a group of men were often sent to other camps, where fellow villagers lived, to deliver the news. For some reason, happy news, like weddings never found its way to the mosque minaret, so those types of announcements still had to be made by the old method of spreading news by one or more volunteers.

Communication between camps worked as follows. Let us say the news was about a funeral. Several individuals, usually relatives of the deceased, but not his children or siblings, would be dispatched separately or together to the various camps where relatives or fellow villagers lived. Each would go to the elders of the *hamuleh* (clan) in their respective camps or to the *mukhtar* or *wajih* (elders) of the village and announce the news. The *wajih* takes it from there. He arranges for the news to be disseminated among all the villagers in that camp, either by arranging for it to be announced over the mosque loudspeaker or by sending a group of his own people—sons, nephews, etc.—to deliver the news to households. If announcement cards had been written, the messenger would give the whole lot to the *wajih* who would arrange for their distribution.

With the rise of political activism in the camps in the late 1960s, the *deeb al-sawt* was used to announce political events. Demonstrations were announced from the mosque about the martyrdom of youths who had joined the resistance in Jordan and about ceremonies in their honor.

Identity in *'Ayyam al-UNRWA*

Villages, recreated in the camps, constituted a point of departure in identity formation, as did nationalism, with all the potency of exilic nationalisms. The desire and organizing for a future were equally significant and squarely situated Palestinian identity within a modernist project of becoming rather than simply being. Out of the foment of dislocation would emerge an imbricated Palestinian identity revolving around the critical elements of home, village, family, camps, and nationalism in the unstable atmosphere of a sectarian host state and a legal identity as refugees.

There is little first-hand research and few secondary sources on camp life during this period. To elicit identity, the ethnographer has to talk to now elderly people, whose memories of the past come from the standpoint of the present. In addition, the currently middle-aged who can remember this period do so from the vantage point of childhood and of course, the present. This was the age of equal measures of despair and hope: hope for the future through a return home and education, despair over life as stateless camp dwellers and every day that passed without return.

Palestinians were acutely aware of the abnormality of their daily lives. Even young children soon began to ask, "Why are we living here and other people live in houses?" They were sensitive to the stares, the rude behavior their parents encountered, the anxiety upon approaching checkpoints and most important, the humiliation of their parents by host authorities. Tales of discriminatory experiences circulated easily. To the Lebanese and to UNRWA, Palestinians were "refugees," which in international discourse and policy implied humanitarian intervention and resettlement rather than political solutions addressing root causes. Palestinians intensely disliked being referred to as "refugees," with its implications of powerlessness, denationalization, and the disdain of being charity cases. Hussein remembered the frustration of being called a refugee: "Being called a refugee, I felt different from the Lebanese, The sense of not having a home, a country was devastating. I always felt insecure and unwelcome here. We were Palestinians and we came from Palestine—this place just over the border."

Rafiq and Abu Nabil recalled that during morning exercises in elementary school they stood in formation and chanted, "Return, Return" ('awda). They adamantly refused the label "refugee" with its explicit reference to a disconnection between place and identity and thus its denativizing impulse. Yet their sense of themselves as "returnees" was quite ambiguous, having little structural force to embody and express it. Identity was referenced to a spatiotemporal past and a nebulous vision of the future. Palestine was becoming more and more distant, not in terms of memory, attachment, or significance in social relationships, but in terms of accessibility and as the locale for the enactment of Palestinian nationalism and sovereignty. What was just across the border was dangerously out of reach. The harshness of camp life, the pain and humiliation inflicted on their elders, and the daily interactions with the host population and refugee bureaucracy were visceral immediacies that directly impinged on identity and subjectivity. Rafiq's recollections of his youth in Nabatiyyeh, relations with his family and local Lebanese, and school days give a poignant insight into daily life.

My grandfather lived in a state of waiting. He was almost certain that the day when he would go home to Palestine would come soon. He believed 100 percent in Nasser's ability to liberate Palestine. In his mind, there was no other course. And he was 100 percent sure that on that day he would go back to reclaim his land. My grandfather, my father, and my mother were always telling us stories about Palestine—what they owned, and how they were going to claim it, how they were going to return.

He was always listening to the Egyptian radio station. He believed in Nasser so much. I remember him telling me that he dreamed he saw Nasser's face in the moon, meaning that Nasser was a saint and was going to accomplish all that he had promised.

Aside from returning to Palestine, the only thing on my father's mind was that we should all be studying hard. At school, we learned about Palestine informally from the teachers and other kids. The kids would tell stories about Palestine. Sometimes it became a competition over whose land was more fertile and whose produced better crops. We also learned a lot from the radio, especially the Egyptian radio during the era of Nasser. We thought it was Egypt's duty to liberate Palestine.

All our teachers in the UNWRA schools were Palestinians. Most were very nice and dedicated. Some were more strict than others but we felt they cared about us. Somehow, you could tell that they were tough on you because they cared. There was a sense of not only giving you an education, but giving you a sense of mission, that part of one's duty and identity as a refugee—as a Palestinian—was to make your life worth something. And one way of doing that was to get a very good education. Dedication to teaching became a part of those teachers; they saw teaching as a national duty. In retrospect, I think about the different ways they educated us.

My parents befriended some of the teachers, who almost always were from different towns. My father felt it was his duty to invite these people to a home-cooked meal occasionally, because they were living on their own. It created some very good, close relationships that have lasted a lifetime.

Most of the time I played with Lebanese kids, in a grassy square. The men from the camp would pass by on their way home from work. The Lebanese kids were very cruel to them. They would chase them and make fun of them because they were darker-skinned, because they were poor. That was hard for me because I identified with the Palestinians as our people and yet we were kids playing. I didn't have the courage to speak up. They would think I was siding with the refugees and would make fun of me. Although I didn't participate in the teasing, I would watch what was happening with a kind of split personality.

For the refugee, the way of being in the world was transformed and the world exterior to family and camp was magnified in importance. In exile the notion of the familiar became strained. Knowledge of place, the built environment, livelihood, community relations, social networks, and arrangements of power had all been part of a familiar routine that peasants engaged in during the course of their daily lives without extensive conscious elaboration. In Lebanon, the terrain, both geophysical and social, had to be relearned and navigated. In spite of similarities in language, culture, and religion, Palestinians were acutely aware of differences from the host population. What set them apart from the host was neither language nor culture but relation to place and the absence of citizenship and the rights it entails. Rafiq recalled an incident while on a school field trip in the 1950s, a stark lesson in just how powerless the refugees were and the contingency of their social world.

Our class went to visit Beaufort Castle in Nabatiyyeh. It was normally forbidden to visitors because it was a military post but our principal had somehow received permission to take our fourth grade class. After we had arrived and were walking up to the castle, our principal stopped and spoke with an officer in charge. They had words—I don't know what they said but suddenly the army officer slapped our principal in the face and cursed at him. To us as students, this was shocking, devastating actually. I thought "There is someone who can slap the principal who beats us." To that officer, we Palestinian students were nothing. It didn't matter to him that we saw our principal being slapped and humiliated this way.

Palestinian identity and subjectivity can be linked to being set apart, to a difference and powerlessness that made them exceedingly vulnerable. All their suffering was referenced to being Palestinians and stateless. The phrase "if we had a state this would or that would not have happened" was almost axiomatic. The Arab component to both Lebanese and Palestinian identity inserted a tension in this process of real and discursive difference. In the 1950s, Palestinian identity was decidedly not at odds with Arab identity. Indeed, Palestinians pinned their hopes on the Arab world, particularly Abdul Nasser, as their savior and many young activists were affiliated with the pan-Arab national movement.

Alienation was doubly meaningful, referring to severance from home but also from the host population who treated them with disrespect and hostility. In a social order where honor accrued, in part, from a recognition of one's grounding in a particular place, displacement meant learning anew how to carry oneself and present oneself to others and compelled the assertion of new forms of identity. A popular Palestinian joke that circulated up to the 1970s, when people still found it sadly humorous, goes as follows: A young Palestinian man boards a public bus heading to south Lebanon. The bus is stopped at a roadblock by the Lebanese police who try to keep the border area free of Palestinians. The police enter the bus and ask to see identity cards. The young Palestinian man, realizing he must have left his wallet at home, says to the policeman: "I left my wallet in my other pants." Astonished, the policeman replies: "What is this? A Palestinian with two pairs of pants!" The joke brings into focus in a self-conscious way refugee awareness of their vulnerabilities as noncitizens, their limited mobility, and the humiliation of poverty. Location in the Lebanese geosocial landscape and a legally imposed identity also worked in tandem to shape Palestinian identities. Marginality, as articulated by Rafiq's memories, honed identity by putting into relief what you were not.

The lack of citizenship worked in a similar way. The role of the identity card and checkpoints assumed paramount importance in their lives, a constant reminder of being out of place, an intruder, an unwelcome guest with no protection. The frequency with which Palestinians discussed checkpoints and identity papers over a fifty-year period was testimony to their ubiquitousness in everyday life. The checkpoint was the bane of refugee existence, approached with trepidation, for Palestinian identity was freighted with significance and as noncitizens they had no rights. Abu Fadi described his feelings as a youth in the 1950s stopped at a roadblock: "In those days, one didn't fear disappearance or death at a checkpoint like now. No, then it was all about humiliation. I watched as Lebanese passed quickly and were treated politely while I was rudely told to wait without being given a reason. When I asked why I was being held, I was told gruffly to 'shut up.' You could wait for hours without ever knowing why you were there or what might happen to you."

The camps were at once productive of similarity and of difference, drawing physical and social lines of inclusion and exclusion. Poverty, dependency, overcrowding, and vulnerability marked the interior and pointed to difference from those on the exterior. Talking about his youth in the 1950s and 1960s, Abu Fadi reminisced, "We didn't know we were poor because everyone was poor in the camps. I only realized we were poor when I started leaving the camp to go into the city. Then I begin to realize just how poor we were compared to many Lebanese and to urban Palestinians." Abu Fadi's friend Abu Munir echoed a similar sentiment.

In the camp, one could speak the Palestinian accent with ease and unconsciousness unlike on the outside. I felt at home. It was easier to be with people like myself—living the same poverty and statelessness, rather than on the outside with the Lebanese where I always felt different. . . . In the camps, I knew where I belonged and I was comfortable with that.

Institutional developments and the legal categories associated with the management of refugeeness played key roles in fostering a distinctly Palestinian identity—*'ayyam al-UNRWA* and *jeel al-UNRWA*—labeling an era and a generation by an institution underscored its significance in quotidian life. "I have been a refugee since the day I was born. I collected rations for my family until I was a teenager. I identify with and feel for every refugee in the world." Now in his fifties and living in Beirut, Issam, an engineer by profession, made this statement at a meeting of foreign NGOs discussing refugee assistance. The enveloping and life-sustaining space of UNRWA cross-cut the fragmented spaces where Palestinians resided, connecting them with one another through the experience of its forms of governance. In short, it was a shared structural feature of life as exiles.

Despite the absence of a specifically Palestinian curriculum, UNRWA schooling was an unprecedented institutional forum, functioning in much the same way that schooling does in the rest of the world, inculcating nationalism and constructing national subjects. Strongly nationalistic, often politically active, and committed to youth and the development of their Palestinian identity, teachers quietly adjusted the curriculum to incorporate Palestinian themes. This was a dangerous strategy, for they could be fired if caught.

Not only did access to secular knowledge and literacy propel a shift in authority and prestige, once based on age and premodern forms of knowledge, from elders to a new corps of young people, it also initiated a transformation in gender relations. Many young girls were becoming more educated than both their parents, enabling them to have a greater voice in family affairs and later in the resistance movement. As we saw in Chapter 3, youth encountered secular modern forms of knowledge. Education facilitated new forms of community, facilitated new kinds of nonkin and nonvillage networks, complicated the relevance of village identities, and fostered new spaces and discourses of interaction and ideology. Thus schools constituted another shared institutional space and new set of practices for refugees.

An investment in the future, educational achievement was also point-edly conceptualized as a form of political struggle and a strategy for personal and collective survival. For the immediate period, education was the route to a secure and viable future. As Rafiq's grandfather and parents recognized—faith in Nasser and the Arabs, but education for the future. If education was conceptualized as a form of cultural capital for peasants-turned-refugees, its centrality to identity and subjectivity comes into focus. Education, it was concluded, would facilitate survival in an uncertain future. Loss of land and country was equated with a loss of honor central to individual and collective identities. Educational achievement, for which the Palestinians were known in the first few decades of exile, emerged as a new component of honor, and like traditional honor, it was a form of cultural capital.

Conclusion

From the vantage point of the present, with its overwhelming problems and sense of despair, there is a nostalgic longing for this era of basic safety and time of cultural, political and intellectual ferment. When I did fieldwork in the resistance period, refugee narratives depicted the 1950s and early 1960s as a dark age, harsh and repressive. The Lebanese authorities were cast as enemies whose task was to prevent political organizing, monitor signs of permanency in the camps, and to keep the refugees politically and spatially contained. Over refreshments at the 'Ayn al-Hilweh home of Um and Abu Kamal, with whom I had worked with closely in the early 1980s, the visit of a childhood friend and class-mate sparked a lively and impassioned discussion of the present compared to the 1950s and 1960s. Um Kamal, now a schoolteacher, reminisced:

Remember how we used to study in 'Ayn al-Hilweh. Our generation (*jeelna*) was so committed to studying! And we knew exactly who we were. If asked we would say we are from such and-such a village. Now the young people only know which camp they are from! These are the worst days I have ever seen and I have been in this work for over twenty years. Children are hungry and search the garbage for food. We have children in the streets rather than in school. They come to school hungry and without proper clothes. Some of them don't even have shoes! There is a new generation of illiterates. UNRWA throws out those who don't perform well and then they are in the streets. Currently there is a Swedish program to take these kids and give them remedial help. In preparatory research, we looked at one [village] area—Hittin—and found 75 street kids.

Those who pass the Brevet[8] are semiliterate, not like in the old days when we studied so hard and were expected to learn. Kids these days are unable to study. Their home environment is lacking. How can they study in a home where no one cares, where there are so many problems! And these days in the camp, no ones looks out for anyone else.

In this early period, the social production of space arose from building the camp and sharing its space, naming its areas, participating in new social institutions and crafting new social relationships, and forging community out of common loss. It was characterized by ambiguity as to the future and a furious running back and forth between hope and despair, chaos and fixity, sameness and difference, security and perilousness. It would give way dramatically to a landscape of imagination and anticipation, of intense hope and a general mobilization of political and social efforts to shape the future.

Place is always in a state of becoming; embedded in local contexts, it acts upon them. These uncertain, accidental, and contested places of violence were to undergo profound and rapid formation and reformation. These were not places that conformed easily to their initial intent. The recuperation of Palestine could only be partial, and its partiality opened an interstice for a landscape of hope and anticipation. Refugees were the driving force in generating places as meaningful constructs within the constraints imposed by structural features and forms of external power. At one brief point in time, the era of militancy and autonomy (1968–82), power shifted to the interior and gave leeway for Palestinians to transform the camps in their own image. Chapters five and six continue the story of the social production of space and reformulations of identity with the coming of the resistance movement when the permanent state of conflict crystallized.

Chapter Five
Landscape of Hope and Despair

> He saw the camp in another way. He lifted his head and began to
> look around. . . . He can't see a gun on a young man's shoulder
> without moving aside and caressing it.
> —Ghassan Kanafani (2000: 132)

> there has been no place for us like Beirut, a city of staggering vio-
> lence and unpredictable resilience.
> —Edward Said (1986: 169)

The camps could be seen as a built environment, as everyday abodes,
and as places where possibilities for the future emerged, took shape, and
were acted upon. Maintaining secrecy about the *fidāʾiyyin* signaled a
community boundary, a defensive line of inclusion in a community of
shared marginality and repression, and of militant action. This chapter
explores place-making and identity in the resistance era (1968–82) and
during the camp wars (1985–87), both periods of extraordinary violence. Rafiq and Abu Fadi's statements evoke this landscape.

Before the revolution, we couldn't stack two stones on top of one another.
When the revolution came, we built in stone, with concrete roofs and we built
second and third stories. Before the revolution we could not do anything. (Abu
Fadi, ʿAyn al-Hilweh camp)

In the early days, the resistance was extremely secretive. Young men disappeared from the camp and nobody knew where they went. Rumors circulated
that so-and-so joined the resistance which meant he went to Jordan because
that's where the training bases were. In Lebanon, the camps were still under the
strict control of the Lebanese Intelligence. Nobody dared to do anything political, let alone militarily at that point and there were no weapons. In the beginning, we heard these fantastic stories about guerrillas. They were the first to go
and in the camps there was a kind of agreement to keep things secret.

With the resistance takeover of the camps, there was a complete rush of
enthusiasm. What changed most was the shift from the belief that the Arab

armies were going to liberate Palestine to the belief in a peoples' war of guerrilla fighting. Although Nasser was still respected and revered by the Palestinians, there was a sense of disillusionment. The gap was filled by the resistance very quickly and very effectively.

In the camp, the idea that you are freed from the reign of the Lebanese Intelligence and police was overwhelming because we had been living under the terror of these people. Our first reaction was to get rid of them in a very humiliating way. So our first sense of empowerment was very localized and then came the larger, more important sense that we could do something to change the prospect for our future. Not only on the camp level anymore, but on the more general level—it was the idea that we Palestinians, not the Arab governments, could inflict damage on Israel. There was the romantic hope that you are the small flame that's going to light the fires of all the others. (Rafiq, 'Ayn al-Hilweh camp)

1968–69: Landscapes of Hope: Spatial Explosion or "Jumping Scales"

In the late 1960s, there were skirmishes between the nascent resistance movement and the Lebanese Army. Regionally, the Palestinian resistance movement was gaining credibility as a political force to be taken seriously. In March 1968, about 300 Palestinian *fida'iyyin* inflicted substantial and unexpected casualties on several battalions of the invading Israeli Defence Forces at the battle of al-Karameh in Jordan. In the aftermath of this stunning military action—what Khalidi refers to as the "foundation myth" of the guerrilla movement (R. Khalidi 1997: 196), Palestinian political offices in the Arab world were flooded with recruits. In the November 1969 Cairo Accords, the Lebanese government accepted the resistance movement's openly armed presence and control over the camps. Immediately, armed resistance forces entered the camps and Lebanese government personnel fled or were escorted out as crowds of Palestinians cheered. The abrupt change in the power equation launched the relandscaping of the camps as well as a new era of institution building and internal autonomy. The resistance movement, commonly referred to as *al-thawra* (the revolution) or *al-muqawameh* (the resistance), engaged in mass mobilization, recruiting thousands of young Palestinian men and women throughout Lebanon. Within a few years, it was under fairly constant attack from Lebanese and Israeli military forces and was eventually drawn in as a central player in the Lebanese civil war. While short-lived, these heady days of ideological fervor and political autonomy and militancy gave rise to a generation, *jeel al-thawra*, and an era, *'ayyam al-thawra*, both marked by new forms of subjectivity and identity. A young guerrilla from Rashidiyyah camp, Abu Salah, who trained in Jordan and returned with the commandos to take over the camps in 1969, described those days:

The consciousness of the people changed in a matter of hours, not just days. There was a tremendous jump from before the revolution to after. The revolution was almost holy, you know. After the Lebanese soldiers left the camps—and relieved the oppression—it was a new kind of freedom. I came back with a large group of *fidaʾiyyin* and we prepared to enter ʿAyn al-Hilwah. We had our guns at our sides and begin to march into the camp. I was very nervous and scared—we were carrying weapons openly and we still weren't completely sure what the military or local situation was. As we entered the camp in military formation, I kept my head stiffly facing forward, too afraid to look around me. Then I heard a growing rumble, a din of noise. Slowly I turned my head to the side to see what it was and where it was coming from. I was stunned! People were lining the narrow streets and cheering our arrival! All I saw were smiles and waving arms greeting us.

The coming of the resistance had an immediate impact on the landscape. The revolution ushered in the permanency of cement, as people began building with stone, expanding their small homes and adding private bathrooms to replace the common latrines. Cement roofs replaced the sheets of zinc, and second floors to house expanding families were added with impunity. Cement homes signified permanence and thus alarmed many Lebanese. When commented upon, Palestinians were quick to explain, "We will leave them to the Lebanese when we leave." As self-perceived guests and seekers of refuge in Lebanon, they thought to reciprocate long-term hospitality.

When the resistance took over the camps and their borders, it remapped the scales of power in space; the microgeography of the camps exploded. As the refugee community jumped imposed borders, the margins imploded into the center. Power exercised from inside the camps swiftly transformed their meaning for host and refugee. The landscape of despair and anticipation was transformed into a new one of hope and struggle. Sites of waiting and confinement became sites of mobilization and militancy. Freed of the restraints imposed by the Lebanese authorities, they became zones of autonomy, militancy, and community self-sufficiency. As spaces in a state, they remained ambiguous, in the territory of the state but not of it.

The camps' geosocial landscape was visibly and experientially transformed. They were now active national spaces. The plethora of resistance offices that sprang up in what were once largely residential areas, the ubiquitous presence of gun-toting *fidaʾiyin*, and the numerous new faces working and living in them transformed the camps' landscape. Every family had some sort of relationship with the movement, ranging from full-time salaried members to employees. National consciousness was spatialized, that is, given territorial status in these small but militant and autonomous islands in the midst of another state. Palestinian flags flew defiantly over the camps and at the checkpoints surrounding them.

In this newly realized atmosphere of autonomy, practices of resistance were on display—military training, openly carrying weapons, wearing military dress, and joining demonstrations, among others.

A heterogeneous demographic shift reinscribed the social landscape. Resistance cadres came from Jordan[1] and Lebanese and Palestinians from the south flocked to the Beirut camps searching for work and escaping conflict. Um Khalid's three-story building in Shatila housed Lebanese and Palestinians from both the Galilee and the West Bank. Although usually single men, some of those coming from Jordan did bring their families and rent housing, further complicating spatiality in the camps. Their particular villages or towns were often not known to Palestinians in Lebanon and in the national scheme of things mattered less than did their affiliation with a particular political faction. Village space and mapping receded somewhat as the camps expanded to incorporate new residents and institutions. Villages were overlaid with other social markers, reworking the meaning of place. Never homogeneous to begin with, village areas begin to incorporate families from other villages as people moved out of their homes and rented to others. Palestinians migrating to Beirut in search of work found affordable housing in the camps. They were becoming cosmopolitan locales as non-Palestinian Arabs and Euro-Americans worked and lived in them as part of an internationally based solidarity campaign.

These foreigners, especially the medical personnel, were known by name to most people. These social relations became indelibly etched into the spatiality and collective memory of the camp. Years later, people still recall them by name and have fond memories of them and what their presence signaled about the Palestinian cause. Eva, a Scandinavian nurse in Tel al-Za'ter during the 1976 siege, lost her Palestinian husband and miscarried her child. She also lost her arm after being hit by shell fragments. Her name is easily recognized in many camps twenty-five years later. In recalling the idealism of this period, Abu Jawad, now a grizzled fifty-five-year-old veteran guerrilla captured the inclusiveness and cosmopolitanism of this era when he said of Tel al-Za'ter camp in the 1970s: "We became one village. Palestine was the name. In the camps, the resistance and one's activities in it mattered more than the village from where one came."

Once fairly well-defined boundaries were simultaneously diluted and strengthened, Palestinians could move from the camp to the exterior with ease and a sense of security. The newly guarded borders kept out strangers (non-Palestinians). Reorganized from inside, they were ringed by the newly formed Palestinian police force, *al kefah al-musallah*, an armed force whose task was to ensure safety by patrolling the camps' borders, defending them from external assault, and controlling entry of outsiders. Nonresidents, including Lebanese military or police, government officials, and civilians could not just enter at will. *Al kefah al-musallah* or *al-fida'iyyin* from Palestinian organizations would ask for an identity card and question where one was going. The fear of spies and infiltration was pervasive. Once foreigners such as myself were vouched for by the resistance, we were free to enter and exit at will.

Where once interior and exterior were antipodal, proximate space on the exterior of the camp moved closer as the borders became fluid and expanded outward; mobility was no longer so constrained. In the Beirut camps, labor migration to Europe and the oil-producing states and inmigration by southern Lebanese and Palestinians made for fluidity in population density and village spatial integrity. By the early 1970s, the once demarcated camps were merging with Lebanese areas in a two-fold process of expansion. For example, demographic growth compelled Shatila to stretch beyond its original borders at the same time as Beirut expanded into the southern suburbs. The Beirut camps and their surrounding Lebanese areas were economic zones providing low-income housing and consumer goods to Shi'a from the south. In addition, the PLO made many of their services, such as free or low-cost medical care, available to poor Lebanese. In 'Ayn al-Hilweh, an earthquake provided the initial impetus for a blurring of borders. Lebanese families displaced from the old city of Saida were housed in a development project next to 'Ayn al-Hilweh called Ta'meer. Camp housing gradually expanded across the railroad lines that marked its western border. A long single row of houses on the other side of the tracks signaled this spatial jumping.

Most significantly, the more open borders symbolized points of overarching interest between the two communities, spatializing a constellation of interests, struggles, and visions of place that contested marginalization, poverty, and displacement. Political relations between progressive Lebanese movements and the Palestinians were at their height. Before the formation of Shi'a political organizations in the mid- to late 1970s, liberals tended to join the Lebanese Communist Party or Palestinian organizations. Close political, economic, and social ties between the communities could be read spatially. In the early 1970s, Um Hassan and her family, Shi'a from the south, moved to Shatila. She rented the apartment next door to Um Khalid and they quickly became close friends. Her husband worked in construction and their rent was relatively inexpensive. Services, particularly medical, provided by the various organizations of the PLO were available to these nonrefugees. Hayy Farhat, a small Lebanese neighborhood on the southern edge of Shatila, had merged into the camp such that it was difficult to pinpoint the exact borders of the original camp from this burgeoning neighborhood inhabited by both Shi'a Lebanese and Palestinians. The resistance exerted control over it, its inhabitants were both Lebanese and Palestinian, and the frequent movement between it and the camp proper was not marked by any visible boundary.

After 1969, camps had a multilayered topography. New forms of place-making and placenaming accompanied the radical shift in the empowerment of the refugees and their relations with their hosts. Arranged by villages and dotted with UNRWA service sites, the camps' spatial organization and landscape was now overlaid with a strikingly different sort of mapping, encoding new sorts of social relations, institutions, and forms of power. In this new landscape the valorization of resistance and the significance of the national were imprinted on space. A host of new institutional sites associated with the resistance such as offices, clinics, nurseries, vocational training and literacy centers, and clubs created a new type of public space. Fateh and the official PLO institutions were dominant, although smaller groups such as PFLP and DFLP did open offices and offer a variety of social services. In Shatila these joined the mosque, the geospatial heart of the camp, and UNRWA service centers as spatial landmarks. While village organization was never as sharp as in other camps, the new resistance landscape was more pronounced than elsewhere. It was close to the bustling and politically vibrant Fakhani area of Beirut, the headquarters of the PLO and its constituent organizations. Burj al-Barajneh's distinctly etched village spaces were multiply marked by references to resistance spaces such as Hayy Sa'iqa (Sa'iqa neighborhood or area) or Hayy Jebhat al-Tahrir (Liberation Front neighborhood or area).[2] Refugees' descriptions of where things were included villages and new resistance institutions and offices.

As the camps and their surrounding neighborhoods merged, external spaces were added to cognitive mappings. For example, a once empty area adjacent to Burj al-Barajneh was called Samed after the factory built there in the late 1970s by the PLO as part of its emerging industrial infrastructure. On the edge of the camp, the Lebanese Vocational School became another reference marker, as did the Sabra market and Dana Mosque for Shatila's northern border. Cognitive maps incorporated and made signposts of these new sites. In giving directions to others or explaining the location of a particular building or area, these new landmarks dotted the former villagescape, accompanying already well-imprinted markers. These new exterior and interior landmarks mapped an expanded terrain of control, mobility, and empowerment for refugees.

Remapping stretched the spatial inventory to include geographically distant Palestinian urban centers. The national was invoked as new institutions were named after Palestinian cities such as Haifa Hospital in Burj al-Barajneh or Gaza Hospital in Sabra, underscoring the national in the camps, their intimate connectedness with places distant and never seen and the spilling over of Palestinian nationalism and cultural space into Lebanese areas. In the 1970s, it became fashionable to name baby girls after Palestinian towns and villages, asserting national rather than parochial village affiliations and identity. When Um Fadi's niece named her daughter Beisan, a town occupied by Israel in 1948, or Jenin as did her sister, a West Bank town occupied in 1967, or after the cities of Haifa and Yaffa, they were asserting a connection to and claiming of Palestinian space as well as proclaiming national unity by consolidating present place and time with Beisan/1948 and Jenin/1967. In the face of fragmentation, naming patterns linked past and present, thus collapsing time and space. In other words, names drew lines of inclusion, linking people, places, and time, past and present, and locating identities in a national landscape.

The exact borders of Shatila camp were apparent to me only in the early 1990s. When I worked in the camp in the 1970s and 1980s I had not paid much attention to the borders because they were simply not much of an issue at the time. And indeed, they were so fluid that I would have had to ask someone to show me exactly where they were. Yet there were some physical and social signs that distinguished space during this period. Over time I learned some of them on my own and generally was aware of when I was, and was not, in the camp. However, there were some areas I was always unsure of. On the north, Shatila is bordered by the neighborhood of Sabra, a quasi-camp and a sizable urban market. A densely populated area of low-income housing, part of Beirut's urban sprawl and poverty belt, it had a distinctly urban feel to it. Urban dress prevailed and Palestinians dressed in their outdoor wear when shopping there. The streets were wider and noisier because of the volume of traffic and the commercial nature of the area. With time, I became aware of the spatial and sociocultural border that separated the camp from this area. At one particular corner coming from the Sabra market, I abruptly left the bustle and din of the market and found myself in a much quieter place. Children played in the quiet, narrow alleys, too small to accommodate cars, and commercial activity was much diminished.

On leaving the Lebanese area and entering the camp, dress codes relaxed and, most significantly, the gendering of space changed. In spite of the fluid borders between Lebanese and camp spaces, refugees still considered Lebanese space urban and dressed accordingly. They did not wear house dresses or a *jelabiyyeh*. Um Khalid would don her Western style dress, patterned, long-sleeved, and shift-like, comb her hair neatly, and carry her well-used but still sturdy black handbag to go outside the camp. In camps with village neighborhoods, space retained private or domestic aspects. Men still sat in front of their houses in their pyjamas, but they would not go into the public space of the camp or outside the camp in such dress. Women might enter houses in their alleys in house clothes, but when visiting other villages in the camps they would make sure their hair was neatly combed and wore a clean *jelabiyyeh*.

The transposition of gendered norms of space and mobility were integral to placemaking. Within the camps, women's mobility was not overly restricted as they visited friends and ran errands, although young girls were supervised and a hasty return was expected. The presence of young single men from the West Bank, Gaza Strip, Jordan, or other camps who were associated with the resistance had an uneven impact. Young girls were moving about the camps more to attend classes, go to meetings, or participate in resistance activities. These young men from elsewhere were not as much of a perceived threat, however, as men outside the camps. Yet parents still did not completely trust their behavior because they did not have family in the camps. However, their resistance affiliation meant they were accountable to someone. Thus mobility outside the camps was more restricted for girls and young women. They went out with parental permission and in groups or, for unmarried girls, with an older chaperone. Mobility within the camp signaled its status as protected space where norms of proper behavior toward women and girls were expected to prevail. In other words, the camps became private space vis-à-vis the exterior. Crowded conditions meant that this was practically a face-to-face society. If you didn't actually know someone personally, you always knew someone who did.

Women's visiting networks constituted a means of placemaking, and as a methodological device they tracked spatiality. Daily visits between Lebanese and Palestinian women, such as those Um Khalid was involved in, brought the former into the political and social orbit of the camp and vice versa. In visits, information was exchanged as to the availability of services and participation in camp political activities was encouraged. Via women, families could cultivate access to the political hierarchy of the resistance (Peteet 1991). These visiting relations nurtured cross-national and cross-sectarian relations with the potential to serve both communities.

The construction of neighborhood, the sense of belonging to and being of a place is integral to placemaking. In the Middle East, one can often read neighborhood boundaries by the street behavior of young men (*shebab*) toward girls and women. Where streets are defined largely as male space and women perceived somewhat as transgressors, petty harassment of women is often commonplace. They face less harassment in their own neighborhoods where they are known and young men fear to bother them because of the potentially serious consequences if male kin are alerted. Moreover, men are assigned the task of neighborhood surveillance and protection of inhabitants. It is when they leave their own neighborhoods, or are in those where they are unknown, that harassment is more likely to occur. It occurs most frequently in urban areas without a sense of neighborhood, those newer commercial areas where people are not connected by ties of neighborliness or kinship. Within the camps, the harassment of girls and young women was negligible. Young Palestinian men might harass women outside the camps, in the anonymity of Beirut's commercial areas or neighborhoods, but they would not dare do so in the camps. I attribute this to the sense of camps as neighborhoods where people felt connected to and responsible to and for one another. These implicit behavioral codes marked community boundaries.

Gender, both masculinity and femininity, was critical to the maintenance of the camps as Palestinian places and their communal boundaries against a hostile exterior. During military emergencies as in the civil war, the *fida'iyyin* defended the camps against external aggression. They were affectionately referred to as *bani al-mukhayyam* (sons of the camp), a cultural technique that inscribed place into male bodies and these bodies onto the camp. Their actions symbolically and in reality did define camp borders. As "sons" of the camp, domesticity was extended beyond one's own progeny and home and incorporated the "sons" of everyone. This was another instance of the camp as a domestic unit and the blurring of public/private spatial schemata.

The interior of the camp home was unambiguously gendered. When male visitors who were not kin entered the home, they were seated in the front room reserved for visitors. They rarely if ever entered the rest of the house. Knowledge of the general rules of space was embodied and they were performed with little conscious thought or effort. Their observation was highlighted by an instance where the unarticulated rules were broken. During the civil war, a French crew was filming in Shatila and Um Khalid hosted them for lunch. The mixed crew of six were served a lavish meal by camp standards in Um Khalid's living room. Located at the front of her house, this room was reserved for visitors. Nonkin males never entered the back rooms of the house, where cooking took place and rooms for sleeping were located. The family took its meals, watched TV, and socialized in one of the bedrooms, which during the day was converted into a family room with cushion-lined walls set up for women visitors. The only males who entered this space were close kin. Once the meal was finished, one of the French men stood up and started carrying dishes down the hallway, looking for the kitchen. Um Khalid's daughters jumped up to protest but he was off. Not only as a guest should he have remained seated, he broke a fundamental cultural rule of thumb: males have access to extremely limited spaces in homes not their own. Um Khalid's teenaged daughters made great sport of the cultural breach, giggling and winking at one another until he deposited the dishes in the kitchen. Um Khalid looked at me with a smile and a shrug, as if to say "what does he know?" They insisted he sit down but graciously never let on that he had violated a fundamental aspect of Arab etiquette.

Where space is polyvalent and its usage multipurpose and contingent, a public/private polarity is a non sequitur. For example, homes doubled as venues for political meetings and informal gatherings. This was more so for women, who conducted political meetings and seminars in each others' homes, but it was true, even if to a lesser extent, for men. Male visits were often to conduct informal political affairs. Mobilization of recruits usually started with home visits (Peteet 1991). In this way, facets of the domestic became public and the public sphere was present and working in the domestic arena.

During the resistance era, villages were somewhat eclipsed as forms of affiliation and their traditional leadership was bypassed, coopted, or merged with resistance affiliations. Abu Salah, from the village of 'Alma, commented:

After 1948, you could say, as a village, we lost our balance for a few years. Initially each family looked after themselves. Every village was a bit different but in 'Alma each family tried to find somebody—the respected elder, let's say—from the village to look to for leadership. But in the late 1960s all that changed for the new generation. In our view, these people had lost their esteem. We were involved in politics. These older people hadn't been involved. We started to see these older people as responsible for what had happened to us.

To disaggregate family/village/resistance affiliations and identities would be to exaggerate and simplify the impact of the resistance. These new and emergent aspects of identity and affiliation such as political organizations did not displace but rather overlaid and interacted with village based affiliations, identities, or rivalries. Abu Salah provided insight into the complexity of these relations:

Before 1969, if there were troubles between people that became violent—say someone shot someone else—there were two ways to resolve it: the Lebanese police would take over or we would have *sulha* [traditional mediation]—so, either a legal solution or a social one. After the revolution took over the camps, most problems were resolved by *sulha*. The PLO tried to set up a kind of court system and prisons. The problem was that it wasn't applied to everyone in the same way. For example, if someone committed a crime in the camps, the camp police [*al kefah al-musallah*] were supposed to arrest him but if he was from a particular organization, or had someone powerful behind him, they would not touch him. So in that sense, nothing much changed. But something had changed in our thinking. If you were to even think of organizing on the basis of your village, people would jump on you saying, "What are you talking about!? You are talking about one village. It is wrong to think about Palestine in pieces, to confine the struggle to one area."

I remember a *sulha* I was involved in soon after the revolution took over the camps. I was based in Rashidiyyah camp, which was my home as well. There was a fight one night between two young men from different families in the village of 'Alma. One of them struck the other, killing him on the spot. The two families began to fight with each other. They lived close to each other—each on one side of an alley—and they had intermarried over the years. One family had an affiliation with the Democratic Front for the Liberation of Palestine (DFLP); the other was affiliated with Jaysh Tahrir [Palestinian Liberation Army]. I was a *masool* [responsible or local leader of a political organization] in the camp and I belonged to the PFLP [Popular Front for the Liberation of Palestine]. The camp police, made up of guerrillas from different political organizations, arrested members of both families to keep things from getting out of hand. And we placed military forces between the two families. We separated them for about a week. And then I was assigned responsibility for arranging a *sulha*. It was not because I was from the same village—but because of my political position. And after about a week, we managed to bring about a reconciliation between the two families. The big Palestinian leaders, "known" or prominent people from other villages, and the elders of 'Alma were the mediators. If the PLO had changed the way we did things, it would have been a different situation. I don't want to think back to that now. They didn't change the traditions or the way we did things. They went back to the old ways like *sulha* but did it in the name of the revolution. Those words "in the name of the revolution" [*bism al-thawra*] were enough to make you forget your enmity, your problems, for the sake of the national struggle and the future. The political organizations involved, DF and Jaysh Tahrir, put pressure on these families to accept *sulha*. The resistance didn't want trouble between these families to escalate to the political organizations and create bigger problems. So they used the traditional system of mediation and brought big name families from other villages to the mediation. During the mediation, the family of the perpetrator said, "We are at fault and we offer our apologies. What can we do for you?" The family of the victim replied: "We want nothing. You have recognized our right [*haqq*] and that is enough." In the past, they would have had to pay blood money; in this case, the perpetrator's family cooked food and fed everybody and that sealed the reconciliation.

In this explicit critique, Abu Salah advocated a legal system with universal procedures and equity where village origins and loyalties would be sidelined. The emerging legal system during the resistance era still had recourse to traditional legal procedures, personnel, and outcomes. The resistance provided a new and powerful source of affiliation, identity, and benefits which, as Abu Salah's legal case illustrates, incorporated those derived from village and kin. In addition, kinship was a primary means of political mobilization, as relatives encouraged and facilitated each others' activism in their particular organizations and thus villages retained their significance as sites of affiliation, identity, and political mobilization. Once fairly common, village endogamy was giving way to increasing cross-village marriages. As elsewhere in the region, village endogamy and exogamy operated simultaneously to strengthen kin and village ties by solidifying social ties within and across village boundaries. Rather than replacing family and village social relations, the resistance worked in tandem with them.

The resistance movement fostered a sense of community among Palestinians in Lebanon and gave it organizational expression. Political activities and duties took people from their camps to other camps; these were new venues for forming friendships and marriages. For example, Maryam, twenty years old in 1976, was active with the resistance in Rashidiyyeh camp. She visited camps all over Lebanon for her work establishing women's vocational training projects. In the process, she forged friendships in other camps that could hardly have been imagined in the preresistance period. When she visited 'Ayn al-Hilweh camp, she always slept at the home of her good friend and coactivist Lamya. For a young single girl to sleep away from home would have been unthinkable before the resistance cast such behavior as nationalist. In her travels, Maryam gained knowledge of each camp and, as she said, "When you travel from camp to camp as I do for my work, you begin to feel a connection to each place. Although Rashidiyyeh is my home, I feel at home in all the camps." With resistance military organizing, there was a coalescing of all camps in particular areas into operational units able to coordinate a military response to assault, giving a material reality to regional communities in south Lebanon, north Lebanon, and Beirut.

Moreover, the resistance movement linked camp Palestinians with the outside world, thus playing a strategic role in the formation of a transnational Palestinian community. Palestinian students from Lebanon, Jordan, and Syria traveled to Eastern Europe and the Soviet Union on PLO scholarships. There they formed student groups linked at higher levels in the General Union of Palestinian Students (GUPS). On another level, the PLO's international diplomatic activity connected refugee camps to other exilic sites, to regional Middle East centers, and globally to networks of solidarity activists. In hosting foreign solidarity activists and delegations, camp residents established linkages with a world far beyond their boundaries. The formation of institutions and social affiliations such as unions and political organizations that cross-cut camp boundaries formed the bases for the emergence of a sense of community as the Palestinians in Lebanon.

By the mid-1970s, as a permanent state of conflict crystallized, camps became known as sites where particular forms of violence unfolded. After its destruction in 1976, Tel al-Za'ter became a symbol of tragedy, a repository of memory of defeat, massacre, and erasure. Now the stuff of lore and poetry, a metonym for disaster, it also symbolizes heroic resistance.[3] Initially Shatila embodied political power as the Beirut camp where all the Palestinian organizations had major offices. Later, after the 1982 massacre and the camp wars, it became closely linked to heroic defense, steadfastness, and tragedy, a metaphor for defeat and trauma.

This resistance period was short-lived, coming to a violent end in the summer of 1982 with the Israeli invasion of Lebanon and the subsequent withdrawal of the PLO. Between 1975 and 1982, Palestinians were heavily involved in the civil war then raging in Lebanon. The civil war was a local as well as regional and international affair. Lebanon was the terrain for regional conflicts with nearby states implicated as sponsors or financial and military backers of local political organizations. In addition, superpower rivalry played out as the USSR, the U.S., and European states intervened to promote their national interests. Locally, the war was a class-sectarian clash in which the Palestinians were aligned with the largely Muslim, Lebanese progressive forces in battling the primarily Maronite Christian right's attempt to maintain their historic hegemony and dilute the Palestinian presence in Lebanon. The civil war launched the beginning of the end of Palestinian autonomy in the camps and remade the spatial arrangement of power in Lebanon. In August 1976 Tel al-Za'ter and Dbiyyeh camps in East Beirut were demolished, "cleansing" Christian East Beirut of Palestinians. The other camps remained in a state of alert from 1975 to 1982 as they faced a series of air and artillery assaults by rightist Maronite and Israeli forces. As the "vanguards" of resistance and cultural authenticity, the camps were exemplars of nationalism and suffering.

Palestinians draw lines of continuity among the civil war, the 1982 invasion, and the camp wars of the mid-1980s. In their view, an Israeli driven and U.S. as well as regionally supported plan was underway to contain Palestinian nationalism and cut down to size the PLO. Disarming the camps, bastions of Palestinian nationalism, was central to this plan. Palestinians understood clearly that rather than posing as a regional military threat they were more a force of ideological destabilization for Arab regimes. Their armed presence did give them the ability to spark confrontations, but the more ominous threat they posed was their revolutionary fervor and exposure of the inability and unwillingness of local government to respond to colonial and imperialistic projects in the region and their ability to politicize and mobilize the street. On the local level, Palestinian political and military clout in the 1970s and the ideological appeal of their anti-imperialist and progressive stances were rallying points for the mobilization of many Muslim Lebanese into Palestinian and Lebanese leftist organizations. The Maronite establishment felt threatened by the Palestinians' ability to mobilize the Lebanese left, largely but not solely Muslim. Because of its nonsectarian and leftist ideology, it posed a patent challenge to the leadership of all sects, indeed to the notion of sect as a basis for organizing the polity.

The refugees' gradual empowerment and ability to jump spatial scales were accompanied by a heightened Lebanese rhetoric of impending dangers. By 1975, sectarian leaders had become increasingly vocal and highly inflammatory in their statements. The Lebanese reference to the refugees in a guest metaphor was replaced by more ominous representations. Immediately prior to the civil war, a Palestinian university student recalled a speech by Phalangist leader Pierre Gemeyal in which he called them the "filthiest of people from the holiest of lands," followed by, "We offered them a half a loaf and they took the other half," a phrase which eventually entered popular discourse.

For Palestinians, the camps embodied multiple, sometimes contradictory and ambiguous, meanings. Social location is crucial in discussing these representations and imaginings. For their residents, they were places of sanctuary as well as zones of cultural celebration in a hostile world. To Palestinians on the exterior, they epitomized cultural purity, suffering, and resistance. Because they housed the resistance and refugees who had previously been peasants, they were places of an authentic Palestinian identity rooted in the land, struggle, and suffering. In the occupied territories, peasants were signifiers of an authentic, rooted past (Swedenburg 1995), while in exile, those now in refugee camps were imagined as being somehow more "Palestinian," more authentic in their capacity to represent key components of collective identity.

The camps also evoked guilt among the urban-dwelling Palestinians because they bore the burden of the national struggle and shouldered the losses resulting from violent assaults. Urban middle- and upper-class Palestinians combined guilt with admiration for the camps' militancy and distaste for their once peasant, now quasi-urban lower-class style of life and standard of living. Many urban Palestinians had never visited a refugee camp, considering them dangerous places.

The mobilization of the Lebanese right in the early 1970s was accompanied by a heightened production of difference and otherness, expressed in representations of the camps and the refugees. Often referred to as guests (*duyoof*) when they first arrived in Lebanon, with the development of hostilities between Palestinians and the Lebanese right, they were reconfigured as strangers (*ghuraba*), a highly politicized term in this context, usually used to refer to Arabs from elsewhere. The guests had violated the code of hospitality by ostensibly behaving ungratefully and attempting to take over the host's home. The ungrateful guests now constituted a menace to Lebanon's unique social landscape and social-sectarian balance (or imbalance). Eventually, the camps were imagined as places harboring Palestinian and foreign terrorists who insulted and challenged the legitimacy of the government and army. The expansion of the camps' borders, which coincided with the resistance's alignment with progressive Lebanese movements, threatened Christian hegemony. I remember tuning into vitriolic Phalangist radio broadcasts in the 1970s and listening to the camps described as eyesores and equated with a cancerous growth blotting the beauty of the Lebanese landscape. The landscape of Lebanon, especially Christian East Beirut, could not contain Muslim refugee riffraff if it was to achieve sectarian and cultural purity. In the quest for sectarian modernity, distance from Arabism, which was exemplified by Muslims and Palestinians, was pursued. In the civil war, the actions of the Lebanese forces suggested an aesthetics of place destruction. Their military moves to erase the camps echoed the rhetoric likening them to eyesores and garbage heaps. To resurrect the purity of the landscape, the right talked of tennis courts and shopping malls, places of leisure and the pleasures of consumption to be built on the sites of obliterated camps such as Tel al-Za'ter.

Identity in 'Ayyam al-thawra

During the resistance era and the civil war, new forms of violence, suffering and heroism began to affect identity. Retrospectively referred to as 'ayyam al-thawra, this period was remarkable for both the violence and self-consciousness of the moment. As Said lamented, "the one thing none of us can forget is that violence has been an extraordinarily important aspect of our lives . . . and [has] exacerbated our self-awareness as a community set apart from others" (1986). He captured the seeming contradiction of Palestinian nationalism: its specificity forged through violence and otherness and yet its flexibility and expansiveness. Palestinians were acutely aware of living in a moment of heightened meaning and historicity where one could act as "a small flame." Identity was the object of conscious action and deliberation, not simply a given. Palestinian leader Shafiq al-Hout underscored the centrality of agency to Palestinian identity when he uttered what soon became a slogan of the times: "Anyone who struggles is a Palestinian!"

Palestinians described the resistance takeover of the camps as "a new beginning" and a new way of being outside the camps. Once vulnerable, they were now empowered by a movement to assert their national rights. The ubiquitous carrying of weapons engendered self-esteem and pride, while military training constituted a rite of passage into militancy, validating their ability and commitment to the nation and community. With its requirement of distance from home, it unsettled family control over youth, especially young women, and emboldened them to challenge it

(Peteet 1991). Forging a militant Palestinian identity was a project of modernity, of lifestyle as consciously produced and enacted.

By 1968, the term "refugee" was avoided in self-characterization and public presentation; it conveyed an image of passivity and denationalization, and suggested humanitarian solutions to a fundamentally political problem. Rafiq's notion of the individual as "a small flame" with the ability to "light the fires of all the others," highlights the insertion of agency and consciousness into identity formation. In the early 1970s, when I first arrived as a graduate student at the American University of Beirut, I casually referred to Palestinians as refugees. My Palestinian roommate chided me for this injudicious choice of words and said in no uncertain terms, "We are not refugees. We are returnees, militants, strugglers, and revolutionaries." Rather than choosing terms of self-definition that indicated where they were—seekers of refuge in—they defined themselves as people seeking to go to where they came from. The distinction hinged on action as well as belonging. The "returnee" implied a political commitment that underwrote agency. "Refugee" undercut national identity, implying a passive acceptance of the status quo and the possibility of resettlement in a third country. Moreover, in this period, it was increasingly less relevant to daily material existence. UNRWA services were being superseded by the resistance's infrastructure, which provided employment and a modicum of welfare and medical services.

During this era, Palestinians referred to themselves as "strugglers," "militants," "activists," "revolutionaries," or simply Palestinians, now a term freighted with empowerment. Identities became caught up with resistance activities. Naturally, the Palestinian national identity of someone not active in the resistance was not denied, it just wasn't marked to the same extent. Instead identity was heightened and exalted by action. Militants were "real" (*haqqiqiyyun*) Palestinians, as were those in the camps whose daily lives were perceived as a struggle in and of themselves. With the PLO headquartered in Beirut, the camps were places of intensive interaction with Palestinians from elsewhere and with foreign supporters. Spatial boundaries were at their loosest. As such, they were cosmopolitan intersections where people joined together on the basis of a common national identity and commitment to a political cause. As an indication of the flexibility of Palestinian identity, foreigners could be real Palestinians. It wasn't "blood," or even place of origin or parental nationality, that counted as much as commitment to the struggle. During the 1970s when the Palestinians were training Iranian opponents of the Shah, on more than one occasion I heard those who excelled in fighting referred to as "real Palestinians." Militancy stretched the boundaries of belonging well beyond any simple national designation.

Honorary or fictitious national membership could be conferred on non-Palestinians by virtue of militancy or active solidarity with the Palestinian cause. So powerful was political action for identity formation and expression that everyday roles and tasks were politicized and redefined to incorporate militancy (Peteet 1991) Women referred to themselves as strugglers and militants for their role in reproducing the nation and maintaining domesticity under often onerous circumstances.

Political action was conceptually broad enough to encompass official membership in an organization as well as the informal activism of everyday life that drew in sectors of society (mothers, the elderly, youth, and children) not easily mobilized into formal political roles. In the context of a militant social movement, what were the contours and intricacies of the relationship between identity and place? The political arena, itself embedded in the shared space of the camps, was a medium through which Palestinian identities were produced, articulated, and lived. Palestinian national identity, used to mobilize people into the resistance, was itself transformed during the course of political participation. In other words, the Palestinian social movement mobilized around and reaffirmed identities; yet it had the potential to transform them as well (Peteet 2000). The resistance movement was identity-giving in several ways. First, it provided a protective shield around public expressions of Palestinian identity. For example, the Palestinian accent could be openly spoken in Lebanese areas without arousing hostility, replacing the linguistic dissimulation practiced in the preresistance period. The resistance transfigured the way of being a Palestinian in relation to others in Lebanon. Individual and collective empowerment was a key component of this transformation. Palestinians described the years before the resistance as ones of insecurity and humiliation. With the advent of an armed movement, they were perceived as so empowered that people were easily intimidated by them, deferring to them in potentially volatile public encounters. Moreover, the resistance movement endowed Palestinian identity with celebratory cultural qualities. A number of new symbols served as markers of identity. For example, the gun, a potent symbol of agency and empowerment, was incorporated into forms of cultural production such as dance, poetry, and the visual arts. Ubiquitous in daily life, the *kalashnikov* (Soviet assault rifle) slung casually over the shoulder or the pistol tucked in the waist, conveyed militancy and the ability to defend oneself and graphically communicated a space of autonomy around their bearers. Second, families and individuals were known to one another by their political affiliations such as Fateh or PFLP (Popular Front for the Liberation of Palestine), or DFLP (Democratic Front for the Liberation of Palestine). Indeed, these affiliations were so well-articulated that endogamy was encouraged among members of particular groups. These affiliations were a primary means of identifying a person, often vying with or eclipsing village or kin affiliations.

Last, the resistance provided the organizational space in which action intended to bring about a solution to their refugee status could be advanced. Palestinian identity became intimately associated with militant action. This is why ordinary camp Palestinians could refer to any *fedaʾi* as "a son of the camp." The resistance mobilized thousands of young Palestinians who were desperately dissatisfied with the abnormality of statelessness and were adamant nationalists. Samiya's story illustrates how the resistance affected her sense of self. I interviewed her in 1979 when she was a member of a commando unit based in south Lebanon:

> Around 1967, I saw my brother beaten several times by the Lebanese police; my father was arrested twice and came home after having been tortured. I knew they were Lebanese and we were Palestinians—we spoke the same language and looked the same but they had rights and we had none. I also knew Palestine was where we would achieve our rights as human beings. I had a vague awareness that our misery was because we were Palestinians—people from another place, who live here, in Lebanon, but are not from here. When the resistance came to the camps, I begged my parents to let me go to meetings and demonstrations. After several years of this sort of activism, I went to the military. I had so many battles with my parents but eventually I won! Being Palestinian means to struggle, to fight for our land and our rights. The resistance made that possible. Before we were in the dark. What should we do? We didn't know what to do. We just sat in these camps for twenty years waiting desperately. We are not waiting any more! It may take decades, but we are active and struggling. I feel a strength in myself that I can accomplish things instead of just waiting for others. This is what it means to be a Palestinian—not to wait for others, to fight for your rights.

Where violent crisis is prevalent, some facets of daily life can become identity-endowing and affirming. The refusal to move, to leave one's home, reverberated among these refugees. They pondered and debated what their parents' generation did in 1948 by fleeing or by not resisting the expulsions more forcefully. What would have happened if people had simply stayed put at the border or in their villages, they wondered. What if they had been steadfast (*samideen*) and not moved? It was not until the generation born in exile underwent similar attacks, massacres, and displacement in Lebanon that they gained insight into the complexity of decision-making and actions undertaken during wartime. The concept of *sumud* (steadfastness) has been central to Palestinian self-definitions. As a way of being in the world, it illustrates some of the problems inherent in the imposition of an overly rigid distinction between formal and informal political activism. In the civil war, resistance leaders visited homes and underground shelters during attacks and counseled camp residents to be steadfast, to remain in the camps. Steadfastness as

a category for interpreting one's own actions and those of others underwrote a cultural and political recoding of seemingly ordinary action as
resistance. Sitting in the ground floor hallway of Um Khalid's building
during the civil war, the walls vibrating as artillery shells crashed into
Shatila, she forced a weak smile, shrugged, and said, "We have to be
steadfast." The women lining the walls, trying to soothe crying babies
and calm frightened children, would nod in agreement. Steadfastness
took on connotations of survival and registered a refusal to acquiesce, a
refusal to be dislocated. As an act of resistance, *sumud* is only meaningful
in the context of an exceedingly powerful, well-equipped other, willing
to unleash horrific violence.

Under the resistance, certain cultural symbols were loaded with new
meanings and served as potent markers of identity to outsiders, and
internally as creative assertions of cultural identity. Although Palestinians rhapsodized the pre-1948 past from the standpoint of the present,
they had little intention of resurrecting it; rather selected aspects of it
were mobilized as "traditional" and elevated to national significance. In
doing so, these symbols took on new meanings and were associated with
novel practices and a new aesthetic. For example, the *kufiyyah*, the black,
or red, and white checkered men's head scarf worn by peasants and
urbanites alike became saturated with meaning as the *fida'iyyin* adopted
it as an emblem of militancy.

The distinctive Palestinian embroidery on linens, cushions, and wom-
en's dresses enjoyed a remarkable renaissance. Northern Palestine was
not noted for the richly embroidered dresses commonly worn by women
in the West Bank and Gaza. Although refugees in Lebanon were only
remotely familiar with these traditions, in the 1970s, the women's sections of several political organizations and some of the urban-based
charitable groups initiated income-generating projects for women in the
camps to produce traditional embroidery. Once highly regional and
class specific, peasant women's traditional embroidery of their own
clothing and trousseaus, a skill taught by mothers to daughters, was now
taken up in the fragmented spaces of exile in the name of the nation.
Further animating and politicizing this revitalizing impulse was the
Israeli appropriation of Palestinian art forms and their repackaging as
"Israeli" for international circulation. In Lebanon, the expensive
embroidery pieces were bought by upper and upper middle class Palestinians, Lebanese, and tourists, and displayed and sold at international
fairs. Reinvigorated to symbolize and display national culture, this traditional art form and skill was transformed from a localized, everyday
domestic use to represent a national aesthetic and cultural past. Once
produced domestically and locally, it acquired a national meaning that
cross-cut regional, class, and aesthetic divides. This rescripted art form

was commodified to serve the cultural, economic, and political needs of the present.

The Palestinian map, inclusive of pre-1948 Palestine and the Occupied Territories, became an ubiquitous icon. The red, white, black, and green Palestinian flag was a prominent feature in all resistance offices and flew over the camps. Paper copies could be found adorning the walls in many houses. In addition, the map logo was made into small gold charms worn by women and young girls on gold chains. In this instance, the map icon was a political statement and claim as well as an aesthetic that was on mobile display. Bodies, and the signs they displayed, proclaimed Palestinians' identity. The map was also a common theme in artisanal works, such as small copper maps mounted on a black velvet background and hung in homes. As jewelry or home decor, the space of Palestine was thus objectified, embodied, and incorporated into a nationalized, domestic aesthetic. The map logo, the mobile, now aestheticized spatial icon of the nation, stated commonality while embroidery celebrated the nation's cultural homogeneity, recognizing and celebrating rather than subsuming difference. Once I received a set of coasters as a gift. On each black square cloth was embroidered in red, green, and white calligraphy the name of a Palestinian city or town such as Nablus, Haifa, 'Akka, Yaffa, or Jerusalem.

Israeli attempts to cast doubts on a uniquely Palestinian identity have been equally significant for subjectivity and expressions of identity. Identities can't be "unilateral" (Jenkins 2002: 120), especially if they are invoked as a basis for national sovereignty. They can only exist and take shape in reference to a spectrum of others who offer recognition. International discourse and public opinion often cast Palestinians as nonexistent, or if they did exist, as terrorists and more recently as Islamic terrorists, each a representation or discourse which located them as beyond the bounds of civilization, international law, and diplomacy, and therefore political recognition and national sovereignty. Identity through militant enactment may be related to attempts at enforced disappearance.

Particular moments in history, especially violent ones, may be appropriated for inclusion in national narratives and identity. The 1976 siege, massacre, and razing of Tel al-Za'ter is one such moment and place. Incorporated into the national narrative, this moment conflates place and murderous events, encapsulating and representing suffering, displacement, and betrayal. It focuses on the heroic in face of the duplicitous and, as we will see later, it was part of a growing panoply of violent places and moments that have been added to the Palestinian national narrative. Refugees can acquire another layer to their identity through intimate association with these specific places and moments. Those who survived Tel al-Za'ter were still known a quarter century later as "Al-Za'ter people."

Although it is a category of persons with international legal recognition, the meaning of refugee status can be a contingent one for both refugees and host. In this instance, it moved in tandem with shifts in the power and fortunes of the resistance movement. Identity became very caught up in militant action, and the resistance ushered in a celebratory attitude to Palestinian culture. With the increasing chaos and the breakdown of the host state during the civil war, coupled with heightened militancy and community autonomy, the term refugee was muted. It was politically suspect, brought few tangible benefits, and was largely irrelevant in wartime, where residency was based less on a legal right and more on the power to be there.

The War of the Camps: 1985–87

The remainder of this chapter explores the placemaking capacities of refugees under the extremely adverse conditions of the camp wars. The 1982 Israeli invasion, the defeat and departure of the PLO and the subsequent Sabra-Shatila massacre, and the camp wars dramatically transformed daily life and generated another seismic shift in identity. In the summer of 1982, Israel invaded Lebanon and besieged Beirut. The PLO negotiated a withdrawal of their forces from Beirut. Huge crowds of Palestinians and Lebanese gathered to send off the leadership and hundreds of *fida'iyyin* at Beirut's port, marking the end of an era. The security vacuum created by the PLO withdrawal left the camps exposed and vulnerable. Within weeks, despite U.S. guarantees for the safety of civilian refugees, Israeli-coordinated and supported rightist Lebanese Christian militiamen surrounded and entered Shatila camp, where they engaged in a three-day blood bath with anywhere from 800 to 3,000 Palestinian and Lebanese civilian victims. It was a portent of things to come.

In the mid-1980s, camps in the Beirut, Saida, and Sour areas were subjected to a sustained campaign of assault and siege by Shi'a 'Amal militia with support from the Lebanese Army's largely Shi'a Sixth Brigade. In Shatila, the camp wars consisted of a series of three sieges of the Beirut camps, 'Ayn al-Hilweh, and the camps in the Sour area: the 1985 Ramadan Siege of 19 May–22 June; the One-Month Siege of 26 May–27 June 1986; and the Five-Month Siege of 25 November 1986–6 April 1987. In 1985, 'Amal (with Syrian support) attempted to complete the process of eliminating the PLO from Lebanon. Although the rightist forces and Israel had succeeded in ridding the Beirut area of the PLO, the camps were still intact, while rumors flew of their remaining weaponry and rearming. Palestinian male civilians were not necessarily distinguished from fighters. Once poor and "dispossessed," Palestinians and the Shiʻa had been seemingly natural allies. Indeed, ʼAmal (*harakat ʼamal*) is the militia for the Movement of the Dispossessed (*harakat al-mahrumin*). The Palestinian narrative of the camp wars posits that they were launched with the intention of simultaneously containing any vestige of Palestinian nationalism or organizing and propelling movement out of Lebanon. Those who would not leave would be corralled in tightly controlled camps. Abu Khalid explained the camp wars as "just the latest plan to fragment us and move us away from the border," an opinion shared by many.

Prior to the first camp war in May 1985, rumors were flying that Palestinian military forces, particularly those associated with Arafat's Fateh movement, were returning to the camps. Ominous warnings of "a return to the days of pre-1982," a refrain that encapsulated the fear of a reversion to chaos, war, and disintegration of the fragile Lebanese state and military, was accompanied by a rhetoric of punishment. For example, Daoud Daoud, a local Shiʻa leader in the south, gave a speech in which he railed against the possible return of the PLO to Lebanon and said, "We want their return, but only to punish them."[4] As a prelude to the camp wars, the rhetoric of "return" was heightened in the press, striking a common chord of dread among Lebanese. The following sort of reporting and analysis in the Lebanese press was not uncommon:

> The expulsion of thousands of Palestinians from Beirut does not mean that all fighting elements were expunged. Organizational cadre left but the civilians in the camps have never distanced themselves from military or paramilitary activity. The majority of them have taken part, at one time or another, in one form or another, in guerrilla activity. They have nearly all been militarily trained.[5]

In the ʼAmal version of the camp wars, they had to ensure that Lebanon did not return to its pre-1982 conditions with the Palestinians running "a state within a state." They had to be "punished"[6] for their misdeeds and for bringing on Israeli raids. ʼAmal talked of "finishing them off once and for all" and of "cleansing the camps," ensuring that the Palestinians would not be allowed to "fight until the last southerner," as they were fond of stating.

What drove the frenzy of ʼAmal violence unleashed on the refugee camps? How did the relationship become unglued between two communities in close proximity, whose spatial and communal boundaries had been fairly fluid and who had similar experiences of poverty and sociopolitical marginalization? In other words, how did Palestinians become the "strangers" and their camps become places of subversion and threats to the Shiʻa community? How did they become objects of a murderous, punishing rage? Why did their presence engender such anxiety at that particular time? The answers lie in a number of areas. Progressive Lebanese support for the Palestinian movement had started to unravel over the course of the civil war, and the LNM was itself devastated by prolonged conflict. The Shi'a-Palestinian political relationship started coming unhinged during the late 1970s. Iran's Islamic revolution offered a new model for empowerment, using a sectarian and religious idiom at the same time as hostilities over turf and Palestinian misman-agement and misbehavior in areas under their control in Lebanon had led to a growing anti-Palestinian sentiment. In the post-1982 period, with the Palestinian political forces discredited, and the Shi'a having developed their own sectarian agenda, they engaged in sustained politi-cal mobilization and organizing. In the vacuum created by the 1982 PLO withdrawal, the Shi'a militias 'Amal and Hizbollah soon emerged as dominant political and military forces in West Beirut and parts of South Lebanon. Formerly economically, politically, and socially marginal within the Lebanese sectarian system, the Shi'a asserted their newfound hegemonic status in spatial appropriations and redesigns in Beirut. To maintain their new dominance in the southern suburbs of Beirut and their still precarious place in the sectarian-political order, 'Amal's cre-dentials as nationalists had to be vigorously asserted and verified. Having once supported a variety of Palestinian and Lebanese political parties and militias, many but not all Shi'a were increasingly drawn into sup-porting their own sectarian-based organizations. However, Hizbollah and 'Amal took radically different positions on the Palestinians: 'Amal decided to launch a war to contain them while Hizbollah, with their more Islamically inspired ideology, remained supportive and refrained from engaging in the battles. A renewed Palestinian military presence and activity would pose a threat to sectarian Shi'a interests. Political affiliations as well as social relations with the Palestinians had to be diluted and new sectarian and national boundaries drawn.

Without forgetting the Syrian role in the camp wars, and the Syrian-'Amal politico-military relationship, concern here is with the question of how erstwhile allies and neighbors, people with similar economic posi-tions and a fairly steady rate of intermarriage, and no visibly marked signs of difference, could arrive at a sense of absolute difference such that murderous violence ensued. The sectarian discourse of the camp wars was all the more remarkable given the near absence of sectarian conflict and tension over a nearly thirty-five-year period. 'Amal's recourse to a sectarian discourse reflected both its political-military maneuverings within a newly reorganized sectarian balance of power in Lebanon and its relationship with the Palestinians. Palestinian political and military power had once eclipsed local Shi'a elites and overshad-owed emerging leadership alternatives. In the new arrangement of power, 'Amal eventually joined forces with those wishing to eradicate a Palestinian presence in Lebanon, having "tired of paying the cost—in blood, sorrow, and wealth—of the armed guerrilla presence in their midst" (Norton 1987: 107).

What were their grievances with the Palestinians? The Shi'a felt they had paid a high price for the Palestinian struggle. Israel's continuous bombardments, raids, and kidnappings in the south were initiated, in part, to turn the Shi'a against the Palestinians with the expectation that the Shi'a would eventually push them away from the border area. On another front, undisciplined Palestinian guerrillas sometimes behaved arrogantly and mistreated local residents at checkpoints and in their villages, and perceptions of their engagement in criminal activity and mischievous behavior fueled resentment. The lack of accountability on the part of the resistance movement and the lack of recourse by the Shi'a residents of the south were leading to an inevitable clash. Finally, the absence of change in the Lebanese sectarian system of political representation meant that sectarian organizations remained the predominant means of ensuring access to state resources. A Shi'a political movement would deliver more to them than would an alliance with the Palestinians. As part of asserting national belonging, the Shi'a adopted the rightist rhetoric of blaming the Palestinians for the disintegration of the state and the anarchy that had become a way of life for nearly a decade.

In the broader Lebanese context, the continuing Palestinian presence disturbed the newly emergent and highly fragile national order, signaling a potential transgression of Lebanon's attempts to forge a national identity that could rein in the multiple political affiliations once available to the cosmopolitan Lebanese. In the purifying quest of Lebanese nationalism, there was no place for refugees. In the post-1982 period, the Shi'a 'Amal movement was vying for a more visible and powerful presence in the Lebanese state where they had long suffered neglect and distance from the distributive powers of the state. To validate their national belonging, they took up the mantle of anti-Palestinianism, attempting to finish what the Lebanese right and the Israelis had started, if not the disappearance of the camps from the Beirut area, at the minimum their political-military control. Shi'a violence against Palestinians began to resemble a rite of passage into national belonging. The Shi'a and Christian right narratives eventually coalesced around the shared commitment to avoid a return of Palestinian forces. In short, 'Amal was going to keep Lebanon safe from the potentially destructive Palestinian presence and uphold the precariously emerging legality and sovereignty of the state. They would restore the state by controlling its potential challengers and thus prove themselves worthy of national belonging.

The camp wars launched a violent project to inscribe, spatially and

legally, a geography of national belonging as a defining aspect of asserting a cohesive national identity. Palestinians embodied and signified a
foreignness against which Lebanese national identity could be defined.
The post-1982 Lebanese national imagination, with its lines of exclusion
and inclusion, had profound effects on the refugees. Rhetorically the
camps were pathologized in medical metaphors. Segregating, or compelling to migrate, the once potentially contagious Palestinians would
facilitate Lebanon's "normalization." The national body and its health
could be restored through the spatial, legal, and social isolation of this
infectious presence. In aesthetic terms, the camps were "eyesores" mar-
ring the beauty of the Lebanese landscape; their removal would set the
nation on the road to recovery and unity. Because the Palestinian presence had once so acutely illuminated the weakness of the state, tight
control of the refugees and their camps would indicate the reestablishment of state sovereignty and a "Lebanon for the Lebanese." 'Amal perceived that if they did not act upon representation of the Palestinians as
a pathological presence to be eliminated or cut down to size, they risked
jeopardizing the Shi'a's precarious position in the volatile national project. Abu Fadi bitterly summarized their logic: "They had to compete
with the Maronites in killing us to prove they are Lebanese."

In his seminal study of violence in Northern Ireland, Allen Feldman
writes that "political relations of antagonism are mechanisms of ideological reproduction but they also carve out autonomous material spheres
of effect and affect that diverge from formal political rationalities"
(1991: 4). His view of how Republican, Loyalist, and state violence "have
fused into an enclosed sphere of cognition, exchange, and symbiotic
representation" certainly echoes in the camp wars. Violence may carve
out and mold spheres, but they are hardly uniform or unperforated.
Indeed, during large-scale violence often perpetrated by quasi-state
actors, internal consistency, logic, and enclosure are not always evident.
In even the most seemingly intractable conflict situations, there are subversive border crossings and leakages. Thus it may make more sense to
seek the simultaneity of distinction and sameness on each side of the
border and consequently of the potential for crossings. Abu Jawad, who
fought inside Shatila during the camp wars, responding to my question
of how they were able to fight without a secure supply line in face of
what seemed to be a tight siege, said,

Do you really think we were completely cut off from the outside? We would
have died! We had Shi'a friends in 'Amal who looked the other way and allowed
us to smuggle in medicine, food and weapons. Others we paid. These Shi'a kids
did not know what they were fighting for and they were terrified. All we had to
do was pay them and they would let us take stuff into the camp. We knew them
well—we had been neighbors and friends for many years.

Figure 10. Street, or border, separating Burj al-Barajneh camp from urban Lebanese neighborhood. The ruins on the left are on the Lebanese side. Julie Peteet.

When I returned to Beirut in 1992, Um Khalid, her family, and close friends shared details of the wars of the camps. According to Um Khalid, in the days immediately preceding the first siege, Shiʿa families who lived in Shatila were quietly warned to leave by their friends and relatives outside the camp. "They knew what was coming, by God," she exclaimed, and indeed their departure signaled impending danger. Members of Um Hassan's (Um Khalid's Shiʿa neighbor) family sent a car to take her out of the camp. With ʾAmal already surrounding the camps, both knew it meant a serious confrontation was imminent. Um Khalid described what happened during the first days of the war in her building—the sorting-out and differentiating of Palestinians and Lebanese and the disruption of their social relationships and shared space:

We were eleven families living in that building; nine of them were Shiʿa. We were living together—no differences among us. We ate together. On the first floor lived a young Lebanese army officer, Muhammad. When the fighting broke out, we went down to the ground floor. There we stayed in a room where the Norwegian volunteers used to stay. Two Lebanese women went down with us, others refused to go, like one of my neighbors. She even had an artillery shell land on her balcony and still she refused to come and be with us. The next day all the Shiʿa families living among us in the camp, and most in the building,

Figure 11. Street, or border, separating Burj al-Barajneh camp from urban Lebanese neighborhood. On both sides of the street, buildings are heavily pockmarked from years of warfare. Julie Peteet.

Figure 12. Western border of Shatila camp. On the left are buildings, once home to Lebanese and Palestinians, destroyed in the camp wars. Julie Peteet.

Figure 13. A main road, Shatila camp. The Lebanese neighborhood of Hayy Farhat is in the background. Only about 40 feet separates the camp from this neighborhood, which once housed hundreds of Palestinian refugees. Julie Peteet.

gathered and got into cars and left the camp. The only Shiʿa women who stayed were Um ʿAli and Um Kamal. Their children were carrying arms with us. They said either we live together or we die together.

The following day ʾAmal came to our building and occupied it. They came and found us on the ground floor. We were all sitting there. Our neighbor, the officer Muhammad, was with them. He was wearing a green headband [a Shiʿa symbol] and brandishing a *kalashnikov* [Soviet rifle], ready to shoot. The children were playing in other rooms, so the women went to fetch them. I approached our neighbor Muhammad and said, "Don't do the wrong thing, I beseech you in the name of neighborliness." He replied angrily "Nobody say a word you so-and-sos, nobody move." He took us all into one room and made us sit there. He was dark and he looked darker that day. Then he called on Um ʿAli—she lived on his floor. She went to him and knelt at his feet, begging him. He kicked her, throwing her flat on the floor. He asked "Where is Nasser [her son]?" Nasser was there. He stood up. Muhammad ordered him to get closer and then to stand beside him. Then he asked "Where is Khalil?" Khalil was the type to scare easily. He fell to the floor. Then he asked, "Where are ʿAli and ʿAbed? Are they also fighting with the dogs?" Um Kamal's sons were carrying arms with us and that is why she did not leave. She wanted to stay and either die with them or live with them. Suddenly we could hear sounds of very nearby fighting. The officer left. As the fighting came closer, we feared being trapped. By some miracle, our fighters, using grenades and explosives, opened the several walls that separated us from our forces. Once they opened the holes, we handed out the children to them and they carried them under fire to the mosque. Then, we adults ran for safety to the mosque.

The boundaries around the camps were at once reinforced by violence and yet transgressed and undermined by the subversive and perilous crossings Abu Jawad referred to. Once seemingly solid social relationships dissolved with remarkable rapidity; others continued subversively. Appadurai notes that "ethnocidal violence between social intimates is not only about uncertainty about the 'other.' Obviously, these actions indicate a deep and dramatic uncertainty about the ethnic self" (1998: 244). The drive to achieve national certainty was no doubt about the uncertainty of the Shiʿa national self, yet it was accompanied in some instances by continuing social relations with their Palestinian neighbors that crossed and thus challenged now dangerous boundaries.

One can read in Um Khalid's narrative an attempt to make sense of an episode that further shattered already battered lives. She talked of a beginning period of closeness, and then the descent into violence where unambiguous categories were imposed (and rejected), and finally, closure by rescue. Her appeal to the idiom of neighborliness was an attempt to assert cultural coherence and order in the face of eroding trust and the unpredictability of violence. She invoked the ethos of neighborliness, with its strong connotation of kinlike relations and obligations. She pleaded with the officer Muhammad not to engage in an atrocity that would open a deep and irrevocable chasm between them. Her narrative juxtaposes essentialized, unambiguous identities (the green headband) with a commitment to intercommunal sociopolitical relations (Um 'Ali and Um Kamal). Terror and fear of reprisal compel some people to move (Um Hassan) and, in doing so, to state spatially their loyalties by physically locating themselves on one side or the other. Equally notable was the way social and political affinities were asserted at the risk of death. Um Kamal and Um 'Ali, both Shi'a refused the enforced spatialization of identities and social relations, asserting the primacy of friendship, motherhood, and political ideology over the sectarian or national.

Um Taher, mother of six and resident of Shatila, left during a lull in the fighting. Occasionally she would come to the camp to try to see her family. She related the following story about her friendship with a Shi'a woman:

> During the camp wars, we were here for the first and second one—the one-month and the forty-five days war. But the six-month war—I took the younger children and went to relatives in the south. Abu Taher and my two older boys were in the camp. Every week, I would come to Beirut to see if the roads to the camp were open, to see if they were still besieged. I wanted to check things out. I would stand near the camp. I did not dare approach.'Amal had their headquarters near where I would have entered—near the Dana Mosque. Once I came with Um Fathi, whose children were also besieged. Um Fathi is one of them originally [Lebanese Shi'a] but she is married to a Palestinian. We walked near the mosque—we had decided not to be scared. They ['Amal militiamen] called out to us, "Where are you going, you so and so?"[7] We said we were coming here to visit someone. One of them said, "You so and so's, your husbands are inside the camp fighting and you want to see them!" Um Fathi said, "No, I am a Shi'a." He motioned to me and barked "And you?" I replied, "I am Palestinian." He yelled, "Are you coming to see your children in the camp?" I said, "No, neither my husband nor my children are inside." I was so scared. Trying to calm him down, Um Fathi said, "I am one of you, so if you are angry, be angry at me." They shouted, "Get out of here!" and they turned their guns toward us. We walked away and just stood around for a while. We waited and waited and nothing happened. Things like that happened many times. I would come and wait, hoping the road would open.

As Shi'a departed, Shatila and Burj became homogeneous spaces and identifiable targets. Spatially legible, both symbolized a Palestinian collectivity. Once they were emptied of non-Palestinians, Shi'a militiamen could be certain of the identity of their victims. About a square kilometer in size, Shatila gives the impression of being easily overwhelmed, which may account for the initial confidence of the 'Amal militia in the first siege. A few hundred *fida'iyyin* tenaciously fought thousands of attacking 'Amal militiamen. Abu Jawad, who had fought in Tel al-Za'ter in 1976 and escaped, explained, "We knew they were killing captured fighters, and that if the camp fell, a massacre would follow." A tight blockade meant no entry or exit, and thus food and medical supplies were scarce. Reports of near starvation and death of the wounded due to lack of medical care circulated widely in local and international media. As in the 1976 siege of Tel al-Za'ter, getting water was to risk death (Peteet 1991: 73–74). Abu Khalid summed up life under constant fire: "Each glass of water was paid for with a glass of blood." Numerous women died from sniper fire or shelling in a futile attempt to fetch water.

How did people survive these prolonged sieges in an area around the size of a square kilometer with daily bombardments and sniping, a high death toll, and no secure supply line? Sitting under a canopy of ripening grapevines on the rooftop of their house, Um Khalid remarked proudly, "We are like a hand—the fingers are separate but the hand works together." The "one hand" drew a line of inclusion and exclusion. Camps were homes to be defended, places from which further displacement was vigorously resisted. Refugees were willing to fight to the death for their homes. When Um Khalid used the metaphor of the "hand" to refer to the camp, she meant that its components were intimately linked with one another and, like a hand, functioned as a cohesive whole. During the camp wars, Palestinians from other camps and multiple political factions with their own lines of division lived in the camp, but under siege, the camp as a whole functioned as a defensive unit. The "hand" (*khamsah*) invoked deeply etched cultural notions of kin responsibility, support, allegiance, and payment of blood money to the fifth degree of relatedness. Some of their neighbors and their children and their friends soon joined us on the roof. They animatedly detailed how the camp organized to defend itself. In other words, they described the "one hand" of Shatila at work under intense external pressure.

Internally, Shatila managed to overcome potentially destructive internal political divisions to fight and organize the camp's defense. A siege is fought on multiple levels—not just militarily; morale has to be maintained and besieged areas have to be brought under internal control in order to ration limited supplies of food, fuel, and medicine. Noncombatants were mobilized into committees to organize the provisioning of water and the production and distribution of bread, care of the wounded, management of supplies and distribution, maintenance of shelters, and building of fortifications. Using simple hand-held tools, both men and women dug trenches and tunnels for moving supplies, fighters, and the wounded, and for military defense. Fayha, a young woman in her twenties, described how at night she dug the "trenches that linked all parts of the camp." With a sarcastic laugh she said, "Didn't you know—they called us rats because we lived underground for so many years. We stayed in the shelters all day and at night we moved around the camp via the trenches." In the first round of fighting, the camp's perimeter of buildings was destroyed, exposing the interior directly to shelling and to gunfire from snipers perched in higher buildings. Trenches were the solution to the problem of exposure and mobility under intense sniping and artillery fire. Indeed, the Palestinians prevented 'Amal's entry into the camp and its conquest even though they were heavily outgunned, besieged, and lacked a secure supply route. The camp rallied fairly well in spite of some internal problems with slackers. War tends to generate heroic narratives of resistance and comradery by both participants and those who write about them. Sayigh's seminal account (1994) of the camp wars elicits the heroic as well as the reality of corruption, selfishness, cheating, and malingering.

In Burj al-Barajneh camp, 'Amni, an engaging young woman who participated in its defense, took me on several walking tours. I had met her at the home of a teacher in the camp. She had dropped in for a visit with his daughter and was eager to talk about the camp wars. Her brother fought in the wars and he and some of his fellow fighters took me on a tour of the tunnels. 'Amni's mother commented that her daughter knew the camp well: "She has always been very social, you see, she likes to visit. So she can tell you all about the camp and who lives where." 'Amni, pointing to the alleyway we were walking down, said, "This street—it is a street of death—so many people died on it. We could peek out and see the bodies. See down there—that was where they were positioned to snipe on us." The street she was referring to ran off a small node and had two names: "Street of Death" and its original name, that of a prominent family from Tarshiha.

During the 1980s, Palestinian mobility fluctuated dramatically with the political-military situation. Indeed, it was a diagnostic of sorts. A sudden increase in harassment signaled eminent clashes. Before each siege, the checkpoints would tighten their control, searching people more thoroughly, demanding information about where they were going and whom they would see, and sometimes robbing them. Men were frequently detained for no apparent reason. As skirmishes and shelling heated up, the checkpoints would begin to prevent entry to and exit from the camps. Although the checkpoints posed a general danger, their intensity and consequences were gender specific. During the height of the sieges men faced certain death or disappearance. Effectively imprisoned by terror, some men did not leave Shatila or Burj al-Barajneh for three or four years.

Relying on cultural notions of the relative immunity of women in war, women risked leaving the camps to purchase food for their hungry families. Sniper fire posed a primary danger and, if they reached the checkpoint, they faced assault, intimidation, and harassment. During fieldwork in the 1990s, I used to enter Burj from either of two entry points. After passing the main Syrian checkpoint, I would choose between two points of entry, one facing west, the other north. To enter the camp on the north, I had to cross an open dusty space of about fifty meters. Knowing I often entered at that spot, 'Amni explained that women who tried to leave from either of those two spots were often targets of snipers positioned in the four- and five-story buildings that bordered the empty perimeter. "Many women were killed by 'Amal sniper fire—they took aim at anything that moved, you see—even cats. Their bodies would lie in the empty spaces until someone could run out and drag them back inside the camp." These death zones dotted the camp perimeter.

Once women managed to cross the dangerous perimeter and reach a checkpoint manned by Syrians or 'Amal, they were often denied exit. Sometimes after being allowed to exit to purchase food, they would have everything taken from them upon their return, especially batteries. Beatings and sexual molestation were not uncommon. Some insults conflated gender and national identity. Desperate for food for their increasingly hungry families, Um Khalid and a group of women decided to try to reach the nearby market. "We were scared to death but our children were starving. What could we do!? We were older women—we figured maybe they would let us through." At the checkpoint, the 'Amal gunman gruffly demanded to see their identity cards. He grabbed Um Khalid's Palestinian identity card, threw it on the ground, and spat on it, screaming, "Those without land have no honor!" which in Arabic involves a play on words. Because Palestinians possess neither land nor citizenship their women have dubious claims to honor and thus are vulnerable to sexual predation. In other words, *mustabaheen* (being without protection) was highly gendered. His furious comment was an ominous warning of the potential dangers of being stateless and without the honor and protection a state can bestow. They might not automatically be killed, as were the men during the height of the siege, but they certainly faced the dangers of sexual assault and intimidation.

Certain kinds of behavior were intended to publicly humiliate women and the national entity they symbolized. Hints of such incidents subtly surfaced in discussions of the siege, but names and details were pronounced only with reticence. In Burj al-Barajneh, women intimated at public head shavings at the checkpoints. When we were alone, 'Amni told me in a hushed tone, "Groups of women would have their hair shorn by soldiers as crowds of Lebanese gathered to jeer and taunt. Old women were made to dance while soldiers shot around their feet. Others were made to insult Abu 'Ammar (Yassir Arafat's *nom de guerre*) and the Palestinian people." Exposure to assaults and insults strained family ties.

If a family was to eat, women had to brave these checkpoints to buy food. Fathers and brothers had to helplessly endure humiliation as well as intense fear for their mothers, sisters, and daughters. In other instances, fathers and husbands insisted their wives and daughters go in search of food. Women bitterly retold such incidents as a betrayal of the cultural code that assigns men protective functions. Their bitterness was directed both at the men and at the staggering depths of the situation facing them that would compel men to abandon such fundamental cultural principles.

In addition, breaching key cultural norms of gender encoded a message that peace would be impossible. 'Amni's father who fought to defend the camp, angrily commented, "They did these things to women so that there could never be reconciliation. These kinds of actions can never be forgiven and they know that. They want to make sure there is no basis for reconciliation later." If reconciliation was not possible because of the extreme shame and humiliation of sexual violation, it was probably assumed that Palestinians would be more amenable to leaving the area, or at least be humbled and pacified.

While the camp wars raged in well-defined locales, Palestinians in urban areas and towns faced a campaign of harassment and terror. The intent was to force them back into the camps and take over their homes. In Saida and Beirut, stories abounded of gunmen storming in and demanding at gunpoint that families go immediately to the camps. Some of this terror can be read as a grab at Palestinian property. Shireen, a middle-aged woman who lived alone in a two-bedroom apartment in Beirut, was kidnaped by a group of 'Amal in the middle of the night. She was kept for weeks in a cell in a bombed out high rise building in downtown Beirut, where 'Amal was keeping hundreds of Palestinians prisoners before killing them by throwing them from the rooftops. Beaten and nearly starved, she recalls, "They never accused me of anything or even asked me for information. When they finally let me go, my hair had turned white. I went to my home only to find a Shi'a family living there. It was the family of one of the guys who kidnaped me. They said this apartment was theirs now. 'What do you need all this space for?' They wouldn't even let me take my things." Simultaneously, as we have seen, Lebanese residing in the camps were cautioned to depart and did so. An unknown number of Palestinian men aged fourteen to sixty-five simply disappeared. In effect, this sorting out campaign relandscaped the camps' national, sectarian, and ideological topography.

This leads to the issue of mixed Lebanese-Palestinian families. When armed hostilities erupt between ethnic/religious communities such as the Hutu/Tutsi conflict and in the former Yugoslavia among Serbs, Muslims, and Croats, intermarriages are put into dangerous relief. Crossing sectarian and national lines, Lebanese-Palestinian intermarriage was not infrequent in the context of blurred of spatial boundaries and cosmopolitan social interaction, as well as a history of earlier intermarriage and the absence of stigma. In ethnic-national violence, mixed families can occupy an anomalous and potentially dangerous position. Indeed, they may be targeted precisely because they subvert ostensibly "pure" categories of belonging. The usual pattern in such marriages was for a Palestinian man to marry a Lebanese Shi'a women. A Lebanese Shi'a with a Palestinian wife would not be subjected to the same kind or intensity of harassment and disdain that a Lebanese woman faced if she were the wife of a Palestinian. These women were less prone to assault, but they did face taunts and accusations of betrayal for "marrying one of the dogs," and of course, their Palestinian husbands were not granted immunity from assault.

Um Fahim, an acquaintance of Um Fadi, told me the story of her brother who had married a Lebanese woman.

My brother was a teacher for twenty-seven years. In the early 1970s, he was living in Tel al-Za'ter camp and teaching in a Lebanese school in Burj Hamoud [a highly mixed Beirut suburb]. He fell in love with one of his students, a Lebanese Shi'a. Her parents turned him down because of the age difference. But she was in love with him and a couple of years later they eloped. She lived with him in Tel al-Za'ter and eventually they reconciled with her parents. Several years later, he left Lebanon and worked in Saudi Arabia and made a good living. His wife was not happy there because she was confined to the house. She convinced him to return to Lebanon. They came back and rented an apartment in West Beirut. During the camp wars, he didn't feel safe in West Beirut where many of his neighbors were Shi'a. So he took his wife and four children to Sour to stay with his family. A month later his wife wanted to go back to their apartment in Beirut. He said they shouldn't move back there because they were still killing people. She convinced him to let her go alone and check the apartment. She found her home in shambles—it had been ransacked. She returned to him, but did not tell him about the apartment. Nevertheless she soon convinced him to move back to Beirut.

A few days later, he wanted to go swimming with the children. She tried to talk him out of it but he took the children and went. She stayed home and cooked okra in olive oil and fish. He came home and sat down to eat insisting that he wanted to eat only okra and not any fish. Suddenly they heard shooting nearby. He ran to the balcony of their fourth floor apartment, looked down and saw the shooting was at his car parked outside the building. The tires were flat and the glass blown out. He jumped over the balcony to the neighbor's apartment and tried to hide. Armed men then came into his apartment and asked where he was. His wife answered that he was in the south. They told her they knew he was there because they had seen him peer from the balcony. In the meantime, he became afraid the armed men might hurt his wife or children so he decided to face them. He jumped back onto his balcony and went in. He was still in his bathing suit and they refused to let him put on any clothes. They said, "Don't worry, you'll be back within an hour." As they left, they cursed his wife for marrying a Palestinian. He never came back. His body was found with a group of Palestinian men next to a wall. They had all been shot.

'Amal and the Lebanese Sixth Brigade violently recrafted Shatila's geopolitical borders. Continuous artillery bombardments and sniper fire were followed by the advance of these forces through surrounding neighborhoods. With the dynamiting and bulldozing of swaths of Sabra camp, adjacent to Shatila and once difficult to distinguish spatially, the way to Shatila was open and, from the tops of the surrounding higher buildings, the advancing militia had a view of the camp which enabled highly precise sniping. As 'Amal advanced, they dynamited successive perimeters, attempting to open up the camp layer by layer. Following the camp wars, the policy of the Lebanese state and the Syrians was to ensure that the camps were spaces of containment and surveillance. Containment was accomplished, in part, by the reestablishment of the camps' original borders. For example, Burj al-Barajneh camp, which had long incorporated poor Shi'a areas in the southern suburbs of Beirut and whose borders were nearly indistinct on the north and east sides, had the perimeters systematically dynamited by the 'Amal militia. Clear, open vistas that rendered the camps visible from the remaining high rise buildings controlled by 'Amal were crucial for surveillance and controlling movements in the camps.

Violence also reconfigured the meaning of internal space. In Shatila, the mosque reemerged onto center stage, spatially and metaphorically, as surrounding layers of the built environment were torn away by 'Amal's attempts to reach it. Once the geographic center of the camp, it had been eclipsed in significance as the camp spread horizontally and political sites became geospatial markers. The withdrawal of the resistance removed most of those spatial markers. Because there were few underground shelters, the mosque became a sacred, communal point of retreat for those whose homes were destroyed or exposed to relentless artillery fire. As shelling intensified and movement became riskier, medical facilities were moved into the mosque's ground level floor, which then teemed with the wounded and the growing number of displaced. With all exits blocked, the dead were buried under its stone floors. Now a sanctuary and the symbolic heart of the camp, 'Amal aimed to capture it. They never did advance that far, suffering heavy casualties that halted their military goals. In the center of the now exposed and constricted camp, the mosque became polyvalent, attesting to the rapid capacity with which a space can acquire and absorb new purposes and meanings.

Conclusion

The period of autonomy was short-lived. Almost from its inception, it was challenged by Israeli air and land attacks, an increasingly alarmed

Lebanese state, and a growing rightist militia movement committed to diluting Palestinian political power or removing them from Lebanon. The camps came under intermittent but consistent attack. Although this era ended in defeat, impoverishment, and incredible human suffering, it left an indelible mark on the Palestinian collective consciousness, identity, and larger national narrative. It signified both an era, 'ayyam al-thawra, and a generation, jeel al-thawra.

While all identity is performative to some extent, Palestinian identity was patently and tangibly more than ever about doing or performing rather than simply being. In an atmosphere of denial and displacement, expressions of national identity were even more performative. The national identity taking shape in exile was patched together from past life in Palestine and the realities of everyday life in exile. It celebrated heterogeneity and inclusion yet it manifested essentialized components. Active participation in the Palestinian struggle accompanied descent and relations to place as the bases of national inclusion. While inclusion was highly rhetorical, it also had a profoundly real dimension. People who worked together in the camps during assaults and sieges developed close bonds. Non-Palestinian nationals were accorded honorary kinship status and were considered honorary Palestinians, an indication of the centrality of activism and struggle to Palestinian identity and belonging.

Spatial borders of the camps were at their most flexible. In this period, territory and social bonds were delinked to some extent. The boundaries between the camps and the surrounding areas were more in the form of gradients rather than lines of demarcation. Cosmopolitan social relations of crossing accompanied this loosening of spatial boundaries as displaced and poor Palestinians and Lebanese progressives came together in a self-identified common cause.

During the civil war, cosmopolitanism and crossings coexisted with assertions of an essentialized Palestinian identity on the cultural rather than the political level in seemingly paradoxical and contradictory ways. Where a large number of Lebanese and Palestinians belonged to a militia and were armed, identities became entangled with national and or sectarian communities in a way that underscored the horrific dangers of essentializing identities, or perhaps more appropriately, the way conflict acts to essentialize identities. Hundreds of people were killed or disappeared at Lebanese roadblocks simply on the basis of the national or religious identity noted on their identity card or according to accent.

There are some interesting parallels between Beirut's city center, destroyed early in the civil war, and the Beirut camps. Both were heterogenous zones of crossing and intermingling by multiple groups and both were violently ravaged. The reconstruction of the destroyed city center in the 1990s sparked controversy and a heated debate over what and whom it should represent, reflecting a fragmented Lebanese narrative of the past and future. A Lebanese consensus on the meaning of the camps provided a source of national unity.

The next chapter continues the examination of the Palestinian placemaking project and identity formation in the postwar period of the 1990s. Refugees faced unparalleled challenges presented by the Oslo agreements and reconstruction in wartorn Lebanon. With the demise of the resistance movement in Lebanon, the camps begin to lose their representivity of Palestinian militant culture in the broader Palestinian arena. Where once they signaled purity, they were becoming places signaling defeat, abandonment, and loss of regional stature.

Chapter Six
The Geography of Terror and Reconfinement

> Fear is most commonly experienced as a distortion and disorienta-
> tion of perspective. It gives everyday life a surreal dimension that
> emphasizes negative aspects to such a large extent that thoughts
> involving the future are flattened and silenced
> —Monique Skidmore (2004: 40–41)

As the millennium came to a close, the inscription of violence assaulted
one at every step: the armed guards ringing the camp, the massive piles
of rubble from dynamited or shelled buildings left by nearly two decades
of war, the open sewage systems, the somber black and white faces of the
dead on posters plastered on nearly every wall, the pervasiveness of the
handicapped, extreme forms of poverty, and the multitude of female-
headed households. Shatila camp was a highly demarcated space; entry
required a lengthy walk through Lebanese Shi'a areas with a profusion
of signs that proclaimed their territorial dominance and reminded Palestinians of a heightened vulnerability. With their crude technologies of
power, the Syrian and Lebanese army checkpoints signaled danger and
contained difference. Each side contained and counter-positioned a
national project. In the wake of the camp wars and the beginning of
postwar Lebanese reconstruction, Palestinian place making abilities
were severely constrained.

The 1990s: Placemaking in a Landscape of Despair

We cry for ourselves. We don't know what is going to happen to us. We are like
a blind person who sees nothing ahead. So where is the future?

Um 'Omar uttered this in tearful resignation, twisting her handkerchief
as she described her fifty-year odyssey from her village of Farah, when

she was eight years old, to the present in Shatila. For her, time stands still, the future is an unknown, a blank. In the aftermath of prolonged war, daily decisions are fraught with anxiety.

I asked Sami, a boy of eighteen, who had spent three years of his youth under siege, to draw a map of Shatila. In comparison with a map of Burj al-Barajneh camp drawn by a young man of similar age and experience, it was remarkably empty. The map of Burj was dotted with homes, alleys, and buildings. It was a landscape of life rather than desolation. The sieges inflicted overwhelming devastation on Shatila, which was still reeling from the 1982 massacre. Nearly depopulated, life returned to it only very gradually over the 1990s.

In the early 1990s, Shatila resembled a ruralized holding center in the midst of a teeming postwar city. Denuded of the services provided by the resistance and heavily damaged, it was eerily quiet; the population was estimated at approximately 500 families or 2,500 people. There was virtually no employment in the camp and men were conspicuously absent, either dead, working abroad, or keeping a very low profile. Given the sieges and the specter of starvation, people were tending animals. Cars were not allowed inside, so everything had to be carried in. In a nutshell, a gendered and ruralized landscape was discernible amid the jumbled piles of ruins. By 1994, cars were allowed in and the population was expanding considerably.

In the 1990s, the borders were more open than during the camp wars but the sense of imprisonment was pervasive. A young schoolteacher commented, "They lock us in at night. It is really like a prison." After almost five years of nearly complete incarceration, residents had only recently begun to leave the camp. Boys and young men did so with trepidation. Um Khalid's fourteen-year-old son came home one day looking dirty, disheveled, and upset. His parents repeatedly quizzed him to see if anything had happened. With barely disguised emotion, he kept insisting he had been playing sports with his friends. Finally his mother approached him and lifted his shirt. His back was covered with welts and bruises. She screamed, "Who did this to you?" He replied, "No one. I was just playing." After much prompting, he conceded that he had been stopped at the checkpoint to the camp. A group of young Lebanese Shi'a men beat him for no apparent reason. They also stole his watch. His parents were helpless to do anything, and there was no one to complain to. His parents comforted him and talked about how dangerous it was for boys to walk about outside the camp. Brutally demilitarized and recrafted as a unidimensional sectarian and national space devoid of internal forms of protection, Shatila was a space of fear and despair.

On a sweltering summer evening I stayed late in 'Ayn al-Hilweh. The young man of the family I was visiting and his friend offered to drive me

Figure 14. Horse-drawn wagon, edge of Shatila camp. Cars were forbidden in the camps in the early days of postwar reconstruction. Julie Peteet.

to a nearby neighborhood. The soldiers at a Lebanese Army checkpoint recorded drivers' and passengers' names and identity card numbers, and cars' license plate numbers for cars entering or exiting the camp between 9:00 P.M. and 6:00 A.M. We stopped at the checkpoint and the soldiers performed the requisite registration. Mahmud, the twenty-six-year-old driver, commented angrily that the purpose was "humiliation more than anything." He continued, "We are monitored as if we were a political threat while the real threat remains the Christian right." His friend had been arguing with him all evening about his plans to join a group of younger activists who wanted to form a new political movement saying it would only bring "more trouble, more controls, longer waits at the checkpoints." Exasperated, Mahmud countered, "I am fed up with this treatment of *shebab* [young men] at the checkpoint. They shout at us, 'Give me your identity card!,' 'Get down,' 'What are you looking at?!' I just want to be treated with respect!" The checkpoint and the registration requirement harken back to the 1950s and their parents' or grandparents' experiences. The intent was the same, surveillance and management, and the effect was similar, humiliation and rage.

Not wanting to call attention to people hosting me, I did not sleep in the camps in the 1990s as I had during the pre-1982 period. Um Khalid insisted on walking me to the exit of Shatila. In previous years she had only occasionally done so. I knew the camp well then and it was a safe place. In addition, she was often busy with young children. Now she walked me to the edge, stopping about fifteen or twenty feet from the checkpoint. The camp was increasingly home to "strangers," so she felt duty-bound to see me out as a guest and friend. She would apologize for not going farther to help me find a *service* (shared taxi). Her sense of duty to accompany me had met its limits. She and I both knew what she was doing and I always insisted I could manage my way out. Sometimes she would find me a Palestinian taxi within the camp and tell the driver, "She's married to one from al-Bassa," stating a kinship affiliation with this particular community to establish trust and therefore an expectation of courtesy and protection.

The way the camps figured in Lebanese political rhetoric underwent a slight shift at the beginning of the postwar period. Now defeated, disarmed, and transformed into places of containment that rendered them impotent, Lebanese representations of them were less dramatic. In a sense they lost their power to engage the imagery of the right or government. However, the camps' potential to resurface as a national threat and danger has remained. The Lebanese interpret any improvement in the refugees' daily lives as renewing the potential for resistance.

In the postwar era, the Lebanese imputed to the refugees a desire for *towteen* (implantation, settlement), which rallied the diverse sectarian communities in their distrust of the Palestinians. For their part, the refugees expressed little desire to implant themselves in Lebanon because it contradicted their national struggle and identity. Once a rallying cry for rightist militias, in the 1990s it resonated across Lebanon's political/sectarian spectrum. Conjuring up the specter of *towteen* voiced a rejection of an Israeli and U.S. agenda to naturalize the Palestinians in Lebanon and reminded the international community of their responsibility for the refugees. Oddly enough, the animosity aroused by *towteen* was directed toward the refugees themselves, who had consistently rejected it. To the Lebanese, *towteen* implied incorporation into the national body of a now demonized other. The sectarian transformation it would entail, significantly bolstering the Sunni Muslim population, would have threatened the dwindling Christian population and posed potential competition to the fast-growing Shi'a. It was the worst case scenario for both the Lebanese and the refugees, yet they were unable to find a mutual accommodation in political ideology or rhetoric.[1]

A coherent postwar Lebanese national, rather than sectarian, discourse was centered on maintaining sovereignty and diluting the number and role of non-Lebanese in the sociopolitical order. The civil war was blamed on "outside elements" or "foreigners."[2] Taking back one's country was a discursive tactic to draw boundaries that excluded foreigners. Imputations of difference descended to the biological level. In a 1999 television interview, Lebanese Interior Minister Michel Murr referred to the refugees' propensity to reproduce at rates greater than the Lebanese population. This was attributed to their owning fewer televisions. Bored, they passed their time breeding.[3] Postwar rhetoric also adjudged the camps as lawless and thus beyond the reach of the state. The enclosed camps, these ostensibly modern disciplinary spatial forms to contain those out of the national order, were instead outside modernity and its forms of restraints.

As an indication of Palestinian respect for Lebanon's sovereignty and to signal a clear refusal of *towteen*, the guest metaphor was revived by Palestinian officials. In the wake of tensions over Lebanon's imposition of the death sentence on a Palestinian brigadier general, Faruq Qaddumi, chief of the PLO Political Department, said, "We respect Lebanese judiciary, law and sovereignty. We are guests in Lebanon and are aware of our duties as guests. . . . Our stay in Lebanon is temporary."[4]

The end of the civil war in Lebanon (1991) was followed by a violent project to inscribe spatially and legally a geography of national belonging succinctly expressed in the popular slogan: "Lebanon for the Lebanese." This unifying rhetorical device encoded a homogeneous and bounded national space and culture. Its emotive saliency derived from a collective sense that Lebanon's woes could be traced to the presence of numerous foreigners. Accordingly the state legislated and put into effect a number of laws to restrict refugees as part of restoring state sovereignty. Palestinians understood these as part of a continuing attempt to compel them to move. "We know they want to transfer us to remote parts of Lebanon or even to Syria and Iraq," Abu Khalid told me. His friend Abu 'Ali, another long-time resident of Shatila, added, "They are strangling us. You know, they want to build on this land." The term "strangulation" referred to the Lebanese authorities' policy to restrict refugees economically and politically. As a Palestinian lawyer cautioned, "The policies of the Lebanese government are going to feed a new round of violence. They are using the violence of the law against us. They have already demonstrated that the violence of war did not succeed in eliminating the Palestinians from Lebanon. I wonder if they will succeed by other means." Confinement in the camps, enforced by widespread harassment and the ever present potential for terror, went hand in hand with a series of legal and administrative measures that isolated and marginalized the refugee community. By the second half of the decade, the fear of transfer was paramount and growing. It framed nearly every serious discussion of Lebanese-Palestinian interaction.

On the economic front, the refugee community was devastated. UNR-WA's proportion of hardship cases in Lebanon, which merited extra services, was the highest in the region, an indication of severe poverty. Several factors contributed to the dire economic situation. The 1982 PLO withdrawal began the downward spiral in income and standard of living. With its once substantial economic, political, and social infrastructure, it was a major employer of Palestinian labor. In addition, it provided vocational training for many refugees, enabling them to compete for skilled jobs in Lebanon and the oil-producing states. Moreover, the PLO had provided a social safety net for the neediest refugees. Their health clinics, nursery and preschool programs, monthly indemnities for families of those killed in war, and educational assistance in the form of scholarships eased the margins of poverty and supplemented UNR-WA's services. Its demise in Lebanon coincided with an economic downturn in the oil-producing countries, sending home thousands of refugees and ending the remittances they sent home. Trust was severely tried by the PLO's inability to provide the promised indemnities. With few other sources of income, widows were desperate and bitter at what they perceived as abandonment and betrayal. With the safety net all but gone and postwar restrictions on Palestinian economic activity, many refugees slipped into extreme poverty. At the same time, UNRWA services were being scaled back. Inflation in Lebanon remained a paramount problem.

A primary point of contention with the Lebanese authorities concerned the issue of work. UNRWA figures put Palestinian unemployment as high as 40 percent, while local observers calculated it as closer to 90 percent (Sayigh 1995: 38). Although international law calls upon host states to allow refugees to work legally, Lebanon legislated severe restrictions on Palestinian employment. Since 1962, legislation had placed the refugees on a par with foreigners, so that employment required a work permit. For nearly two decades, Palestinian refugees circumvented this requirement because demands for labor were high. In addition, the 1969 Cairo Accords gave Palestinians the right to work.

Since 1982, however, these laws have been enforced, and the Cairo Accords were abrogated in 1994. The Minister of Labor and Social Affairs issued a decision on 18 December 1982, setting out the areas of employment—ranging from banking to barbering—closed to foreigners. The Ministry also issued a circular detailing the areas of work open to foreigners with work permits, which were menial and low-paid. These include construction and its ancillary tasks (except on electrical installations) and sanitation, agriculture, tanning and leather works, excavation, textile and carpet works, smeltering, domestic labor, nursing, and automotive repair and cleaning (Natour 1993: 44). Refugees understood these restrictions as a means to make life miserable and pressure them to leave. Syrian or non-Arab labor, cheaper and more transient, was preferred. It would be difficult to see these restrictions simply as a response to Lebanese unemployment, because of the vast number of Syrian workers currently employed in construction and a host of unskilled positions. Even those classified as the neediest Lebanese would rarely take the jobs currently filled by these workers, nor would many Palestinians. I asked Abu Khalid if Palestinians were competing with the Syrians for construction jobs:

Most Palestinians wouldn't take these jobs. The work is too dangerous and too heavy. Few Palestinians can do such heavy manual labor. They are not used to it. And for the Palestinian workers, these jobs do not pay enough. The Syrian worker can take this job because he is not supporting a family in Lebanon—paying rent, sending children to school, and feeding a family. He lives in a building with a lot of other workers and sends all his money home. All he eats every day is bread and tomatoes.

Administrative measures ensured that the camps did not expand in space. Rebuilding was restricted and heavily regulated. Most significantly, no rebuilding was allowed by those not registered as refugees in a particular camp, nor could homes be expanded beyond their initially designated boundaries. Refugees from camps destroyed during years of conflict were classified as "displaced refugees." The right to organize politically was severely hampered by the abrogation of the Cairo Accords and the general hostility to any manifestation of Palestinian organizing or nationalist activity, which faced swift reprisals by the Syrian or Lebanese Army.

In the late 1990s, As'ad 'Abd al-Rahman, responsible for refugee affairs in the Palestinian Authority (PA), presented a memorandum to the Lebanese government calling on it to grant refugees civil and social rights (Suleiman 1999: 78). This was not a call for integration or *towteen*; rather, it was intended to mitigate the debilitating marginalization and destitution of the community. A former political leader explained the desire for civil rights:

It touches directly on everyone's daily life. You cannot imagine what it is like. A Palestinian cannot work! For example, if he graduates from the American University of Beirut medical school, he is forbidden to work or open a clinic, while a Lebanese graduate can find a post in a hospital or open a clinic. If he is educated and wants to work, he will have to leave the country, which means that family relations are strained. This is a huge challenge to the continuity of everyday life.

Administrative measures to isolate the refugee camps physically led to social isolation as well. With less mobility, there was less communication between camps. In addition, without the resistance movement to bring them together socially, politically, and militarily, one primary context for relations between the scattered camps diminished. Visiting patterns reverted to a kin basis, as families continued intercamp visits when possible. Certainly there was less interaction between Palestinians and Lebanese; few Palestinians had Lebanese friends. Um Khalid's visiting network had shrunk considerably from the pre-1982 period, when it encompassed a wide range of areas exterior to the camp. Social relations had been severely strained by prolonged conflict.

Traveling abroad on Palestinian travel documents, a *laisser-passer* issued by the Lebanese government, did not guarantee reentry. In September 1995, the Lebanese Interior Ministry issued a decree that Palestinians carrying these travel documents must obtain a visa to reenter Lebanon.[5] In effect, numerous Palestinian refugees were prevented from reentering Lebanon, thus conveying the government's intention to reduce their numbers. Rumors abounded that the government was canceling the *laisser-passers* of those who had obtained passports from other countries, reportedly about 16,500 refugees. Rumors circulated that UNRWA would drop them from its rolls and they would lose their right to reside in Lebanon. Yet many refugees who returned to Lebanon that summer found that UNRWA had not removed them and they were able to register their children born abroad.

Another means of reducing refugee numbers was through selective naturalization. Official Lebanese policy and public opinion adamantly rejected Palestinian naturalization. However, in the 1990s moves by the government suggested that Lebanon might be facing external pressure to do so. While no precise figures were made public, it was commonly estimated that 28,000–30,000 refugees were naturalized in the mid-1990s and that sectarian considerations were in the forefront. In 1994, the first group to be naturalized were Shi'a from seven border villages, who since 1948 had been classified as Palestinian refugees. A year later, an unknown number of Sunni refugees were able to obtain Lebanese citizenship. The few remaining Christian Palestinian refugees were also naturalized due to pressure from the Maronite establishment to enhance their numbers.

With neither villages nor the resistance as internal controls built into the fabric of Shatila's social relations and spatiality, it was perceived by its own inhabitants as an insecure place. In the postwar period, poor Lebanese once again moved into the camps in search of cheap housing. Um Khalid would sit on her roof and cautiously nod to Lebanese neighbors in the windows or on their balconies and turn to me with a shrug and a sweep of her hand and, in a hushed tone, say, "That family is Lebanese. They are all strangers now," she would sigh, implying mistrust. In casual greetings, I often asked people how they found the camp in the aftermath of war. Invariably, the response was "Too many strangers [*ghareeb*]," indexing both the number of newcomers and the absence of protection. "Strangers" referred to other Arabs—Egyptian and Syrian—and Palestinians from other camps who were unknown to them personally. The absence of knowledge about people cast them as potential risks to one's safety. In 'ayyam al-thawra, there were plenty of foreigners (*'ajanib*) and "strangers," speaking different languages or Arabic, but they were hardly perceived as potentially threatening. Indeed, their resistance affiliation and sponsorship gave them a welcomed niche in the community. A viable resistance presence had conditioned a landscape of order and security in this heterogeneous camp. Now "strangers" (other Arabs) were perceived with mistrust. In other words, Palestinians had lost the ability to control who lived in the camp.

When a five-year-old Palestinian boy was raped and murdered in Shatila, a Syrian worker was apprehended by outraged camp residents, who were compelled to turn him over to the Syrian authorities. The camp leadership requested that he be turned over to the Lebanese police as the representatives of the legal order. They were angry because they feared he would not be punished by the Syrians In the aftermath, the alleyways, usually full of noisy children, were eerily silent as people forbade their children to play outdoors.

Um Khalid and I visited Um Nabil, an elderly resident in a small apartment in one of the new buildings on the very edge of the camp, actually outside the borders, constructed to house "displaced refugees." Um Nabil complained, "In this camp, you can't hang a pair of pants out to dry without someone stealing them!" a common way of voicing distrust. Her neighbor Um Bilal chimed in, "A girl can't go for a visit and walk home by herself like we used to in Tel al-Za'ter. This camp is not a safe place for girls to go about on their own." Women's mobility was an easily referenced barometer of community disempowerment and vulnerability.

In the civil war period, women's mobility expanded as they were required to move, act, and work outside the home. Resistance ideologies supportive of women's political participation lent nationalist legitimacy to their newly enhanced mobility (Peteet 1991). With the end of conflict and the defeat of the Palestinians, a retraditionalization of space was evident, particularly in heterogeneous Shatila. Village quarters had not marked its spatial organization, and in the 1990s it was again increasingly home to Palestinians and Arabs from elsewhere with no kin ties in the camp. Without an overarching sentiment of community and a common structure of governance, a social landscape of unknown and strange people made it difficult to establish trust in the environment.

Figure 15. Shatila camp. A new apartment building for "displaced refugees" is on the left. In the background is the small street dividing the camp from the Lebanese neighborhood of Hayy Farhat. The donkey-drawn wagon is delivering building supplies to an area where cars were forbidden. Julie Peteet.

Figure 16. A new apartment building on the edge of Shatila camp to house "displaced refugees." Julie Peteet.

Families were more hesitant about allowing young women and girls to move as easily as they did in the era of the resistance when protection was assured and a sense of community prevailed. The Palestinians lost the ability to craft an environment of safety and protection.

The loss of internal autonomy markedly diminished the refugees' capacity to fashion place in their own image, as the following encounter underscores. I was snapping photos in the small street in front of Um and Abu Khalid's house when a man approached and gruffly asked, "Who are you and what are you doing here?" Abu Khalid saw the encounter and came quickly to talk to the man. He explained that I was a friend of the family and that I was writing a book on the camp. The man accepted his explanation and walked off. Visibly annoyed, Abu Khalid muttered angrily, "This man is an Egyptian! He's here in *our* camp, asking *our* guests what they are doing? What have we come to!?"

The camp wars had tested the cross-sect and national friendships formed during the resistance era. Vestiges of these friendships suggested that the Palestinians persevered in their heterogeneous social relations, refusing a withdrawal into a national and sectarian outlook. Um Hassan and Um Khalid had occupied neighboring apartments in Shatila since the early 1970s and had raised their children together. Over time, their friendship had solidified through a pattern of exchanging services and support, an indication of the kinds of cross-sect and cross-national relations once extant in Shatila. Um Hassan's two teenaged sons and husband joined the 'Amal militia and fought against the camp. One of her sons was killed. Puzzled by this affiliation, I asked how it had transpired that her husband and sons had joined 'Amal. Um Khalid explained that Abu Hassan had never really supported the Palestinian struggle and lived in the camp simply because they were poor. He was a quiet sort, but she was sure he had always disliked the Palestinians: "He was never really with us, you know." Um Hassan now lived a few hundred feet away in Hayy Farhat, an area once merged with the camp that had now reverted to being Shi'a space. Um Khalid used to point out that the olives served at lunch were from Um Hassan's family in the south, who frequently visited, bringing gifts of home-processed goods such as olives and yoghurt. References to such friendships, exemplified by acts of giving, were daily reminders of past amicable and supportive relations. Invoking them, as Um Khalid did, was a commentary on the violence done to these relationships. This quotidian giving of simple foodstuffs and continued pattern of visiting were a means of crossing over a boundary that seemingly had all the ingredients of the irrevocable—a son had been lost and a community devastated.

When I first returned to Shatila in the 1990s, I asked Um Khalid if we could visit Um Hassan. In spite of the camp wars, they had maintained their close friendship. Just before we reached Hayy Farhat, Um Khalid told me not to speak or look at anyone, in other words, not to call attention to ourselves in this area. Before we left the house, she cautioned me not to ask Um Hassan any questions about the war or Shi'a sentiments if her husband or sons were home. I was carefully instructed to pretend it was a simple social visit. Luckily, she was home alone, and after the requisite greetings and catching up on news I could proceed to ask questions about Shi'a attitudes toward the Palestinians and the war. However, I soon became frustrated. Each time I broached the topic of how the Shi'a had turned against their former neighbors and one-time political allies with such ferocity, Um Khalid would interpret Um Hassan's responses of seeming bewilderment as to why relations had degenerated. Um Khalid persisted in repeating, "There are no differences between us! We are all the same. We all live in this wretched place. We are poor people fighting the same enemy. It is others who have made trouble between us." Um Hassan kept nodding her head in agreement. At first annoyed and impatient to talk with Um Hassan, I soon realized that they were not just talking to me. Um Khalid was affirming, and Um Hassan was agreeing, that despite belonging to warring communities, they still shared poverty, marginality, and the suffering inflicted by war.

Maintaining and nurturing relations of crossing were highly gendered; women performed the often overlooked work of sustaining peaceful relations. Indeed, their crossings met with less danger than men's. Like other camp women, Um Khalid walked through Shi'a neighborhoods, although with trepidation. The fear of potential violence was communicated in her bodily movements. Her eyes cast down, she would pull her scarf tightly around her face, draw in her shoulders and hurry, trying not to look too conspicuous. She always reminded me not to talk when we walked through their areas. Occasionally she would nod her head in a certain direction and say very quietly, "Remember when that building was ours—it fell during the camp wars and so-and-so's boys were killed in the battle." Lebanese men did not enter the camp, fearing revenge attacks or the potential for a fight whose consequences could reverberate well beyond the camp. Conversely, Palestinian men were much more hesitant about entering Shi'a space in the years immediately following the camp wars. With time some of this reticence has abated.

At Um Khalid's house, when I commented on Shi'a women moving through the camp on their way to the local market, there ensued a discussion in a family gathering as to the issue of Shi'a men walking through the camp. With the humor of those who did not "win" the war but who fought well and inflicted heavy casualties on their foes, they avowed that Shi'a men were too afraid to walk through the camp. The fear of revenge loomed large and suggested that the idea of mobility as an enactment of power needed to be complicated and context-specific. Women now crossed these boundaries because they were fairly certain they would not be harmed. Um Hassan visited frequently but her husband dared not walk into Shatila. Violence radically disrupted and rearranged intercommunal social relations, yet did not completely shatter them. Crossings subverted the communal and spatial absolutism imposed by violence and might provide the seeds of collective and individual recovery.

Thus Palestinian abilities to construct place were exceedingly impaired, overwhelmed by the crush of animosity and deadly attempts to contain their national movement. They could not build nor did they have any control over the borders or who was able to live in the camps. In short, military and political defeat and their disempowerment on the local and regional scene seemed to effectively weaken their capacity to shape their environment. However, even the harshest conditions do not entirely denude communities of the ability to craft meaningful places. To argue otherwise would be akin to suggesting that displacement and mass trauma give rise to deculturalization and a complete lack of agency. Palestinians continued to produce places of intense meaning through the elaboration of a moral community, through reinvigorating pre-1948 forms of association and corporate action and through the enactment of memory.

During the period of Palestinian empowerment, Palestinians and Lebanese were amiable and involved in various forms of exchange. Differences were often glossed over, if not indeed minimized, although a subtle Shi'a resentment of Palestinian power and misbehavior, particularly in the south, had become evident by the late 1970s. Hostilities effected a tightening of spatial boundaries, and differences were rhetorically elaborated and put into relief. In short, violence unscrambled and rescrambled social and spatial boundaries in ways often not immediately apparent, generating new lines of difference where previously sameness was avidly declared. As the next section illustrates, the elaboration of difference around an imagined moral divide helped make sense of the hardship and continuing violence that plagued their collective and individual lives and was pivotal in constructing a sense of place.

Moral Geographies, Moral Communities

The violently imposed border was invested with meanings that firmly etched a cultural rift, marking each side as fundamentally different. In the process, identities were recalibrated, in a way that magnified minor differences. The construction and reproduction of difference is a dynamic and historically embedded process. Notions of the moral, of propriety, and acceptable comportment drew a line of inclusion and exclusion, establishing a cultural ethos of both distinction and similarity with respect to others. Yet their imagining and magnification can have real and often horrific consequences. The other, the Lebanese or the Palestinian, was difficult to distinguish physically, culturally, or linguistically, and yet expressions of distinction became more pronounced as tension between the communities mounted. A polarization of interests and identity between Lebanese and Palestinians was spatially enacted with astounding violence. Essentially political differences were transposed into cultural differences that rested on a perceived moral/immoral distinction.

Othering was neither consistent nor totalizing, but it did reach a stage where Palestinians, in camps or not, were openly discriminated against and physically and verbally attacked without arousing much sympathy. A consensus that the Palestinians had to be contained and eventually settled elsewhere had become a common denominator among formerly warring Lebanese factions. Indeed, they were a demon other, a thorn in its side, an ever present threat to Lebanon's national well-being. The Lebanese proprietor of my neighborhood laundry typified this when she complained to me one day about all the 'ajanib in Lebanon and how they stole, got into fights, and generally made life difficult. When I asked who were these foreigners, she replied: "Palestinians, Syrians, Sri Lankans, the Filipinos, the Kurds"—all foreign sources of cheap manual labor.

However, rapidly shifting Lebanese/Palestinian political relations over several decades undermined an easy propensity to organize and make the world knowable through a dichotomized series of absolute categories of moral/immoral and us/them. Thus profound distinctions enunciated in one breath could easily be followed by avid proclamations of sameness. After a tirade against both the Lebanese government and the populace for their post-1982 treatment of Palestinian refugees, Um Ghazi, a mother of three martyrs, told me with conviction, "Between Lebanese and Palestinians—there are no differences. There are good people and bad people among each. They are not all the same—just like your fingers—each looks different. Your own children, if you have three or four, some are good and some give you trouble."

When conflict broke out and space was violently rearranged, moral distinctions became rhetorically pronounced. Palestinians did not present a totally coherent moral narrative of self, community, enemy, and host. Each community could find in the other qualities they claimed were fundamentally contrary to their own and each could equally find similarities. A multitude of cross-linkages, from friendship to political activism to marriage, meant the moral community was porous and negotiable. Within the flux, however, the making and working of a discursive and practical moral community could be discerned. What components of difference and sameness played into its elaboration? A major aspect of modern Palestinian national identity and subjectivity has been its formulation against a variety of "others." The Israelis were a felt but often unseen force; the "other" power to affect their life choices was pervasive but not face-to-face. The immediate and face-to-face other was the host population. The Palestinian narrative of difference with the Lebanese posited a beginning period of good relations; current difference was almost always juxtaposed to a past of peaceful, mutually beneficial relations of solidarity and support. We can recall Um Khalid's narrative of the camp wars. "There were no differences between us. We ate together." Thus the potentially oppositional quality to modern Palestinian identity has not engendered a world view tightly organized around polarized qualities of difference. In other words, while Palestinians constructed and enacted difference from the Lebanese, it was not a *consistently* organized, always dichotomized hierarchy of worth. To further complicate matters, internal divisions positioned some Palestinians as the other as well. In refugees' narratives of 1948, they typically represent themselves as naive, morally upright, and trusting peasants, deceived by a self-interested leadership as well as the Zionist movement. Such narratives point to internal features of class and regional difference as well as external forces, further undermining attempts to construct a deeply polarized, nationalized moral world view.

On a larger scale, the refugees were wedged uncomfortably between a pan-Arab discourse of belonging, identity, and cultural affinity, or Arabness, and a keen awareness of Arab state interests and actions that undercut their struggle. They situated themselves uneasily in the interstices between metanarratives of Arab unity and the sentiments and enactment of Palestinianism. A morality discourse spanning both the Arab and the Palestinian acted coevally in drawing lines of inclusion and exclusion. National exclusion set them apart from other Arabs, particularly the Lebanese, and yet Arabness included them in a more encompassing geography, history, and culture. Shami writes, "As any other identity, however, Arabness has to be constantly reinvented and is constantly threatened. Its discourse is reshaped by historical events as it simultaneously provides the vocabulary with which to interpret these events. . . . 'Arabness,' as any other identity, obtains its power through its very ambiguity and ability to contain different meanings at the same time" (1996: 11, 13). Depending on the situation, Palestinians oscillated rapidly between Arabness and Palestinianism—from "We are not Arabs any more," when reacting angrily to Arab policies, to the ubiquitous "This is Arab culture," to explain cultural practices. The very ambiguity of Arabness crafted a space for Palestinians simultaneously to profess historically and culturally deep linkage and belonging and yet separateness and distinction.

Predictably, gender was called forth as a real and symbolic marker of community; a gendered moral domain formed a bedrock around which to structure, narrate, and reproduce difference. Contrasting images were emphasized as the moral was mapped onto the bodies of women and men. Gender and sexuality constituted a moral fault line, a barometer of sorts indicating lines of distinction but also similarity between Palestinians and the Lebanese. The Lebanese were deemed potentially sexually transgressive. Palestinian narratives suggested that Lebanese men and women were sexually "loose." In casual conversations, girls were advised to avoid marrying Lebanese men because they are unfaithful to their wives and not as committed to their families as were Palestinian men. Practices that might cast doubt on the narrative of Palestinian morality, such as the growing problem of prostitution and drugs in the camps, were spoken of in hushed tones. They signaled the fragility of the moral fabric.

In the postwar period, distinctions also focused on domesticity and socializing. Camp women considered urban Lebanese women rather deficient in the domestic arena. These "social butterflies" were criticized for participating in "morning coffees" (*subhiyat*), leisurely occasions for socializing with friends and relatives. Um Khalid and her friends and neighbors made their visits in the late afternoon or early evening; the morning hours were devoted to housecleaning, cooking, and child care. Not tending properly to one's domestic duties was a sign of slovenliness and indicated a lack of morality and hard work, arenas where femininity was enacted and reaffirmed.

In the Palestinian national narrative, women had the dubious honor of representing suffering and sacrifice along with tradition. Camp women took pride in their reputation for struggle and sacrifice. For example, patterns of consumption were an index of sacrifice and thus purity and superiority. Suha, a twenty-five-year-old graduate student in literature at the Arab University and long resident in Shatila, said with an air of certainty, "Palestinians sacrifice financially for the sake of their children's education and for their families in general. The Lebanese will buy clothes in order to dress in the latest Paris fashions yet their cupboard might be bare." Two related issues are caught up in this critique. First, the Lebanese were perceived as overly concerned with superficial appearances, the constitution of a public face through conspicuous consumption, while through self-restraint Palestinians constructed honorable selves, families, and community. Second, generosity and an ability to provide hospitality, key components of prestige and honor, were compromised by a "bare cupboard." To put one's own needs above those of potential guests by having an empty cupboard and putting one's appearance before the needs of children and family conveyed a blatant lack of self-discipline and thus honor.

Actions in wartime Lebanon gave Palestinians further grounds upon which to map and assert a heightened morality. In their narratives of the civil war, they were on the defensive, reluctantly dragged into conflict. A group of young fighters in Burj al-Barajneh camp took me on a lengthy tour of the series of bunkers and trenches dug around the perimeter. We talked about military strategy and inevitably the topic of atrocities came up. Several of them said repeatedly and with conviction, "We didn't do such things," in reference to 'Amal atrocities. They viewed their own military actions as honorable, and indeed Palestinian forces were seldom if ever implicated in atrocities. Palestinian men assumed the moral high ground and the mantle of honorable masculinity in war in contrast to what they perceived as the Lebanese willingness to go on the offensive and commit mass atrocities.

Women's culturally assigned task of upholding the moral community freighted their behavior with dangerous powers and increased the constraints on them. Women's potential to define the moral outlines of community and simultaneously subvert them through culturally inappropriate behavior on the one hand, and cross-sect friendships, on the other, underscored that the category "women" embodied substantial symbolic and real flexibility.

Sectarianism also denoted a Palestinian moral community. Camp inhabitants are nearly all Sunni Muslims. In Lebanon, Palestinians did not organize politically on a sectarian basis; indeed they often referred jokingly to sectarianism as the "Lebanese disease." Given that Zionism is a form of sectarianism whose logic compelled their displacement, they were particularly attuned to sectarian issues. Their calls for a democratic and secular state in Palestine had been largely ignored and, in an ironic twist, made to appear obstructionist rather than as a possible form of the modern liberal state and citizenship. As the civil war progressed and sectarianism became more entrenched, Palestinian secularism took on a heightened significance in highlighting difference. To them, it signaled a modernity that differentiated them from the Lebanese.

Stepping back a decade, in the summer of 1982 in besieged West Beirut, the outlines of a moral community that transcended narrow Lebanese and Palestinian nationalist and sectarian lines were visible. In West Beirut, whose boundaries had been precisely defined by the civil war and the 1982 Israeli siege perimeter, people came together in solidarity against the powerful military force bearing down on them. The lack of electricity, water, and medicine, the shortage of food, and the intensive daily bombardments brought people together in the practical and every-day search for these basic components of human existence and shelter from the massive and indiscriminate bombardment of their neighbor-hoods. A commonsensical realization that aerial and artillery bombard-ments could seldom accurately pinpoint targets on the basis of sect, ethnicity, or nation meant that everyone was a potential victim. West Bei-rutis were acutely aware of these relations and sentiments of solidarity. With hindsight, the sense of moral community in the summer of 1982 takes on a singular poignancy. Once again, this alerts us to the need for a historically and politically situated framework that can capture and render meaningful both the fleetingness and contingency of imaged and practical moral communities and their ability to cross-cut poten-tially divisive social terrain.

Within the refugee camps themselves, multiple moral boundaries were apparent. First, the camp itself brought together people from dif-ferent villages. As we saw in the last chapter, stereotypes of different vil-lages were bandied about, although humorously. This memoryscape of pre-1948 Palestine formed a spatially and experientially bounded moral community set against an exterior of Lebanese and urban Palestinians. When I asked Um Ghazi what it was like in Shatila camp with people from so many other camps living there during reconstruction, she reiter-ated the stock phase, "We are all of one hand." Yet she, like others, fre-quently complained about "strangers," referring to Palestinians from other camps. The problem of petty theft was blamed on them (and to some extent on the influx of Syrian and Egyptian workers). When Abu Bilal's new radio went missing, consensus among his family and immedi-ate neighbors was that other Palestinians had stolen it. They lived in the newly constructed multistory housing project on the edge of Shatila. They had left their door open while visiting friends down the corridor and upon their return the radio was gone. Um Bilal lamented that these "strangers—Palestinians from who knows where!" had taken it. Um Khalid and her friends were extremely hesitant to discuss persistent rumors of prostitution involving both women and children, yet they openly and avidly discussed the rape and murder of a camp child by a Syrian worker. To acknowledge moral violations by Palestinians would be to undermine the reality and fiction of a moral community.

At times, the camps' moral boundaries stretched to include urban Pal-estinians. Many of them had never been in a refugee camp. During the resistance era, social relations between camp and urban refugees were not nearly as distinct as they had been in the 1950s and early 1960s. The resistance brought together Palestinians from vastly different social classes in a common project of struggle. Intermarriages began to occur, as did a more general pattern of visiting and social interaction. For the urban middle and upper class, trips to the camps validated their Pales-tinianness, ostensibly shrinking moral and class lines of distinction. Thus the guiding assumption was that the camp's authenticity, purity, and capacity for struggle would virtually rub off on the visitors. Visitors also felt they were supporting and participating in struggle by visiting. Rela-tions organized around the idiom of resistance defined a kind of moral community, one whose boundaries were certainly larger than the spaces of the camp itself.

In the post-1982 era, fearing for their safety, almost no one visited the camps and there were hardly any relations to bring together the various sectors of the Palestinian community. The rate of intermarriage, both between Lebanese and Palestinians and among different Palestinian social classes, was noticeably lower. Palestinians rarely left the camps, and when they did it was mainly for daily necessities rather than to socialize. This withering of relations was a direct consequence of the tightening of the camps' boundaries in the wake of the defeat. The boundaries of the moral community thus cannot be delinked from larger regional political events.

Village Matters

I was photographing the alleyways and small shops in Shatila in 1999 when a shopkeeper came out, gestured questioningly, and asked Um Khalid, "Where is she from? What is her nationality?" Um Khalid responded, "She is married to one from al-Bassa." Now smiling, he looked at me said, "'Ahlan was 'Ahlan" (welcome), and readily posed for a picture in front of his small grocery shop. Such an incident under-scores the way the past in the present collapses notions of time and space and informs identity. At the turn of the century, villages still figure prominently in refugees' cognitive maps of the world. Indeed, fifty years after *al-nakbah*, camps such as 'Ayn al-Hilweh and Burj al-Barajneh remain spatially organized in village clusters.

A few days later, on my way to the home of friends in Shatila, I saw two middle-aged men wandering around. From their searching glances and halting steps, it was apparent they were lost. I paid them little attention and went on my way. Half an hour later, they knocked on Um Khalid's door and asked to see the man of the house. When Abu Khalid came to the door, they introduced themselves, "We are from Baddawi camp and originally from Suhmata" (a pre-1948 village). Invited in for the requi-site offerings of hospitality, they explained their visit. Their niece was considering marriage to a young man whose family was from 'Akbarah. "We are her guardians," they explained. "Her father, our brother, is a *shaheed* [martyr] who was killed in battle in 1976." Out of respect for their brother and to follow the proper course of action as her guardians, they wanted to make sure they thoroughly investigated the young man's background. They told Abu Khalid, "We have heard the people of 'Akbarah are good people," and they initially referred to the young man neither by name nor by profession but as a fellow from this particular village. The hosts, themselves from 'Akbarah, were not related to the young man and had only a passing knowledge of who he was. The girl's two uncles were traveling from camp to camp asking to be directed to families from 'Akbarah in order to gain information that would help them determine the young man's suitability as a marriage partner.

In the 1990s villages mattered in multiple and complex ways in the construction of place and in the contours of social relations. They were metonyms for places that existed in memory yet they had a contemporary social existence. Villages had a particular, embodied meaning for each generation, for those who knew them and lived in them, and those who knew and imagined them from the standpoint of exile. Each generation lived in a web of village-based social relations and the spaces in which they had been reconstituted. They were cognitive and social maps that facilitated the location and recognition of others. As people deployed these frames, they produced and reproduced place through practice, in a real sense as well as discursively. They conformed to what Pile and Thrift have called "wayfinding" (1995: 1), the positioning of self and others in a spatially meaningful way. These positions were highly situational depending on the past and present location of the other with whom one was interacting. For instance, when Palestinians meet in chance encounters, there is a fairly standard exchange referenced to present location and the pre-1948 origins. "Where are you from?"/ "Kweikat. Where are you from?"/ "Safed and we live in Burj al-Barajneh" is the kind of dialogue heard frequently among Palestinians in Lebanon. Shifting location, when two Palestinians meet in the United States the dialogue is more apt to be as follows: "Where are you from?"/ "I am a Palestinian from Lebanon. And you?"/ "I am from Jordan—we are from the Jerusalem area." How one locates oneself spatially depends on where one is positioned in the present and where the other person is located.

Within the camps, village affiliation was so integral to locating self and others that it could be deployed routinely with few other references to identity. In the summer of 1995, battles erupted between competing political factions in 'Ayn al-Hilweh. Um Khalid and I slept at her brother's house as gunfire and explosions reverberated throughout the night. The next morning, neighbors came for coffee and to exchange news after a sleepless, anxiety-filled night. Someone announced that in the course of the battles "three from Saffuriyyah died and one from Loubia." Later in the day a young man and his mother came to visit. In the course of exchanging news, his mother announced "He is going to marry one from Saffuriyyah." My host jokingly interceded, "I can get him one from 'Akbarah," her village in Palestine. The boy's mother, from Balad al-Sheikh, retorted, "It doesn't matter where we come from. We are all a family." Thus the conversation ricocheted between village and Palestine, local and national, in the immediate aftermath of a pitched battle between Palestinian factions.

The village as spatial locator was accompanied by the vicissitudes of exile. Um Khalid often referred to her friends by their village of origin or camp residence. Her new friend, Um Bilal, was always referred to as "Um Bilal—from Za'ter." Her tone of voice when she said "Za'ter" intimated a problem, a sense that all was not well. When talking of her in more detail she would refer to Khalsa, her village of origin. "Za'ter" circulated easily as a metonym for calamity and displacement that resonated collectively; people sadly nodded their heads in shared recognition of its meanings.

In the 1990s villages were openly reasserted as a site of both social organization and cultural affiliation, with implications for the meanings of space and identity.[6] Under the resistance, village affiliations, although certainly not muted, had receded somewhat in self-identification. They had been deeply overlaid with political affiliations in locating and categorizing individuals and families. Village protective functions had been supplemented by those of the resource-richer resistance movement.

In the post-1982 period, the void in social and welfare services was compounded by the precipitous decline of remittances from the oil-producing states, with profound repercussions. In this atmosphere, the village took on renewed meaning as a locus of social organization and functions. Village-based associations, loosely knit groups whose membership cross-cut camp boundaries, sprang up. Abu Salah, formerly a guerrilla commented:

Now you have to have somebody behind you, supporting you. In the past, it was the political organizations who would help you in time of need, offer protection and provide *waasta* [connections]. Now it is the family and village. With the resistance gone, people are looking to the village and the big families in their villages. Because of our weak situation in Lebanon, we have been pushed to return to smaller and smaller units, away from the national level.

There are associations for 'Alma, al-Bassa, Dayr al-Qasi, Saffuriyyah, Suhmata, and Um al-Faraj, among others. However nebulous, they were a form of corporate action hardly seen since 1948. Akin to mutual aid societies, they mobilized resources along village lines, collecting money from member families and maintaining a common fund (*sanduq*) from which those in need could draw in the event of an emergency such as death or illness. Indeed, the costs associated with funerals were the spark that led to their formation. During this time of unparalleled poverty, families increasingly faced difficulties paying for the mourning rituals in which visitors were received at home and served coffee, juice, and cigarettes. Few could afford to buy enough chairs to seat guests during the days of mourning. One of the first associations began in Rashidiyyah, when a few senior men of 'Alma solicited donations from fellow villagers and purchased chairs for a funeral. The chairs now rotate among 'Alma houses for funerals and weddings. The leadership of the associations was drawn from middle-aged men, often sons of former *makhater* in Palestine, sons of rivals of former *makhater* in Palestine, and former militants.

A question that pervaded discussion about village associations concerned their potential to reaffirm inequities. Larger villages provided members with a far-flung network of resources, support, and influence. Saffuriyyah was often brought up as a prime example. As a demographically substantial, historically influential village whose members settled in large discernible clusters, Saffuriyyis were clearly able to muster more resources than those from smaller villages. Small, geographically dispersed villagers found it difficult to mobilize people and resources to form an association. For example, when Um Samir found herself in dire financial straits and her house falling to pieces, she could not turn to fellow villagers for support. Her village, Balad al-Sheikh, did not have an association; in 1948, villagers scattered to Lebanon and Syria, and they did not form spatial clusters in the camps. Um Samir lamented, "If I were from Saffuriyyah, I would have people to help me."

Two small neighboring villages discovered an alternative coping strategy. With a history of social exchange and marriage, al-Zeeb and al-Bassa jointly formed an association. Neighboring villages in Palestine, they remained situated next to each other in 'Ayn al-Hilweh. In the 1990s they formed an informal joint insurance company to provide money for members involved in auto accidents. Four older men handled an account comprised of villagers' contributions. Each member of the insurance fund contributed LL 5,000 (about U.S.$ 3.30) a month.

Well-known associations tended to be demographically large and powerful villages, such as Saffuriyyah.[7] The center of the 1936 revolt, its reputation also hinged on its former status as a regional trade center. Belonging to this village endowed an individual with more access than others to jobs and services; its sheer numbers meant that it could provide a larger network of social ties to draw upon. If exile extended villagers over a wide space, village associations reconnected them in a new context and for new purposes. With quarters in a number of camps from Nahr al-Bared in the north to 'Ayn al-Hilweh in the south, they could collect money for a funeral, for example, by sending someone to other camps with an appeal.

Headquartered in 'Ayn al-Hilweh, the association produced a calendar in 1995, attesting to its resources and ability to mobilize collective memory, but also its sense of itself as a community, however dispersed. The calendar says much about the past in the present. The yellow cover is graced with a black-and-white photograph of the mosaic floors in the village's well-known ruins, on which a map of Palestine is superimposed. Nazareth, the district of which Saffuriyyah was the capital, is highlighted in the map. On each succeeding page, a village photograph asserts an intimate link between refugees and the pre-1948 village. The cover page title is twofold: well-known Palestinian writer and artist Ghassan Kanafani's calligraphic "Palestine" and below it, in bold script, "We Will Return Today." The end page contains an array of four photos situating the village in a historical, geosocial, and political landscape. The first photo is the city of Nazareth, now home to a number of Saffuriyyis who have formed a village association there. The text states, "We shall not forgive, nor forget and shall not accept an alternative homeland. We shall remain while the lives of occupations are short." The next two photographs, the pre-1948 village and al-Aqsa Mosque, assert Saffuriyyah's Islamic character. In the last photo stands a lone house in 1987, unconnected to the past, cut off from the deep history of place.

The intervening photo/texts depicts a pre-1948 culturally heterogeneous history. "We will leave the pictures to tell the true story of Saffuriyyah" acknowledges the contested history of nearly every Palestinian village now in Israel and points to photography as a medium that captures the "true" nature of place. The calendar informs the reader that the built environment and the stones used to construct homes and religious buildings will offer the truth. The first page is a photo of a monastery with the caption "Saffuriyyah—Home (*balad*) of Virgin Mary: Hannah's Monastery." Noting that the town was never abandoned, the text gives a historical rundown of the town's inhabitants: Romans, Jews, Christians, Byzantines, and Muslims, and the significance of the town to each of these groups. It was a command post for Salah Eddin, the Kurdish leader who vanquished the Crusaders in the twelfth century. Conquest by Zionist forces in 1948 was the cataclysmic event that displaced its indigenous inhabitants for the first time. The next page features the Crusader-era castle, built on a Byzantine structure, later used as a girls' school. The text narrates the fall of the village, quoting Israeli historian Benny Morris as to its fierce resistance. As headquarters to al-Qawuqji's forces,[8] and before that Salah Eddin, the calendar presents a version of history in which Saffuriyyah played a prominent role as militant defenders of Islam and Palestine. The choice of a photo of a Crusader castle is not serendipitous. In Palestinian narratives, Zionists are often equated with the Crusaders—a short-lived foreign presence that will be defeated through heroic resistance.

Another picture presents the famed mosaics from the third-century house. The text states that the ruins "testify to its importance as a city for all ages where man left his immortal message to future generations." The built environment captured in the photos visualizes continuous occupation and an Arab identity. Having outlasted various occupiers, the buildings stand as witnesses to its history. Photographs of peasants at work accentuated the agricultural and peasant identity of the village, a dominant theme in the nationalist narrative. The calendar was a collective assertion of indigeneity in face of the village's transformation into Tzippori,[9] giving visual reality to a conscious construction of relationship to and claim to place. Colonialism complicates Tuan's distinction between "knowing" and "knowing about" (1980: 8); Palestinians indeed now "know about" their villages.

Acrimonious debates about the meaning of these associations and their political implications stemmed in part from the fact that it was regionally dominant villages which had initially formed them. During the resistance era, smaller villages' lack of power and resources was offset somewhat by access to PLO-based resources. With the safety net pulled out, people from smaller villages had a harder time coping with poverty. I listened to a heated debate between two former resistance cadres, both of whom have advanced university degrees, which revolved around a discourse of "primordialism," "survival," and "identity." Salim, now middle-aged and writing a history of the resistance in Lebanon, argued that these associations reflected a reactionary and atomistic turning inward to pre-1948 primordial ties and away from progressive political ideologies and movements. His friend Sari argued that they were not a return to primordial ties at the expense of national identities but were a means of ensuring survival during a critical time. Indeed, he claimed they reiterated pre-1948 identities and ties to Palestine.

The village associations were remarkably gendered, in contrast to the resistance era, when some efforts were made to bring women into the political process. Although the associations met in homes, women were not visibly active participants. The gender composition of the associations articulated with a retraditionalization of space and activities. With the end of the war, public space was regendered in ways that marginalized women. Although utilizing domestic space for their activities, village associations were a largely male activity. Domestic space thus remained polyvalent, characterized by multiple uses.

The emergence of the village associations signaled a renewed role for the extended family, clan, and now multisited village as a unit of action, affiliation, and loyalty. It remains to be seen whether these associations fit in the framework of Middle Eastern forms of modernity, where the past is invested with culturally potent meanings and mobilized to meet contemporary challenges. Rather than a return to a past, they are alternative political and social strategies, derived from village life, transfigured for the particular circumstances of the present.

Palestinian villages retained their capacity to socially enact and represent the imagined homeland. Village clusters reconstituted Palestine and endowed exilic space with its initial and long-term meaning and organizational form. In the new millennium, villages continued to provide cognitive and social maps as well as a safety net. Just as importantly, villages were a primary form of identification of self and other. Memories of the intricacies of village social life and detailed descriptions may be fading as the *jeel filasteen* dies off, but village remains critical in the making of place and the fashioning of identity.

Community

If we assume that the geosocial spaces of the camps shaped the contours of social experience, what are we to make of postwar isolation? With limited mobility in the 1990s, there was little overt sense of cohesion as a community of refugees in Lebanon. Each camp lived under a slightly different set of authorities (Lebanese, Palestinian, or Syrian), had a different history of violence and struggle, and had developed a highly localized leadership, sometimes intersecting uneasily with the external PLO leadership. Each camp had a set of lore about its history and its heroes. A small group of former leaders spoke occasionally in the name of the refugees as a whole. The story of the "smurfs" illustrates the isolation. A group of displaced refugees were resettled in Baddawi camp. When the children settled in and began to play on the playground, local Baddawi children taunted them and called them "smurfs," after the popular cartoon characters. Parents and community leaders explained that these were fellow refugees who had the misfortune to have been forcibly displaced from Tel al-Za'ter. Isolation meant that refugee children were unaware of, and unsympathetic to, the sufferings of other refugees. One of the community leaders, who intervened and organized a session where the children heard about the history of 1948 and the various places Palestinians had sought refuge, commented that the "smurf" incident was a telling indication of the growing insularity of each camp.

Along with violence, isolation had contradictory effects. As a consequence of marginality, refugees forged a localized sense of community and identity. Sameera, a fifty-year-old schoolteacher who was visiting Um and Abu Khalid in Shatila, said,

In the past, everybody worked together. Before the camp wars, more precisely before the 1982 war, the camp was a million times better. Everyone knew everyone else. You knew everybody and everybody knew you. Now it is different. Everybody is a stranger. There are so many people I don't know. Now we have Lebanese, Kurds, Syrians, and Palestinians. When asked to go on a demonstration or any other activities, not everybody is willing to participate. Maybe you will get two or three people to go with you. Even these will go without real conviction. In the past, over half the camp would come out and participate, and do so with conviction. The original population of Shatila has been dispersed. Those who could have rented outside the camp or bought property. Now that reconstruction has started, and the population is 25 times what it used to be, the noise is unbearable. And the camp is much dirtier now. Before, the alleys and roads were clean, the electricity was secure, water supplies were good. Now electricity is not secure, water shortages are prevalent, especially in the summer, due to the large population. The same water that supplied 200 households now is distributed among 700. So you get much less.

The Palestinian martyr evoked sadness and pride among all the people in the past. They all participated in mourning him and referred to his family proudly. Now, the martyr is forgotten overnight. We have around 850 martyrs buried in the mosque. In the past they would have been mourned by everybody. Now they are mourned, but it is felt it is our destiny. The catastrophe borne by one individual is different from that borne by a whole people. It is easier when it is shared by everybody. That is the difference between now and the past.

Sameera's summary of the camps, in a now and then fashion, encapsulated a sense of community and place defined by social action and collective experience. With prolonged violence, Palestinians withdrew into their individual suffering. The future held no hope because to suffer and die is "our destiny." One can read a loss of agency in such a designation of place. Once sites of potential and hope, the camps spelt only a bleak future of despair.

Refugees conceptualized camps as living bodies with collective experiences and histories and as capable of collective action. As rumors flew that Shatila residents were to be transferred to the interior of Lebanon or even Iraq, Abu Khalid said in a highly rhetorical, yet adamant voice,

We hear the camps in Beirut will be removed. This is supposedly the state's plan—to remove the pockets of misery and poverty around the city. We will resist this plan by all means because we in Shatila have a particular character and experience. We are surrounded by enemies, be it the Israelis, or former allies in the national movement, or those who massacred us. We have 850 martyrs buried in that mosque! We consider ourselves committed to the memory of our friends and comrades and our children. We will not abandon this camp easily. We will only leave to go straight to Palestine.

He pointed to an uncertain future and action connected to honoring a past of suffering and loss. Through memorialization of its suffering and attributions of character, he endowed Shatila with identity, a collective history and honor, and the possibility of collective action.

The effects of spatial fragmentation and isolation were equally evident in the following incident. In trying to help a camp family apply for a scholarship for their daughter, I suggested they seek help from the office of a Palestinian philanthropist. I told them specifically to see the office manager. They spoke with her and came back and told me they hesitated to talk to her because "she was Lebanese." I told them, "No, she's not. She's a Palestinian. What made you think she's Lebanese?" They replied, "Her accent. She spoke like a Lebanese." I said, "That's because she lives in Beirut and can speak that accent and probably does so most of the time." I was stunned when they said plaintively, "There are hardly any Palestinians now in Lebanon except in the camps." They had been so cut off by the camp wars that they hardly believed that urban middle and upper class Palestinians still lived in Beirut.

Violence research raises the issue of the relationship between suffering and the constitution of community. Violence and suffering have been integral to the Palestinian national narrative of displacement and exile. Once in the center, so to speak, of national politics, the Palestinians in Lebanon have shifted to the margins. As the center of gravity in Palestinian politics shifted to the West Bank, for the Palestinians in Lebanon their relationship to the dominant, contemporary national narrative and sense of belonging to the nation took on ambiguity. They saw themselves as sacrificial victims to the resistance movement which had seemingly abandoned them (Peteet 1995b). Yet having lived through these years of violence, and now being on the margins, their particular experiences etched a moral community and narrative distinct from, and indeed occasionally at odds with, the larger national one.

The chaotic brutality directed against a community may be replicated in the capricious and turbulent effects it sets in motion. In addition to fostering communal solidarity and collective memory, violence can equally fissure experience and drive a wedge through communities, fracturing national identity and belonging. For example, refugee camps may figure prominently in the Palestinian imagination and collective consciousness, yet not all Palestinians reside in them nor do they all suffer equally. This complicates attempts to elaborate idioms of suffering and pain as emblematic of national experience. For example, memories of past violence and suffering serve to bind the community in an understanding of contemporary violence, a way of making sense of it and talking about it. Initially I asked people in the camps about the war in a general sense. What was it like? What happened to you? A strikingly specific pattern was apparent in the way they framed their stories. The camp wars were introduced by reference to past instances of violence. For example, Um Fahim in Burj al-Barajneh stated, "It was like Tel al-Zaʿter. And we didn't want to be another Tel al-Zaʿter." Um Khalid said, "It was Dayr Yassin all over again." Recourse to past violence as a framework for making sense of the contemporary is an aspect of inherited trauma, the transmission of memories from one generation to another (see articles in Robben and Suárez-Orozco 2000). Contemporary experiences were articulated to a national narrative of trauma that began over fifty years ago. Yet camp Palestinians were aware that certain forms of suffering pervaded their lives and not necessarily the lives of Palestinians residing elsewhere. Here, suffice it to note that Palestinians outside the camps shared the collective national sentiment in which violence and suffering were paramount. In other words, there was a broad nationalization of the meaning of suffering.

How does suffering give rise to collective memory and intensify feelings of belonging yet concurrently rupture and dilute community sentiments of belonging? First, after episodes of violence, internal differences could become more acute and visible. The rhetoric and reality of "we are all the same here" referred to a general level of poverty, the shared spatial and experiential medium of the camp, and a past involvement in the resistance movement. This could give way to a heightened sense of difference referenced, for example, to well-being, ability to feed, clothe, educate, and provide medical care to children, and past sufferings. Um Khalid's attempt to help a family in Shatila was indicative of these lines of difference and their expression.

One day, I went with Muna, a social worker, to help a family fill out a form to receive emergency UNRWA assistance. This was the first time I had entered the house of these people. I found a man sitting with his children on a blanket. He had the contents of one or two cans of UNWRA meat in a plate and was feeding his children, five of them. The mother was not there—five children and two small cans of meat! He was feeding them with his hands shaking like this. I told Muna, "Let's go." She said, "Aren't we going to have the form filled out?" I thought this man was shaking because he was drunk. I asked where his wife was and he said she went to collect rations. I asked about the children—their ages and such. He said, "When I was wounded, this boy was just three days old." I said, "What do you mean, wounded?" He said, "I wish you had seen how I was before I was wounded." He had been hit in the head and was suffering from a brain injury and his whole body shook because of that. Once he was wounded, he said nobody cared for him anymore. I took his papers and went to an office in the camp where the Popular Committee was meeting. I marched in and I said to all of those men sitting there, "You are sitting here, your presence or nonpresence is the same thing!" They said, "What is wrong, Um Khalid?" I said, "We just ignore the poor and don't care for them? When he is strong he is ours and when he is weakened we throw him away?" Later I went to one of them to appeal for money for this family. I said, "You have only one child and he is fed. You don't know how others are living. This man is feeding his children like little chicks from a can!"

Um Khalid's story called attention to the way poverty drew a line of distinction. The men on the Popular Committee continued to receive a salary from the resistance, which, however paltry, put them above the edge of absolute poverty.

Women like Um Khalid who had honed their skills at community work during the resistance'era continued to use them to help those in need. In addition, Um Khalid often shamed men who in her view "just sat around." Her friend Um ʿAli, a mother of four martyrs, was a case in point. Um Khalid had told me matter-of-factly, "Um ʿAli is a 'problem' or case." One summer I spent many afternoons at Um ʿAli's house. Um Khalid visited her several times a week. Visiting widows and "mothers of martyrs" was an integral part of Um Khalid's informal social work in the camp. In these visits a particular kind of narration occurred with some frequency. In what amounted to a critical commentary on the revolutionary era and leadership, women's experiences of loss were told metaphorically in terms of "blood and milk," bodily substances associated with birth, nurturing, and death, thus evoking maternal sacrifice and conflating life and death. "We gave our blood and milk," Um ʿAli shouted angrily, "and look how we are living—we are barely able to feed ourselves." Mention of the recent Palestinian/Israeli peace accords, which were supposed to pave the way for the establishment of a Palestinian entity in the West Bank and Gaza Strip (and postponed discussion of refugee issues to a later date), were punctuated by a host of comments such as "We have been abandoned! We gave our children, and they—the PLO—have left us!" "They [the leadership] took our milk and blood and left us here" (Peteet 1995b, 1997).

Um ʿAli was in despair. She was eight months behind on the rent for an unfinished two-room cement structure she shared with her son (her own house awaited repairs) and had not been paid her monthly martyr's family indemnity from the PLO Office of Social Affairs for nearly two years. "If I had my sons and they each gave me money, I would be living comfortably," she cried. Um Khalid took her to ask for financial assistance from one of the few remaining Palestinian political leaders in Lebanon. He told them frankly, and without hesitation, that his office could not help. Next, the two women went to seek help from the PLO representative in Lebanon. They met him as he was leaving his house. Um Khalid asked him for money to repair Um ʿAli's house so she would not have to rent. He agreed and told one of his aides to give her $200 when she returned the next day. When they returned to pick up the $200, the aide told her they did not have any money. According to Um Khalid, "Um ʿAli squatted on the ground and started crying. She could not walk from his house to the street. I calmed her down and told her, 'Do not ask for any more—have faith in God and he will provide.'" In talking about Um ʿAli's plight and her attempts to help, Um Khalid engaged in a running critique of the leadership and their abandonment of the refugees in Lebanon and those who had sacrificed so much for nothing.

In the near absence of a social service sector, women like Um Khalid have taken upon themselves the task of identifying those in need and relaying this information to Shatila's Popular Committee. Um Khalid's husband served on it and she conveyed to him her concerns about particular widows. A small French delegation visited the camps and gave Abu Khalid several hundred dollars for the Popular Committee to assist people in need. Um Khalid was present, and the minute they were out the door, she firmly told her husband: "That money is to go to Um ʿAli. She gave four sons to the revolution and look how she lives—in an unfinished shack!" Abu Khalid nodded in agreement. Reproductive tasks were elevated to the communal and deployed by women as a platform from which to put forth strident demands and a virulent critique of the leadership. Their trust in the revolution to effect a positive outcome for their sacrifice was betrayed. Indeed, the rhetorical centrality of maternal sacrifice underscored female political agency.

The loss of children, the most traumatic form of violence and pain, also indexed subtle fractures in the community of suffering. Um Khalid's family was one of the few not to lose a child in the years of conflict, and she was very careful not to draw attention to it. Whenever I mentioned it, she subtly changed the subject. Occasionally, however, it was unavoidable. Late one afternoon, three middle-aged women dropped by her house and were introduced to me as "mothers of martyrs." After the requisite expression of sympathy I broached the topic of how their children had died. Um Khalid's daughters served tea and brought out the *argeeli* (water pipe). In the hot stillness of an August afternoon, one by one, they recounted how their children had been killed. The room was unbearably quiet as each spoke. No one uttered a sound except to interject an occasional "By God!" Each had tears streaming down her face. Um Khalid turned to me and said softly but matter-of-factly, "See what we have suffered. Everyone has lost someone." One of the women turned, took the pipe from her mouth and looked Um Khalid straight in the face and uttered bluntly: "You didn't lose any of your children." After a few seconds of stunned silence, everyone chimed in at the same time—"May God keep them for you." This exchange encoded collective memories of trauma and loss, but it equally excluded and explicitly hinted at awareness and resentment of others' good fortune.

The more immediate one's proximity to suffering, especially the loss of children, the more one embodied the nation. In a subtle ranking of identities, a core is constituted of those who have suffered and an outer edge composed of those who have witnessed but not directly experienced suffering. These lines of inclusion and exclusion, not necessarily stable or well defined, coincide with class and regional tensions in Palestinian society, and sometimes, as in Um Khalid's case, with pure serendipity. They carry into the present components of pre-1948 Palestinian social organization and relationships and a national narrative of the peasants (now camp dwellers) as the true embodiment of Palestine (once for their closeness to the land, now for inhabiting the camps and their endurance of pain and suffering) and the middle and upper class as those largely responsible for the loss of Palestine in 1948.

Second, as a consequence of the camp wars, the social bonds that once vibrantly connected these communities to outsiders, whether Lebanese, Palestinian, or foreign, contracted considerably. Violence imposed an association between territory, place, and identity. Yet isolation simultaneously enabled and thwarted a sense of community. Each camp had to draw upon its own resources, both military and human, to defend itself. Blockades and the absence of communication networks made coordination exceedingly difficult. The walkie-talkie and underground supply lines did not have the capacity to facilitate intercamp defensive strategies. Five years of isolation effected a social turning inward. The daily defense of the camp in a terrifying atmosphere of siege, hunger, and imminent death instilled sense of a common purpose in the project to stay alive. Violence enabled sentiments of community solidarity and was identity-affirming on the level of the individual camp and for the individual as a member of a group now violently categorized as the enemy. It was an attempt to subvert the community of refugees in Lebanon, hindering communication and social relations, and forcing camp residents into narrow social worlds. Highly localized, camp-based identities were closely linked to isolation and collective trauma. Youth in particular were expressing camp-focused identities. Shatila's children often responded to the question "where are you from?" with "from Shatila." In camps with village quarters, children replied more often with their village of origin as well as with the camp. Having grown up in and having rarely left their camps, these were their geosocial points of reference in the world as the incident with the smurfs illustrated. Their teachers noticed it and were concerned that these narrowly conceived identities posed dangers for the future.

Third, and moving to a regional level, with the camp wars over and the Oslo peace process unfolding elsewhere, the refugees felt cut off from the national body. Women railed against Arafat and the resistance for abandoning them and leaving them exposed to violence: "They took our milk and blood and left us here!" "Arafat fattened himself on our milk and blood"—"All Arafat did was dig our graves," in reference to the 1982 PLO withdrawal from Beirut and shift in focus and resources to the occupied territories. "Even if they built houses of gold for the 'mothers of the martyrs,' it wouldn't be enough!" gestured an elderly woman (see Peteet 1995b, 1997). Connerton's notion of social memory as "images of the past that commonly legitimate a present social order" (1989: 5) in this instance was undercut by violence and abandonment. Violence forged a crack in the national narrative and fragmented the local from the larger national body (Peteet 1997). Geographic marginality and feelings of exclusion from the then emerging polity (Palestinian Authority), with its readiness to negotiate away the right of return, unsettled the idea of a unified nation or community.

A new means of producing and maintaining community, that extended beyond camp and host state boundaries, was under way via new communications technologies. At this stage only questions can be posed. Are technologies such as e-mail and the Internet potentially productive of new forms of locality? Are new ways of being a national community fostered by such technologies? Can community be constructed and maintained in cyberspace? Spatially distant camps could now be linked across national boundaries by the internet. Communications technologies have the capacity to expand the borders of community and redraw them to include those once firmly on the outside, complicating the relationship between place and community. At the beginning of the millennium, Bir Zeit University in the West Bank launched a project to create a web page for each Palestinian camp. The Ibdaa Cultural Center in Dheisheh camp in the West Bank set up a youth center with computers for children to communicate with Palestinian children elsewhere.[10] Camps developed web pages so residents could communicate with other camps. The Internet facilitated interaction by diluting spatial and temporal barriers. For example, when the Israeli army withdrew from its nearly twenty-five-year occupation of south Lebanon, Palestinians in Lebanon flocked to the border to look across and try to find relatives who had remained in 1948. Children in Shatila communicated with children in Dheisheh to coordinate a border meeting. This medium was positioned as another level of community of camps. The production of locality through communicative technologies could facilitate the emergence of a transnational Palestinian refugee camp locality on the one hand and strengthen the national imaginary on the other. In these virtual spaces, refugees could speak to each other across once formidable geopolitical borders.

Memory and Metonyms: Sacred Geography

Omnipresent signs surrounded the perimeter of Shatila. A cacophony of Shi'a symbols—black flags, green or black banners imprinted with

Qur'anic verses—flew from nearby rooftops, and posters of Ayatollah Khomeini and Imam Musa Sadr[11] reminded of Shi'a power and the potential for mayhem. These ominously visible icons of militant ascendency and the capacity to inflict terror emphatically announced a boundary between the camp and the exterior with little geographic or symbolic space for graduality in meaning.

Inside Shatila's scarred landscape, particular locales reverberated with the violence now etched into collective and individual consciousness. Streets and alleys had been renamed to incorporate and reiterate violent events, so that when moving through the camps one was constantly reminded of what had occurred in particular spots. At one end of Abu Hassan Salami Street, a wide street running between the camp and surrounding Lebanese areas, there was a mass grave for the victims of the 1982 massacre. It had been renamed Street of the Massacre. The appellation Snipers' Alley in Burj al-Barajneh camp all but replaced the former name of the alley, that of a prominent family residing in the quarter.

In the Palestinian collective consciousness, past and present places and sufferings were strung together in a time/space litany, as in this leaflet from the first *infitada* (#25):

In these days, you remember with bitterness the massacres of Black September and Sabra and Shatila, which cut down thousands of our people in the diaspora and sought to finish off what was begun at Deir Yassin, Qibya, Duweima, and Kafr Kasim, with the aim of obliterating our people's distinctive national identity. (Mishal and Ahroni 1994: 124)

Dayr Yassin, Qibya, and Duweima were places where Palestinians were massacred in 1948, Kafr Qasim later in Palestine under Israeli rule.[12] Black September (Jordan, 1971) and Sabra-Shatila (1982) were massacres indelibly etched on the Palestinian collective consciousness. In this leaflet, these incidents were invoked rhetorically for mass mobilization against occupation, as each place carried semantic density and resonance, uniting an otherwise fragmented national space through suffering and struggle. Places of suffering possessed metonymic qualitites in both a generic and specific sense. Invoking their names sacrilized points of connections for Palestinians far beyond them by embodying and representing the suffering that was central to the popular and official national narrative. They circulated as metaphors for particular kinds of events. Tel al-Za'ter and Sabra-Shatila were prime exemplars of camps as semi-sacred sites of violence perpetrated by Arabs and Israelis and thus of suffering and martyrdom. Tel al-Za'ter lived in collective memory and in the social relations it continued to generate. Sabra-Shatila was also a living symbol, part of the texture of daily life for its inhabitants.

Invoking these places concentrated powerful collective memories and served as a call to action.

In his book on Holocaust memorials, literary critic James Young uses "collected memory" rather than "collective memory" to refer to the "many discrete memories that are gathered into common memorial spaces and assigned common meaning" (1993: xi). Collected memory opens the door to examining individual subjectivity. He contends that "By maintaining a sense of collected memories, we remain aware of their disparate sources." The notion of collected memories encompasses both group and individual meanings. Collected memories may be a particularly apt notion for a geographically fragmented society without a state in which to institutionalize and ritualize memory. It has been exceedingly difficult for Palestinians to construct memorials, for both spatial and political reasons. (Palestinian memorialization is probably best collected and given aesthetic form in literature, poetry, theater, and in the nonfiction genre of memorial books.)

Yet through quotidian practice, the mass grave of the victims of the 1982 Sabra-Shatila massacre and the camp's mosque became sites of remembrance and commemoration. Both were living symbols, integral to the local landscape. Neither had been designated as a memorial site or set apart from other space. Only the mosque had visible signs indicating its recently acquired memorial status. Um Khalid recounted to me how in April 1998 she commemorated the 1948 Israeli massacre in Dayr Yassin by marching in a group to the mass burial site of the 1982 Sabra-Shatila massacre. Two events, nearly forty years apart, Dayr Yassin, Palestine, April 1948 and Sabra-Shatila, Lebanon, September 1982, were simultaneously remembered in the same space; commemorating at Sabra-Shatila performed the memory work for Dayr Yassin.

Palestinians commemorated Dayr Yassin in the present, where it was inextricably linked to the 1982 massacre. In the national and local narrative, both were interpreted as distinct but connected episodes in a lengthy and relentless campaign to effect Palestinian dislocation and denationalization. At these memorial sites, Palestinians situated collective meaning at the heart of a common identity. The Sabra-Shatila massacre was now solidly implanted in a national narrative that combined heroism with suffering, sacrifice with martyrdom. The 1982 massacre site has no official recognition because there was little official Palestinian national presence in Lebanon and the Lebanese did not opt to recognize it. Indeed, local Lebanese children played soccer on it. Palestinians and Lebanese visit the site in September to mark the anniversary of the massacre and on religious occasions when Muslims normally visit the graves of loved ones.

Most sites embodying Palestinian national memory and history were in places beyond their control and exterior to national space. Those buried at the 1982 massacre site could be mourned as victims of Dayr Yassin, potent metaphor of the Palestinian tragedy, and thus this particular site embodied other massacres, other victims. Spatially and temporally distinct events could be simultaneously memorialized in a context where the state was absent and specific spaces designated for remembering were lacking. Thus Palestinian memory and memorialization transcended the limitations imposed by the absence of a state and national space that in most instances unify by their very insistence on memorializing specific events and places.

Fears and anxieties were commonly expressed euphemistically. "We didn't want to be another Tel al-Za'ter," 'Amni's mother in Burj al-Barajneh occasionally interjected while talking about the camp wars. Fighters recalled the 1982 massacre when discussing why they fought so ferociously to defend the camp, against heavy odds. A young man, seventeen years old at the time of the camp wars, said: "We knew that if they entered the camp, 'Amal would slaughter everyone just like in Sabra-Shatila."

Shatila camp as a locale is saturated with meaning in the collective Palestinian memory. For those outside, it is a metonym for suffering and vulnerability, for the totality of the Palestinian trauma. For those inside the camp, it is a living and lived memorial. The mosque is illustrative of an interior memorial site. Located at the geographical center of the camp, the mosque was barely discernible in the crowded jumble of buildings. While there was no elaborate or decorative entrance, just a simple door opening from a small street, it was critically important in the memory work of the camp. People passed it daily on their way to the market or to visit. During the 'Amal assault it was the camp's nerve center, functioning as sanctuary, hospital, and burial ground. Families took shelter in it, emergency medical care was set up in it, and it served as morgue and cemetery when the siege obstructed removal of the dead. Hundreds of the dead were buried beneath its floors, speaking to the horrific abnormality of Palestinian life under siege. 'Amal aimed to capture the mosque, since that would signify the camp's fall. Early in the first siege, the press announced that 'Amal was in control of Shatila.[13] Palestinians continued to deny it, conceding that although 'Amal entered the camp, they never captured it because the mosque did not fall into their hands.

Located at the intersection of space, place, and cultural-religious practice, the mosque became a site of memory and collected meanings through daily practice. Like rituals, a site's status and meaning depend on its audience. Lacking a planned narrative or set of artifacts, its memorial status was generated in part by the Muslim practices of remembering the dead. Thus the mosque became as a shrine of sorts, a site of national mourning and commemoration, literally embodying suffering and heroism. It is visited by hundreds on Islamic holidays. It was not designated as a memorial site in a conscious or deliberate process of memorialization, although visiting foreign delegations are taken to see it as part of their camp tour. To move any distance in the camp, one has to pass it; Friday prayers are said on its second floor. Yet there was no narrative emplotment of the tragic experiences of Shatila at the actual site. They were remembered in situ, as a part of everyday life.

Similarly, quotidian routines were saturated with sites of memory. Walking through Shatila and approaching the mosque, Um Khalid pointed to an open space near the mosque where several alleys converged and remarked, "I remember the person who was killed at that place. Even if you don't know the person well, when you walk by that place, you say to yourself 'Here is where so-and-so was killed.'"

The suffering/heroism dyad was dramatically expressed in the somber black and white photos of martyrs hanging on the white walls of the mosque and on the tombstones arrayed across the floor. For the families of the deceased, the photos offered recognition and remembrance. These 'human maps' embodied collective memory of Shatila's ordeal. Similar to memorial books that make public claims to obliterated places, or histories suppressed, the martyrs' graves and photos proclaimed resistance, sacrifice and heroism.

The visual texture of camp walls and home interiors rendered death ever present. The posters, with their black-and-white photos of the deceased and verses from the Qur'an dotting the walls, preceded one at every turn, forming an integral part of the scarred landscape, grim everyday reminders of the imminence of death. The poster-lined walls, with old, peeling ones plastered over with those of the recently dead, spoke to continuous layers of trauma. Those honoring the dead of the civil war were overlaid with those from the 1982 war, overlaid with those from the camp wars. Interspersed were *fidaʾiyyin* who died in guerrilla warfare in south Lebanon or those killed in intermittent Israeli air raids and assaults.

In the interior landscape of homes, the photos of the dead on the walls and in frames on tables were graphic reminders and silent witnesses. Um ʿAli shared with her only remaining son the depressingly dark and sparsely furnished temporary house. The walls were unpainted, casting a dark pall over the room, and the unfinished windows were covered with dark squares of roughly cut cloth. A framed, glass-covered mat on which were affixed black-and-white photos of a middle-aged man and four young boys hung high on the wall above the cotton mats on the floor. I knew it was a picture of death. She had been

Figure 17. An entrance to the graves in the Shatila Mosque. Inscribed on the marble plaque is a Qur'anic verse: "Think not of those who are slain in God's way as dead. Nay, they live, finding their sustenance in the Presence of their Lord" (Sura 3: 169). The last line reads: "The graves of the martyrs who fell defending Shatila camp, 1985–1987." On the door hangs a poster of martyrs from the camp wars. Palm fronds mark a grave. Julie Peteet.

Figure 18. Pictures of martyrs from the camp war hanging over their graves in the Shatila Mosque. Julie Peteet.

forced to watch her four sons and husband shot by the Phalangists in the massacre of 1982. They told her she could keep her youngest son, who was then about twelve years old.

In sparsely furnished homes, pictures of dead husbands, fathers, sons, and daughters were ubiquitous—a painful reminder of Shatila's tumultuous history. These artifacts of death provided a visual catalogue of ravaged lives. In the near absence of other textures, one of the first things to rivet the eye was these photos of the dead hanging on the otherwise bare walls. Could their ubiquitousness, their repetitiveness—the same poster could be seen in multiple spots—speak to an anxiety about being forgotten by the world? Were they perhaps a means of documentation by those on the margins, in the news yet rarely in control of their image?

Reincarceration: Spatial Constriction and Identity

"Arafat? Arafat is not a Palestinian! A Palestinian is one who struggles." Khalid, a former commando and leader in the resistance movement, spat with contempt. "She's a Palestinian!" he said with a triumphant wave of the hand, indicating Christina, a foreigner who had long worked in the camps. In 'Ayn al-Hilweh in the summer of 1995, well after *'ayyam al-thawra*, the three of us had been discussing the Oslo accords. Anti-Arafatist forces in the camp were critiquing Arafat by denying him, rhetorically, the status of belonging to the national community. "He's not a Palestinian any more. He gave that up when he started conceding everything to the Israelis," Ahmed, a young guerrilla who had joined us, utterly disdainfully. This brings to the fore, in a particularly pointed fashion, the way political agency continued to figure prominently in formations of Palestinian identity, etching lines of inclusion and exclusion. It intimated not simply the flexibility of identity but also its location in specific junctures of power. If space was a medium for the formation and reproduction of identities and subjectivities, then dramatic and striking changes in the spatial, prompted by violence and terror, should have an effect on identity.

With the defeat of the resistance and the reestablishment of the camps as tightly bounded spaces of containment, the shift in publicly iterated identities was striking. With a heightened consciousness of the historical moment and a skewed balance of power, Palestinians were referring to themselves as "refugees" and practicing dissimulation in Lebanese public space. With the safety net provided by the resistance movement pulled from beneath them, claims of refugee status were quickly resurrected. This brings up the role of law in the formation of subjectivity and identity. The meaning of legal refugee status, that is, UNRWA registration and identity documents, was not constant over a fifty-year period. Although it was a category of persons with international recognition, local meanings shifted in tandem with alterations in the power of the resistance movement. Before the resistance era, Palestinians detested the term "refugee" and avoided it in political discourse and self-reference; empowered by the resistance, they were able to reject the term.

In the 1990s, I was struck by how people were referring to themselves as refugees. Suha, the graduate student, came home in tears one day. Her advisor told her he had to drop her as a student. The professor explained that the university administration instructed him to give priority to Lebanese students. Once his graduate students numbered ten, he was to drop any Palestinians among them. When I asked what she was going to do, she lamented, "What can I do? We are Palestinians and refugees. We have no rights. There is no one to appeal to." The new discourse of "refugees" and "rights" intimated a strategic recourse to a legal identity. I sat in on a meeting when Abu Hussein, a member of Shatila's Popular Committee, met with a Lebanese official to negotiate the return to Lebanon of a former guerrilla whose wife and children had not seen him for nearly a decade. He framed his appeal in the discourse of refugee status and legal rights of residence in Lebanon. With the Palestinians powerless to negotiate all but the smallest details of daily life, this was the only discourse available and the one that had some, however negligible, legal power of persuasion vis-à-vis the state.

Self-characterization as "refugees" was a barometer of sorts, indexing power, dependency, and, more ominously, vulnerability. The term no longer aroused much animosity. The wider political frame was one in which the category of refugee was being reconstituted through restrictions on work, residence, travel, education, and political organizing and expression. With the absence of alterative structural and institutional services and high levels of unemployment, belonging to the category of "refugee" was a strategic necessity.[14] Refugee status offered some services, however minimal, from UNRWA. In my previous work in the camps in the 1970s and 1980s, I had rarely participated in picking up rations. In the 1990s, I did so numerous times, an indication of their renewed significance. In addition, refugee status constituted a legal starting point for negotiating with the Lebanese government for rights. Thus invoking "refugee" as a legal category highlights some of the ways in which identities, individually and collectively, were intimately hitched to mutations in the structures of power that framed everyday life. Indeed Palestinians' political intuition that "refugee" meant they were a humanitarian issue rather than a political cause was not far off the mark. In their precarious position they called forth their status as refugees with all its attendant humanitarian components as a mean of ensuring basic physical survival. This is not to imply that national identity was diluted or bypassed, but to point to the way elements of identity, in this case a legal one, can be situationally called forth and highlighted when critical for survival.

Self-identification as refugees assumed a new international political saliency. Most importantly, in presentations of self and community as refugees, they invoked the right of return enshrined in UN Resolution 194 (III) of 11 December 1948. The refugees in Lebanon hold to this resolution as the way to resolve their status as refugees. Indeed, Oslo was cast as a betrayal, since the refugees from 1948 were not on the agenda and the issue of the right of return was postponed. During the 1990s, Palestinian activists and international supporters rallied around the right of return, holding conferences and publishing widely on the topic (see, e.g., Aruri 2001; Quigley 1998; Zureik 1996).

"Without struggle—without the resistance movement—we don't know who we are. It was through struggling that we found our identity," Muna, a Palestinian administrator in a foreign NGO, said with exasperation. Speaking of the Palestinian community in Lebanon as a whole, she continued,

Of course, we know who we are, but we struggled for years and made all those sacrifices—all those people killed and displaced. We kept 'Amal out of the camps. Now, we have no sense of belonging. We don't know who we are! What will happen to us?! Are we animals to be moved around? They talk of moving us to various parts of Lebanon. The Lebanese authority is always giving statements against implantation [*towteen*] and naturalization. Where do we belong?

Muna said this plaintively in the summer of 1994, when Arafat entered Gaza and Jericho, the Lebanese government publicly stated their refusal to consider naturalization of Palestinians, and rumors were flying that the camps were to be moved to remote parts of Lebanon. Her statement captures some of the tension inherent in the term "resistance" in this, and perhaps in other, anticolonial movements. The "resistance" she referred to was the institutional, organized national movement under the PLO umbrella but also the mass-based national movement that all Palestinian felt they belonged to. Action in support of the resistance is "struggle" (*nidal*), which embodied an expansive meaning. Everyday existence was perceived as a struggle (Peteet 1991). A standard refrain was "We are all in the resistance. Just to sit in these camps is a way of struggling," registering a refusal to accept permanent denativization. It must be kept in mind, however, that these sentiments were possible largely in the context of an organized resistance movement with a set of institutions to mobilize and channel political sentiments and provide both protection and services.

"Resistance" evoked different meanings after 1982. Camp Palestinians continued to conceptualize themselves as "true" strugglers, embodying the qualities of suffering and steadfastness. Since 1982, the meaning of Palestinian identity has been reconfigured to focus even more intensely on suffering and disempowerment, compounded by abandonment by their own movement. That is why they could exclaim, "Arafat has given up the struggle" and thus "He is not a Palestinian." They feared the Palestinian leadership would bargain away the right of return. If UN Resolution 194 were ever to be implemented, proof that one is a refugee, found in UNRWA registration records and documents, would become vital.

Rather than Palestinian identity being a source of pride and public display, they now lapsed into dissimulation. In the face of hostility from their hosts, cultural symbols of national identity carried risks. The map logo jewelry was put away. In homes, artifacts celebrating the nation were replaced by those that marked death. Poster photos of the dead dotted the otherwise stark walls, replacing the map and pictures of political leaders. Islamic symbols—Qur'ans, mounted calligraphy, pictures and plastic models of the Dome of the Rock—were now more visible on the exterior as well as in interiors.

Identity became the object of a conscious project of negotiation, manipulation, and dissimulation. Refugees spoke openly about disguising their accents to go unnoticed. A Palestinian *service* (shared taxi) told me how he disguised his accent. After I asked him to drive me close to the entrance to Shatila and he fired off a series of questions about what I was doing in this part of town, he then spoke to me openly about how he disguises himself. As a foreign female I must have been perceived as harmless and distant from Lebanese-Palestinian animosities.

Once passengers realize I am a Palestinian I can feel them looking at me with distrust and sometimes revulsion. One lady tried to scoot as far away from me as possible, as though I was polluted. So now I try to use a Lebanese accent when I pick up passengers. Once I picked up some young 'Amal men; I was badly beaten. See where my nose is so crooked—they broke it.

He was hardly the only one attempting to pass as Lebanese by dialect switching. Raja, Um Khalid's nephew, told me he left 'Ayn al-Hilweh only with great trepidation and when compelled to do so by family visits. Then, he pretends to be a Lebanese. "I don't let them know I am a Palestinian—I am too afraid. So I speak with a Lebanese accent. I don't mention where I live either. Basically I just keep my mouth shut as much as possible." Once back in the security of the camp, accents were switched. Like Raja, people were aware of their switching ability. Raja and Um Khalid's eldest daughter spoke of how the elderly found it almost impossible to switch while for the second and third generations it was fairly easy. Language is a significant component in marking identity. It is an acknowledgment of having being raised in Lebanon yet not belonging there.

The Past in the Present

The past is never dead. It's not even past. (William Faulkner)

Always a marathon visitor, Um Khalid announced: "We must pay a visit to Um ʿOmar—you'll find her interesting—she will have lots of stories. She's from Tel al-Zaʿter and from there she went to Damur and now she lives in al-Zaʿter quarter." We called on her friend, an expansive middle-aged woman, just returned from a month-long visit to her natal village in Palestine, what Slyomovics has called a "variant of pilgrimage" (1998: 14). Before she died, she wanted to see her home and visit with relatives who stayed in 1948. Since the early 1980s, Israeli authorities have granted visas to elderly women to visit Palestine if they still had family there. On their return, family and friends flock to welcome them home and listen to their stories of Palestine. Um Khalid introduced me as a friend from ʾayyam al-thawra, giving me a meaningful location in the social world of the camp. She then quipped, "She's come to talk about ʾayyam filasteen [days of Palestine]." As I settled myself on the plump and colorful cotton cushions lining the walls, Um ʿOmar's son, sipping a small cup of Turkish coffee, calmly but with conviction, looked up at me and announced rather flatly that ʾayyam filasteen are here—in this camp. We are living the days of Palestine." This seemingly simple statement brought home the immediate sense in which place, for refugees, was a lived experience that was carried from one site to another in exile. Experienced from afar and yet never distant, place was more than memory and the imaginary. It remained deeply resonant in everyday life. The daily lives of third and fourth generation refugees were enmeshed in structures and systems of meaning in which places, past and present, far and near, figured prominently. By narrating these visits, refugees such as Um ʿOmar contributed to Palestinian collective memory.

Once we were comfortably settled and I was introduced to the other women visitors and tea was served, Um ʿOmar tearfully related the details of her visit to the hushed audience:

I still knew it even though it looked different. I remembered where certain houses were and some of the fields. I was able to find my way to our house. I rang the doorbell and a Yemeni woman answered. Immediately she understood who I was and invited us in. I asked her if I could look around the house and she agreed. She offered us coffee and we sat and talked. As I left, I lamented that I wished I still lived here and she said, "We feel the same way about Yemen. When we go back there, you come and take back your house."

Um 'Omar's descriptions of the interior of her former home, the agricultural fields, the well, and myriad details about the village were not unusual for returnees. What was a bit unusual in this case was the connection Um 'Omar claimed she established between herself and the new occupants, the transplanted Yemeni Jewish family. She spoke as if the latter were simply tending to her home in her prolonged absence. To her, they were displaced as well. Remembering, narrating, and publicly sharing these details asserted a claim to place through an active, detailed memory of textures, smells, sounds, and the emotions it evoked. These vividly detailed and emotional narrations, and their awed audience, posed counter-claims. Land may be confiscated, places renamed and inhabited by settlers, and histories denied, but the memories of these particular places remained Palestinian possessions inherited by successive generations.

In narratives of exile, the present was often juxtaposed to a sentimentalized bucolic village past, glossing over social tensions, economic insecurity, occasional drought and famine, and class discord. In this refugee version of "paradise lost," food and security stood out as key, interrelated themes. Now elderly Um Issam stated eloquently in reference to her family's past in Palestine, "We had olive oil like water." Control over the production and distribution of food provided material security and a level of household autonomy that were strikingly absent among refugees. The following statements came up in conversations about the present and the past with the elderly: "We had our land, our homes. We planted and we reaped. We grew wheat, okra, melons, and cucumbers. We grew everything on our own land. How could we ever say Palestine was not beautiful?" "We used to plant grains, tomatoes, squash, okra, and melons. The smell of the cantaloupes was wonderful. We had figs, olives, apricots, and plums. Here we have nothing." "In our homeland, we had fruits and orchards—we had land. We were well-to-do in our homeland. Now, here, we hardly find anything to eat. That was our homeland! Who would easily surrender their homeland? Nobody! We should have stayed. It would have been better than what has become of us here living like gypsies. We are not gypsies. We are people. Gypsies are beggars and we have become like them. Is that not *haram* [a pity]?"

Landless, moving from place to place, gypsies perform low status tasks such as peddling and performing at weddings and festivals. This constellation of attributes makes them vulnerable and open to dishonor. The gypsies embodied what the refugees feared becoming. References to food were not surprising given the near starvation diets of the years of siege. When I asked 'Amni's mother if the war of the camps was truly over, she replied: "Yes. I am no longer keeping *mooneh* [provisions]."

Decades of exile have added a multiplicity of places to the notion of the past. Continuing pressures and uncertainties propel emigration and new displacements so that the refugees are in a nearly steady state of becoming, while simultaneously being, refugees. Current displacement sagas have affinities with 1948 but without the sense of hope refugees initially possessed. Indeed, now Palestinians have memories of and nostalgia for past places and times that are themselves part of an exilic trajectory. Um Khalid cried when she saw me after a decade because I reminded her of the good days—of *'ayyam Beirut* and *'ayyam al-thawra.* Widowed and alone, Um Riyad was incredibly angry and bitter. She lived in a newly constructed building in Shatila and longed for life in Tel al-Za'ter:

We have passed through such times. We still are. You think this apartment here counts as a home? I was happiest in Tel al-Za'ter. Those were the sweetest days! I was young and unmarried and there was no war. I was happy. People were living in security and stability. Young women like me could go all the way to the Biqa' and came back at night by herself. It was safe for her. Nobody would bother her and she would be treated with respect. Not like these days. Now if your daughter stays after dark at the neighbors, you have to go to walk her back home. There is no more security. We have people from all over the place living here. Not the same group of people as used to be here. Now they are very mixed. They belong to fifty different factions. In Tel al-Za'ter, it was all Palestinians and Lebanese living together as one group. You could not tell who was Muslim and who was Christian. They were all living together. You could have your girl friends sleep over and their parents would not mind. Not today—people won't allow that. They won't let their daughters visit for more than a few hours. There are so many strangers here now.

Conclusion

When asked by outsiders how they bear their situation, Palestinians often respond with a shrug of the shoulders "Shu bidna n'amal?" (What can we do?) Being Palestinian embodies an undeniably constricting set of daily life circumstances and inexorable collective suffering. Within these constraints, Palestinians have creatively crafted place and produced and reproduced their identities. Saturated by a violence deeply etched into the physicality and everyday life in the camps, trust and a sense of hope have been crushed by the uncertainty left by decades of violence. Structural violence and the always present threat of violence have contributed to a high level of indeterminancy.

Exilic space has been a site for the continual reordering of the meaning of place, identity, and social relations. Always in formation and contingent upon a nexus of others' identity—a fragmented, multiply cross-cut sense of self and community with fluid boundaries, yet simultaneously a highly marked and bounded category highly dependent on exclusion as well—can be tracked along shifting lines of power. Palestinian identity was a terrain of inclusiveness extending well beyond the national, ethnic, sectarian, and local to incorporate ideological bedfellows and participants in struggle. There are enough signposts in Palestinian history to suggest that identity can be formulated in ways that challenge the narrowness of nationalism. Indeed, the irony of the refugees, excised from the nation, is that they become critics of the national at the same time as they strive for a national homeland of their own. In the modern era, however unbounded our identities are from particular places, we live in a world of states and derive our rights from being citizens of those states. The original vision of a democratic, secular state provided an alternative narrative for both Palestinians and Israelis. Such a vision pointed to a common humanity rather than separation and exclusivism.

Fifty years after displacement, place remains a point of departure in formulations of identity for Palestinians. The relationship between place and identity is more about the future than the past, more about where they are now and where they are going than simply about where they have been. Moreover, identities are not neatly tied to places in an unproblematic way. Indeed, recovering the past is not always an object of desire. What the past does represent, however, is what has been denied—a safe location, recognition of rights, and a sense of belonging in one's own homeland, and a process of justice.

Although a nostalgic longing for pre-1948 Palestine, which most of this third generation of exiles have never seen, was not pronounced, they can describe their villages, having internalized the details of the landscape, its configuration and smells, village history, and daily routines from their elders. Socially, they were intimate with the village because they had lived its spatial and social recreation in the camps. But they were also aware of the transformation of their villages. Palestine was envisioned not in a nostalgic longing for pre-1948 lifestyles but rather in the longing for security of place and the rights entailed in being a citizen.

Conclusion: Refugee Camps and the Wall

> Where should we go after the last frontiers, where should birds fly
> after the last sky?
>
> —Mahmud Darwish

Dreams: Going and Returning

A curious story circulated in the refugee camps in the 1990s and in the
wider Palestinian exile community. A young boy from the Shatila refugee camp has a dream of the long awaited and fought for return to Palestine. All the refugees board buses and head south for the border.
Once in Palestine, the people of the village of Tarshiha return to Tarshiha, the people of the village of al-Bassa return to al-Bassa, and so on.
A busload of refugees from Shatila choose not to return to their places
of origin. As former Shatila residents, they stay together and build a new
village.

The dream story has a genealogy and a political and cultural resonance well worth exploring. It was elicited by Syrian director Mohammed Malas while filming a documentary on Shatila in the early 1980s.
Faysal, the eleven-year-old boy whose dream it is, is later killed by gunfire, in Elias Khoury's novel *The Kingdom of Strangers*. Khoury writes, "he
knew he would never return to Palestine—he would go there. No one
will return. Return is a fantasy. We return—that is to say we go" (1996:
26–27). Immediately before relating Faysal's dream, Khoury writes
about Emil, an Israeli student in New York City. Emil relates how his
father, a Polish Jew, fled the impending Holocaust and ended up in Palestine. "'My father didn't want to return to Palestine,' Emil said. 'You
mean go,' I said. 'He didn't want to return,' he said. 'You mean go,' I
said. Albert Azayev [the father] was not like Faysal" (1996: 25).

Khoury explores the difference between the Polish Jew who is ambivalent about going to Palestine, whose son, fifty years later, dubs it a "return," and Faysal who dreams of going to Palestine. Yet to Khoury, in the present context, Faysal's dream is about "going" rather than "returning." It evokes the unmediated linearity and points to the ways Palestinian exile and the social movements generated in it forged new relationships and contoured identities and ideas of community. I heard this story first in Shatila in 1994 and subsequently among Palestinians in Beirut. In the camp, it was told both with amusement and as a commentary on who they are and the overwhelming significance of exilic place and experience on their identity and aspirations. By the time I heard it told by a Palestinian acquaintance in Michigan a couple of years later, I began to realize its potency. A narrative whose currency crosses multiple borders, it locates the refugee camps in a border zone, not just spatially between Palestine, Lebanon, and Israel, but as sites where confinement and collective suffering and experiences mediated the seeming linearity of exile between points of departure and points of return/going. The dream encapsulates the refugees' transition from Palestinian village to a more inclusive vision of place, nation, and identity. It suggests a local knowledge and pointedly objective recognition of the new kinds of identities and social affiliations exile has spawned. This futuristic narrative of return does not evoke nostalgia for a past that is certainly no longer attainable.

For Palestinian refugees, return, or going to, is still imagined as to the geographical space of Palestine, but the social relations and the political arrangements such a return entails have been fundamentally and inevitably reconfigured. They are not based on an unmediated, bucolically imagined past organized around kin, village, and localized identities; rather, the experience of exile and life in the seemingly narrow spaces of refugee camps have recreated the world, expanding the boundaries of community and lines of inclusion. Exile forged new social bonds and sentiments and new ways of locating oneself in the world. Of these sentiments and relationships stretched over multiple places, Edward Said wrote, "We live in comradely communication despite the barriers. Today the Palestinian genius expresses itself in crossings-over, in clearing hurdles, activities that do not lessen the alienation, discontinuity, and dispossession, but that dramatize and clarify them instead" (1986: 41).

Over fifty years ago an ill wind blew over the lives of Palestinians, and they have been living in a maelstrom ever since. In a matter of months the majority of Palestinians—peasants, craftsmen, and shopkeepers—became refugees, their daily lives intimately bound up with an international system that both contributed to their displacement and has been unable to resolve it. Facing a formidable enemy bent on their containment and silencing, a project Israeli sociologist Kimmerling (2003) aptly calls "politicide," they have resisted with the means at hands, from stones and *sumud* (steadfastness) to guns, from political organizing and militancy to international diplomacy and scholarship. Most significantly and poignantly, they have resisted by surviving, by not ceding their Palestinian identity. Their mere existence is a critical commentary on the Zionist project to settle Palestine and claim indigeneity. This whirlwind of displacement and a violence-ridden and prolonged exile projected Palestinians onto the international arena. As the longest refugee situation in the world, "Palestinians" and "Palestinization" have become code words in international organizations for hopelessness and for the impossibility of finding a solution to a protracted and desperate refugee situation.

The dream underscores the ways in which exile and the vicissitudes of fifty years of life in refugee camps have refigured a relationship between place and identity and the elements of community. In Shatila and in exile, the story circulates as a commentary on the camps and their "one-hand" nature, conveying the sentiments of solidarity among those who have endured exile and its murderous events. It registers a refusal to telescope time to 1948, a return to an unmediated past, and thus it is a recognition of profound change in the Palestinian community. The dream captures the consciousness of a disconnection, those intervening years of life events and social relationships, as well as the Israeli transformation of Palestine, that make a return impossible. "Going to," however, is still possible, and this possibility has animated the Palestinian vision of a democratic secular state of its citizens rather than an exclusivist ethnonationalist state. Palestinian refugees in Lebanon can describe their villages, having absorbed their landscape, smells, history, and daily routines from their elders' narratives, and socially they are intimate with the village because they have continued to live its spatiality and sociality as they have been recreated in the camps. Yet they are vividly aware of their villages' transformation. Palestine is envisioned in the desire for the security that place can provide and the rights entailed in being a citizen. As the first-hand transmission of knowledge of the homeland fades for the younger generation, their knowledge is increasingly locally and experientially derived.

Palestinians are keenly aware of the complex relationship between place and identity, animating as it does their daily lives and struggle for recognition. The certainty as to where one is from and who one is, in all its complexity, incorporating multiple places, undercuts postmodernity's sometimes celebratory approach to contemporary nomadism. The grim conditions of refugee life—physical hardships, pronounced uncertainties, the suspension of trust, persistent vulnerability, and ever present specter of violence render refugees, in general, a vastly different category of nomad from migrants and elite travelers.

Palestinians do not always fit easily into anthropology's contemporary theoretical frameworks. In an era of postcolonial studies, Palestinians remain in the throes of modern colonialism's grip. Thus they provide an opportunity for a sustained and probing engagement with theory, its possibilities and limitations, and an opportunity to plumb, critique, challenge, or carry in new directions contemporary theoretical themes such as postcoloniality, nationalism, the nomadic subject, the relationship among place, territory, and identity, diaspora, and transnationalism, among others. Palestinians have made lives in new local contexts, but they desire a state and citizenship for the sense of belonging, protection, and recognition it would provide and the sense of justice it would register. Palestinians in Lebanon retain a deep attachment to the concept of Palestine and a desire for home. Local integration is not as possible for them as it has been for refugees in Jordan, where the state granted them citizenship. Palestinian refugees in Syria have been endowed with the same rights as Syrians except for citizenship. They are able to work and own property and have access to government services. Although political activities are monitored and repressed, their camps are not sites of terror and insecurity. Palestinians in Lebanon are cosmopolitan nationalists, which suggests that the two concepts cannot always be neatly opposed. Indeed, they can operate in tandem. The nature of host state-refugee relationship is critical in determining not just the rights of the refugees and their living conditions, but also their sense of the past and future and their attitudes toward citizenship and return. The lack of citizenship poses serious problems for Palestinians in Lebanon. For them, going home remains more than just an issue of belonging and justice. Lebanon's constitution forbids Palestinian settlement, and the state has engaged in concerted attempts to make life so unbearable that they will leave.

The focus in this book has been on the mutuality between place and identity in exile mediated by structural aspects of refugee life in Lebanon and an aid regime that constituted the Palestinian refugee as an object of intervention. Palestinian refugees used space in the camps in ways not intended by those who devised them. Through ordinary practices of daily living, the refugees made and remade spaces not their own, and in the process reconfigured their identities. Palestinian identity took shape as a cultural product of sociospatial location and practices within a violently shifting field of power arrangements. For the refugees, location has been a beginning, not necessarily an end, in the trajectory of identity. I highlighted the historical and spatial rather than the cultural because culturally specific frames for grappling with identity can gloss over the complexity of agency and history. I showed that identities can shape social movements and yet are themselves, in the process of this interaction, sites of rearticulation.

The spatiality of the camps encodes a tumultuous fifty years of refugee life in Lebanon. Refugee periodization articulates with a mapping of the camps' shifting borders, their changing meanings, and the kinds of social relations they contained and enabled. Rapid reordering in scale indexed shifts in the empowerment of the refugee community. The scattering of the refugees, their confinement, and the imposed invisibility characteristic of the 1950s and 1960s gave way to hypervisibility as Palestinian militancy transformed the camps into spaces of autonomy. Eventually, they reverted to spaces of misery and confinement in the post-1982 period. With the camps as a device of biopower to reformulate and denationalize Palestinian relation to place and identity, these spaces, designed to be repressive, were inevitably politicized in contrary ways. Indeed, their disciplinary features guaranteed that they would become spaces of resistance. Thus this study also examined the relationship between individual and collective actions, that is human agency, and the social structural constraints imposed by host states and aid regimes. Through oppositional practices and the practices of building lives and homes, individuals exercised the capacity to accommodate and shape the larger structures that marginalized and constrained them.

Once glossed over by a militant Palestinian identity, a publicly iterated refugee identity has resurfaced as a strategic asset, a means of access to resources, and a plea for protection in a world of nation- states which effectively leaves refugees, particularly those not under the UNHCR mandate, without protection.

Forms of Violence

On a larger front, the latest round in the Palestinian-Israeli conflict has been characterized by the reoccupation of the West Bank and Gaza and the violent containment of the Palestinian National Authority (PNA) and its embryonic state institutions. Under the guise of "security," Israel has been constructing a wall deep inside Palestinian territory to fragment the West Bank and obstruct a contiguous and viable Palestinian state. Thousands of acres of Palestinian land have been confiscated in the process. The policy of closure, with its checkpoints, permit system, and wall, is akin to a camp, an exercise in biopower, a spatial device to contain people and transform their bodies through the imposition of new and extreme disciplinary measures and routines. Even with mass military might, well-developed techniques of surveillance and containment and pervasive structural forms of violence, the wall has an inordinate influence on Palestinian mobility, work, access to land, family relations, education, nutrition, and health status.[1]

Intended as a spatial device of containment and denationalization, refugee camps continue to be sites for the production and reproduction of Palestinian militancy and nationalism. Will the wall, an "open-air prison," function in the same way? It has mobilized substantial media commentary and international opprobrium and has become a highly visible and critiqued commentary on the Israeli occupation and their long-term plans for the West Bank. In subduing the Palestinians, Israel has deployed a destructive combination of modern and premodern forms of violence such as mass imprisonment, curfews, land confiscations, assassinations, torture, economic devastation, and the pronounced immobility imposed by general closure of the West Bank since 1993 and Gaza since 1989, their increasing internal closure, and now the wall. While routine in the sense of occurring regularly, violence and subordination cannot be characterized as "routinized" in the sense of alluding to acceptance and resignation. To use such a term flies in the face of the resistance Palestinians mount and sustain.

Palestinians live in a "state of emergency," recalling Walter Benjamin's statement that it is "not the exception but the rule" (1968). To them, violent events and spatially restrictive devices are not a series of discrete events uniquely encapsulated in their own set of meanings and consequences. They simply form key elements in a new chapter in an ongoing saga that began well before 1948. Indeed they narrate it in the same terms—the desire of Israel to expand and claim indigeneity at the cost of Palestinian land, lives, and abuse of human rights. With unqualified U.S. support, they proceed apace in this agenda. Ariel Sharon's assumption of power unleashed the extreme right-wing expansionist sector of Israeli politics. In what Kimmerling calls the second instance of "politicide"—the first was 1948—the containment of the PNA, enhanced settlement activity, assassinations of suspected leaders of resistance, and a policy of closure indicate a renewed attempt at expansion with an accompanying shattering of daily lives and gross human rights violations. Sharon and higher levels of the Israeli military confirmed a Palestinian understanding of the relatedness of these events when they dubbed the second *intifada* "the second half of 1948" (Reinhart 2002: 10).

Unrivaled U.S. power and its unconditional support of Israeli actions, buttressed by a vocal and active alliance with Christian fundamentalism, have created a climate of unlimited possibilities for pursuing an expansionist agenda and crushing the hopes of Palestinians for statehood or even basic human rights. Some members of the Israeli Parliament have suggested transferring the Palestinian population to Jordan. Chief of

Staff Moshe Ya'alon described the Palestinians as a "cancerous manifestation" and military actions against them as "chemotherapy" (Kimmerling 2003: 30) a discourse indicative of ethnic cleansing.

The wall, bypass roads, ubiquitous checkpoints, widespread practices of collective punishment, arbitrary arrests and detentions, school closings, and denial of work in Israel in an economy that has been appended to it are intended to induce Palestinian subordination to the Zionist colonial project, to crush resistance through mass retaliation, and to make emigration attractive. In the second instance of politicide, a high level of emigration would be a "miracle" akin to that of 1948, when Israel was able to expand the territory allotted to it under the 1947 UN Partition Plan and clear it of the native Palestinians.

What impact will this new form of ethnic cleansing, drawn out over time, slow-motion, if you will, have on the concept of refugee status? This kind of silent transfer avoids international condemnation and puts Palestinians in the category of voluntary migrants rather than refugees with international recognition. Can one be a refugee as a result of a prolonged campaign to make life so miserable that people leave? Is the definition of a Palestinian refugee flexible enough to include this new category? This is occurring at the same time as pressure is being put on UNRWA, which has long defined Palestinian identity in the international legal arena, to scale back its operations. The UN has been a key player, defining who is a Palestinian and who is entitled to relief and refugee status. Suggestions to diminish UNRWA operations are attempts to deinternationalize the Palestinian issue. Continuing budget cuts, which signal a further move in the dismantling of UNRWA, have been met with vocal protests and demonstrations by the refugees, who understand that more is at stake than simply receiving rations. In addition, the claim that Arab Jews who left their homes in various Arab states to emigrate to Israel should be classified as "refugees,"[2] to give the two populations some kind of parity and thus make the expulsion and denial of return appear to be a population exchange, is an attempt to dampen, if not strip, the category of "Palestinian refugee" of any moral and legal standing.

The Lebanese Arena: Permanent Crisis

"'You're aliens here," they say to them *there*. 'You're aliens here,' they say to him *here*." Darwish's seminal *Memory for Forgetfulness: August, Beirut, 1982* (1995: 13), as the title indicates, recounts the story of the Israeli invasion of Lebanon and the siege of Beirut. Time/place races between Lebanon/Palestine, here/there, and, like the dream story, casts the past, or Palestine, as irretrievable. In short, Darwish captures the dilemma of exile—one is neither here nor there in terms of belonging; whether in Palestine or outside it, Palestinians are aliens. For the refugee, life is carried on in a borderland—a vulnerable betwixt and between—without the assumed comforts and ease of being at home.

In Lebanon, the Palestinians have been on the sidelines of both the battles being waged in the occupied territories and internal Lebanese politics. Yet each arena provides the framework in which policy and thus daily lives unfold and each tends to exacerbate the vulnerability of the refugees. The affirmation of a cohesive Lebanese national identity has been paramount to Lebanon's reconstruction and national reconciliation process. Although politically marginal and silenced, the Palestinians occupy a salient position in this project. They have become an "other" on which a Lebanese national identity and sense of territorial sovereignty are being constructed. Containment of and control over the Palestinian community in Lebanon, and the adamant refusal of their permanent settlement in Lebanon, are agreed upon by all sects and political factions. Harsh measures that deny the refugees basic rights to health, education, civil rights, and security are designed to remind the international community of their responsibility for the Palestinians and keep them in a permanent state of crisis. Keeping alive the image of the camps as armed and dangerous—ticking time bombs, as they are called—serves the same purpose.

Contrary to local expectations, Lebanon's economy did not rebound in the postwar period. With a generalized descent into poverty, the middle class is struggling to maintain a semblance of their former standard of living while the poor barely survive. A small but visible sector of the population lives an opulent lifestyle with the financial means to enjoy Beirut's glittery nightlife and resorts. The Palestinians are living in dire conditions with high unemployment, declining literacy and education rates, and a high rate of emigration. A recent study found that refugees in Lebanon "stand out as having the lowest levels of educational achievement both relative to refugees elsewhere and others in Lebanon" (Jacobsen 2003: 79). With unemployment rampant and levels of poverty escalating, we may once again see a point of connection, a common interest, between Palestinian refugees and a sector of the Lebanese populace. The same economic, although not political, marginality that produced a Lebanese-Palestinian alliance in the resistance era could spawn another such alliance.

The refugee camps are once again clearly marked spaces of containment. In postwar Lebanon, the refugees have been spatially confined, legally marginalized, and socially outcast. One could characterize the fifty-year Palestinian refugee experience in Lebanon as a perpetual state of emergency. The initial trauma of dispossession, statelessness and exile was followed by war, sieges, and massacres. The latest crisis involves multiple forms of violence. Spatial and legal marginalization ensures that the refugees remain isolated from the Lebanese population and signals an anticipation of emigration from Lebanon because of acute and prolonged misery. The continuing refusal by Israel to repatriate the refugees, which make normal life impossible and consigns a population to a stateless existence, is itself a form of violence.

The Palestinian political movement is in a profound state of crisis. Without a viable leadership, it lacks vision and strategy. Early in its inception, the movement's constituent units were united by a common goal: implementation of the right of return and a democratic secular state of its citizens in Palestine. By the early 1970s, political realities on the ground derailed the Palestine Liberation Organization (PLO) call for such a state in favor of pursuing a strategy of Palestinian/Israeli separation, or a two-state solution. The brief moment when the vision of a democratic secular state was on the Palestinian agenda has been completely overshadowed by the dehumanizing violence of an exclusivist vision and political organization of the Israeli polity. The progressive nature of their vision was roundly rejected by Israel and the U.S., who preferred instead to continue along the course of an expansionist, exclusivist, ethnoreligious state. By the mid-1970s, the Palestinian political leadership had traded this progressive vision for a truncated state in part of historic Palestine (the West Bank and Gaza Strip). As part of the Oslo Agreements of the early 1990s, Palestinians ceded to U.S. and Israeli demands and begin to dilute their insistence on the right of return. In short, Palestinian leader Yasir Arafat was bargaining away a fundamental right of the Palestinian people without a mandate to do so and with little of substance to show in return. With the failure of Oslo to bring about peace, the Palestinians once again turned to the right of return as a fundamental right and a goal to be pursued. The secular character of Palestinian nationalism has been severely challenged by the rise of Islamist movements on the political scene in the occupied territories.

Little can be said with certainty at this time concerning the long-term situation of the Palestinian refugees in Lebanon. The flurry of scholarly and political activity on the right of return has subsided somewhat in the wake of Sharon's ascension to power. A defunct peace process and an impotent leadership suggest that the refugee issue will remain on the back burner for some time. Indeed, there is a new worry that Israel's demographic vision is to significantly thin the Palestinian population in the occupied territories and impose a solution that will close the door to any negotiations over the refugee issue in Lebanon or Syria. Lebanon encourages emigration through a policy of economic and political marginalization. In the face of hopelessness and despair, human smuggling is flourishing as Palestinians seek asylum in the West. Those who have an opportunity to leave do so. An international study reported that "nearly 80 percent of refugee households in Lebanese camps have relatives residing abroad" (Jacobsen 2003: 51). Thus the thinning of the Palestinian population is occurring on two fronts, although in both cases reliable and accurate numbers are difficult to come by.

Palestinians are aware that neither residency elsewhere for a lengthy period of time nor citizenship in another country negates a sense of self and identity strongly linked to a particular place of origin. Cosmopolitanism and attachment to a particular place are not mutually exclusive. One can be a citizen of a state and still retain an attachment to and an identity strongly connected to another place. In other words, citizenship and nationality need not be isomorphic. On the one hand, the conditions facing the refugees in Lebanon foster narrow nationalism, while on the other, being stateless and identifying with other refugees and people who live on the margins of states compels a global view of one's position in the world and a pointed awareness of the instability of place. As an analytical construct and sociopolitical practice, Palestinian nationalism can accommodate a progressive imaginary. It is transnational and cosmopolitan, and the elements of time and space render it dynamic while illuminating the way it has continuously evolved within the limits and possibilities set by particular sociopolitical fields.

The Lebanese have faced little international pressure to ease the restrictive conditions under which the refugees are currently living. With the refugee negotiations delayed indefinitely, the official Lebanese position will likely remain one of refusal of resettlement of the refugees and Israel will continue a fifty-year pattern of trying to absolve themselves of responsibility and insist that the internationally sanctioned right of return is unreasonable.

Notes

Preface

1. In pre-twentieth-century warfare, armies on the move, or besieging communities, depended on the local population for food. Thus, it was in their interests that populations stayed put.

2. See *World Refugee Survey* (2003), Table 3, p. 3.

3. Ibid., Tables 5, 6, p. 6.

4. I use "displaced" rather than "diaspora," which may be an ideological invocation with less relevance in this instance. For a critique of Palestinians as a diaspora see Peteet (1999).

Chapter 1. Introduction: Palestinian Refugees

Epigraph: Charles (Carel) Sternberg headed the International Red Cross from 1965 to 1985. A Czech, during World War II he was a refugee fleeing Nazi persecution (U.S. Committee for Refugees 2003: 17).

1. United Nations General Assembly Resolution 194 (III) of 11 December 1948 states, "*Resolves* that the refugees wishing to return to their homes and live at peace with their neighbors should be permitted to do so at the earliest practicable date, and that compensation should be paid for the property of those choosing not to return and for loss of or damage to property which, under principles of international law or in equity, should be made good by the Governments or authorities responsible;"

2. For an example of such an argument, see Curtis et al. (1975).

3. See Zerubavel (1995) for a critical discussion of how Israeli histories and relation to place have been constructed and circulated.

4. R. Khalidi counters the notion that Palestinian nationalism emerged as a response to Zionism and the establishment of the State of Israel by noting, among other things, that "an increasing identification with the new states created by the post-World War I partitions, one based on preexisting loyalties as in the Palestinian case, was a universal process in the Middle East during this period. Moreover, Lebanese, Syrians, Egyptians, Iraqis, and Jordanians all managed to develop their respective nation-state nationalisms during the same period without the dubious benefit of a Zionist challenge" (1997: 203). While the identity-as-derivative approach has been bypassed by a new scholarship, it retains its hold on the popular imagination.

5. Palestinian refugees are thus outside the mandate of the UN High Com-

missioner for Refugees (UNHCR). The mandate of the UNHCR is to provide aid and protection to refugees; UNRWA's mandate is to provide aid. In effect, this means Palestinian refugees lack international protection (see Jabri 2003).

6. UNRWA figures may not be accurate. Untold numbers of UNRWA card holders are out of Lebanon, as laborers, immigrants, or citizens of other states. A census has been difficult to carry out and generates anxiety that it is a prelude to settlement of the refugee problem through transfer abroad.

7. Increasingly, environmental impact is a concern, as refugees can quickly strip a region of its natural vegetation and put pressure on water and electrical resources.

8. 'Amal was a sectarian movement dedicated to extending the interests of the Shi'a community in Lebanon. It grew out of *harakat al-mahrumin*, the Movement of the Dispossessed, a Shi'a political movement formed in the mid-1970s by Imam Musa Sadr. Its political and military fortunes expanded once the PLO withdrew from Beirut in 1982. They were violently anti-Palestinian and spearheaded the camp wars of the mid-1980s. Hizbollah (Party of God), by contrast, was a religious-based organization, promoting Islamist politics in Lebanon.

9. For a detailed account see Rosemary Sayigh (1994).

10. With the birth of a first son, the parents commonly become known as the "mother (*um*) or father (*abu*) of so-and-so," the son's name. The resistance leadership adopted these as *noms du guerre*, so Yassir Arafat is popularly referred to as Abu Ammar. In some cases, leaders did actually have sons with these names; in other cases, such as Arafat's, the name was fictitious.

11. In the fall of 1995, to protest the Palestinian-Israel peace agreement, Libya expelled nearly 30,000 Palestinian workers, 10,000–15,000 of them from Lebanon. On 22 September 1995, the Lebanese Interior Ministry issued a decree (number 478) requiring entry and exit visas for those holding the Palestinian *laissez-passer*. Many holding these travel documents were denied reentry. The timing of the decree was clearly intended to prevent large numbers from returning to Lebanon.

12. Fateh, the acronym for *harakat al-tahrir al-watani al filastiniyya*, is a political and guerrilla organization headed by Yassir Arafat. As a broad-based nationalist group, it is the largest and most dominant group in the PLO.

13. For example, a once standard academic source on refugees, with chapters on regional refugee-producing areas of the world, addressed them in barely a paragraph or two. See *Escape from Violence: Conflict and the Refugee Crisis in the Developing World* (Zolberg, Suhrke, and Aguayo 1989).

14. The cross-cultural appearance of narratives of deep connectivity captures the profoundly historical and spatiotemporal similarities of terror and displacement. A Mayan refugee "tied the exploitation of the Mayan people by the Spaniards to the terror he experienced at the hands of the Guatemalan Army" (Manz 1995: 155). He commented on the conquest: "It brought us the terror of destruction of a culture, of a people, and of a social organization. It was also the first step in the imposition of a system of exploitation and humiliation that persists to our day and under which we still live and suffer."

15. There are antecedents to anthropology's involvement with displacement. For an ethnographic and applied approach to resettlement and integration into the urban U.S., see Donnelly 1994 and Burns 1993. Going back further in time, anthropologists were professionally involved as research staff and consultants to the internment of American citizens of Japanese ancestry, and Japanese residents, during World War II (Leighton 1946). See the Acknowledgments for the

names of those anthropologists involved, and "Appendix. Applied Anthropology in a Dislocated Community" in Leighton (1946: 371–80).

16. In the mid-nineteenth century, when large numbers of Irish immigrated to the U.S., relatives often held wakes to mark their symbolic death in those communities (Metress 1990). A common theme in early American immigration narratives has been rupture with the past, the awareness that leaving meant never returning or seeing family again (Coan 1997). The pervasive American cultural sentiment of the possibility to remake the self in new geosocial terrain is apparent in narratives from the Ellis Island period.

17. Vietnamese camps in Hong Kong in the 1980s are a prime example. Designed for "humane deterrence," they were spatially and administratively modeled on prisons, and indeed were operated by the Hong Kong Correctional Services Department. Severely overcrowded, they offered the minimum in terms of protection, food, and shelter.

18. To this day, one still encounters the argument that responsibility for Palestinians residing in refugee camps can be laid at the feet of the host Arab states. In this argument, refusing to integrate the refugees and naturalize them was a component in a regional Arab plan to keep the refugees cooped up and miserable.

19. Three camps were built on land owned by the Maronite church and leased to UNRWA: Tel al-Za'ter, Jisr al-Basha, and Dbiyyeh. These have been excised from the Lebanese landscape, and the Church has refused to allow them to be rebuilt. Nabatiyyeh was built on land leased to UNRWA by its owner, a one-time mayor of the town. The land has now reverted to its owner and has been divided into plots that have been sold to wealthy buyers. Their villas now dot the landscape. The former inhabitants of Nabatiyyeh and Tel al-Za'ter are categorized as "displaced refugees." Nabatiyyeh residents migrated to the camps in the Beirut area, especially Tel al-Za'ter before its destruction in 1976. With its demise, they were again displaced. During the war, those displaced from destroyed camps often squatted in urban Lebanese areas. Their homelessness was finally addressed in the late 1990s. Some have been resettled in Nahr al-Bared and Baddawi camps in the north with funds provided by the Canadian government.

Chapter 2. Prelude to Displacement: Producing and Enacting Knowledge

1. The new Israeli historians have challenged historical narratives once sacrosanct to the state and its ideologues. See Beinin (1998); Lockman (1993, 1995); Morris (1987); Segev (1993, 2001); and Shafir (1989, 1996). For an overview of Israeli revisionism, see Pappe (1995).

2. Anthropologist Joel Bauman analyzed his tour of "so-called Western Wall Heritage Tunnels," during which "a large mechanical model reveals an overview of the temple mount. . . . The visuals effect a removal of the surrounding layers. A replica of the Second Temple remains fixed to the spot where, in actuality, today stands the mosque of the Dome of the Rock, which is not shown. As the layer with the modern Muslim quarter splits open and disappears, guides comment that 'originally, there were no Muslims in the Muslim quarter. They were moved in at a later date.' The process of removing successive layers of the model until the 'original' Second Temple is reached taps visitors' imaginations in such

a way as to engage then in a metaphorical conquest and displacement of Palestinians" (Bauman 1995: 23).

3. Native Americans were forcibly relocated and then tamed, domesticated, and civilized, in other words, reconstituted as new individuals. Biolsi argues that in the reservation system, "empropertying" the Lakota certainly "opened up their subjectivities to the penetration of the state, its sovereignty, and its law" (1995: 35).

4. Lockman notes that in the pre-1929 period there did exist a "sort of Jewish proletarian *mission civilisatrice* toward Arab workers in Palestine" (1995: 227).

5. The Middle East was often depicted in Western scholarship as frozen in time. It was described as a place where "one can find people living today as they did in the time of Christ, or even Abraham" (Coon 1951: 2). Under the Ottoman Empire the region was "relatively constant and relatively homogeneous." Only with the advent of Western technology and forms of governance was the "metal-age culture of the East irrevocably shaken" (8). As with time, so with space. Anthropologist Raphael Patai characterized the region, in spite of "localized developments and variants," as "the domain of one basically identical culture" (1962: 5–6).

6. Colonial powers frequently appropriate and refashion native time through the imposition of work and production schedules and laws defining and regulating vagrancy (see Merry 2000).

7. This is not to eschew complexity in contemporary Zionist reckonings of time. In his article on time in Israel, Paine observes that Israelis "experience different temporalities within the same country" (1992: 150).

8. See Ella Shohat for a discussion of the tripartite division of labor, space, and rights in Israel. She argues that the Askenazi Jews conceptualized the reformation of the Arab Jew in an "orientalist rescue trope." While the Muslim and Christian Palestinians could be relocated, the Jewish Palestinian embodied the potential for rehabilitation, but only to a certain level, one that could not catch up with Askenazi Jews. As labor replacements for Palestinians, the Arab Jews occupied a different time zone, but not a national-spatial one. They were part of the national space of Israel but assigned to the margins. Indeed, Shohat argues that in the Zionist "stagist discourse," the Arab Jews "would hobble along toward modernism" while the European Jews would "reach the stage of post-modernism" (1997: 8–9).

9. *Newsweek*, 20 September 1993, provides a good example.

10. In his interpretation of South African colonial landscape painting, Bunn brings forward the "association between sight and surveillance" and further notes that "the African landscape is conceived as a liminal zone between self and savagery, and rendering things visible is a necessary prerequisite to administrative control" (1994: 128). For a comparative examination of U.S. policy, practice, and landscape discourse on Native Americans with Zionism and the Palestinians see Finklestein (1995).

11. For example, the media routinely refer to the Haram al-Sherif (Noble Sanctuary) in Jerusalem as the Temple Mount, displacing a Palestinian and Muslim presence in, or claim to, the area. Settlements in the West Bank and Gaza Strip, illegal in international law, are now often referred to in the media as "neighborhoods"; Gilo, a settlement in the suburbs of Jerusalem, is a common example.

12. In the Hebraicization project, renaming encompassed individuals as well. For example, David Gruen of Poland becomes David Ben-Gurion; Golda Meyer-

son (nee Mabovitch) becomes Golda Meir; Ariel Scheinerman becomes Ariel Sharon.

13. Not only were the vast majority of Palestinians not nomadic, this discourse embodied little understanding of the actual nomadic land use patterns and the meaning attached to place. Indeed, for colonialists and states as well, nomads were often conceptualized as "economically inefficient, illiterate, and uncultured heathens, living in abject poverty and disease" (Gasteyer and Flora 2000: 129).

14. A study of Jewish settlers removed from the Sinai Peninsula upon its 1982 return to Egypt is ironic. The relocation of the settlers "initiated a process of community disintegration, the material destruction of places, and a process of displacement and deracination" (Kliot 1987: 43). Their removal precipitated the collapse of the "taken-for-granted world" and the settlers' security in and familiarity with place. Settlers then experienced alienation and few were able to feel rooted back in Israel. Having lived for twelve years in the Sinai, the settlers had established a deep sense of rootedness and belonging to place highly related to their ideological motivation and pioneering spirit.

15. The Stern Gang, or Lehi, called for the transfer of the indigenous population of Palestine. Parts of Syria, Lebanon, and Transjordan were envisioned as integral to Israel. Masalha's source was Heller (1984: 225).

16. "Veteran Israeli Hawk Tries out Wings of a Dove," *New York Times*, 21 May 1996, 3.

17. Zionism was hardly a homogeneous movement with a singularly united vision of Palestine. The writings of, among others, Achad Ha'am and Judah Magnes called for integration and coexistence and posed questions about the implications of Jewish nationalism.

18. The Universal Declaration of Human Rights states: "Everyone has the right to leave any country, including his own, and to return to his country." UN Resolution 194 stipulates the refugees' right of return. In defense of the Israeli position, legal scholar Donna Arzt (1997: 64) has raised the question: "But what if, at the time of initial departure, one's own country did not exist?" She also points out that the Declaration's language was "later modified in its treaty form in the International Covenant on Civil and Political rights, to read: "No one shall be arbitrarily deprived of the right to enter his own country."

Chapter 3. Aid and the Construction of the Refugee

1. *Al-shaheed*, the martyr, has a particularly pointed political-nationalist, and more recently religious, meaning in Palestinian society. It refers to any Palestinian, regardless of age or gender, whose death is related to the struggle for Palestine or to defending Palestinians from attacks. It is not necessarily a religious term as it is often depicted in the media, although its origins are in the notion of sacrifice for the cause of Islam. The rise of Palestinian Islamist movements in the 1980s and 1990s has produced a number of martyrs in the name of Palestine as a Muslim cause. The martyr can be cast in a religious/nationalist idiom or a more nationalist one. Indeed, its early usage in the Palestinian movement was a largely nationalist, secular one with Islamic overtones invoked largely for burial rituals.

2. In order to determine eligibility for aid, UNRWA had to formulate a working definition of a Palestinian refugee. In 1951, it provided an initial definition:

"a needy person who, as a result of the war in Palestine, has lost his home and his means of livelihood." In 1952, this was amended to read: "a person whose normal residence was Palestine for a minimum of two years preceding the outbreak of conflict on 1948, and who, as a result of this conflict, lost both his home and means of livelihood and took refuge in 1948 in the countries [Syria, Lebanon, Transjordan, and the Gaza Strip] where UNRWA provides relief" (Arzt 1997: 23). Descendants were also included in the definition. This definition has no standing in international law; it was a working device to determine the organization of aid, access to it, and its zones of delivery.

3. American Middle East Relief (1954: 10–12). The Report is quoting *al-Kulliyah* (published by the AUB Alumni Association), January 1955.

4. The archives I examined were American Friends Service Committee (AFSC) in Philadelphia, American Middle East Relief at the offices of the American Near East Refugee Agency (ANERA) in Washington, D.C., and the Musa Alami Foundation, whose archival material is housed at the Institute for Palestine Studies, Washington, D.C. UNRWA records were not accessible in the mid-1990s.

5. With few exceptions (Voutira and Harrell-Bond 1995; Hyndman 2000; Long 1993; Malkki 1996), anthropologists have not focused much on refugee bureaucracies and personnel. Long's (1993) outstanding ethnography of a Thai-Laotian border camp explores the role of aid and the relief worker in everyday life. As both an ethnographer and an aid worker, she brought a practical reflexivity to her writing. Her work serves as a counterpoint to the characterization of participant-observation as oxymoronic (see Behar 1996: 5) and points to the possibilities for a socially engaged ethnography.

6. See Kerr (1993) and Barton (1930) for accounts of the Armenian refugee situation and relief.

7. "Excerpts Concerning Suffering in Palestine from Reports of the International Red Cross Workers in the Field," December 1948, 1. AFSC Archives.

8. W. de St. Aubin was the delegate of the League of the Red Cross Societies to the Middle East and was on the staff of Count Folke Bernadotte, the UN Mediator for Palestine in 1948, and his successor Ralph Bunche.

9. "Excerpts Concerning Suffering," 3. AFSC Archives.

10. Memo, "To John Kavanaugh—Background Material" 28 January 28, 2. AFSC Archives.

11. On 20 May 1948, Count Folke Bernadotte was appointed UN Mediator for Palestine. This former Red Cross official, a well-known and respected humanitarian, and an aide were fatally shot by the Stern group in Jerusalem on 17 September 1948. This followed the release of his report to the UN Secretary General in which he recommended some revisions of the Partition Resolution of 1947. His calls for Israel to reduce immigration and modify the new boundaries of the state and for the refugees' right to return and/or compensation for lost or damaged property created widespread indignation in Israel.

12. UN General Assembly Resolution 212 (III), 19 November 1948, Establishing a Special Fund for Relief of Palestine Refugees.

13. Today, as a consequence of global communications, rapid air transport, an international relief infrastructure and administration, and the stockpiling of relief supplies for ready transport, aid can be delivered in a matter of days.

14. In 1947, the AFSC and Friends Service of Britain were the recipients of the Nobel Peace Prize for their work in relief and reconstruction in post-World War II Europe. They had a well-deserved reputation for efficiency and compassion in dealing with the displaced.

15. Letter from Delbert Replogle, Field Director, Palestine Relief Unit, to Colin Bell, AFSC, Philadelphia, 12 January 1949. AFSC Archives.

16. Oral History #604, 14–15. Interview with Alwin Holtz. Interviewed by Joan Lowe, 19 September 1992 for AFSC Oral History Project.

17. The Nineteen Points, drawn up by Bell and agreed to by the Egyptian authorities, detailed AFSC responsibilities and rights in Gaza.

18. AFSC, Operational Report of AFSC, December 1949, Annex II, "Population by Village of Origin and Family Groups of Refugees Receiving UNRPR Rations in the Gaza Area," 31 December 1949, 16–23. AFSC Archives.

19. "Background Material on Nuseirat," 15 March 1949, 2. AFSC Archives.

20. Letter from Frances Morrison to Corinne Hardesty, 12 September 1949, 2–8. AFSC Archives.

21. Letter from Charles Read, Field Director, to Colin Bell, Associate Secretary, Asian Activities, Re: UNRPR, 11 October 1949, 1. AFSC Archives.

22. Letter from Charles Read to Colin Bell, Bronson Clark, Jim Read and Julia Branson, 15 October 1949, 1–2. AFSC Archives.

23. The AFSC ran the well-known Friends School in Ramallah, which is still in operation.

24. In 1938 the Tennessee Valley Authority (TVA) was organized to provide electricity to the Tennessee River basin area, improve flood control and navigation on the river, enhance farming by introducing new methods, and aid national defense by developing government nitrate and phosphorus manufacturing sites in the area. It also aimed to improve the well-being of the local population.

25. "First Interim Report," UN Economic Survey Mission for the Middle East, November 1949, Department of State, 4. AFSC Archives.

26. In the 1930s, Roosevelt's New Deal organized programs to alleviate mass unemployment. The Works Progress Administration (WPA) created projects to build new schools, post offices, roads, and bridges. Employment was found for 2.1 million workers between 1935 and 1941.

27. "Gordon Clapp Speaks on Work of the UN Economic Survey for the Middle East," Press Release PAL/534, Department of Public Information, United Nations Geneva, 13 October 1949. AFSC Archives.

28. UNRWA had no protective mandate for Palestinian refugees. Sparked by the first *intifada*, UNRWA began to provide "legal assistance and human rights protection" in the West Bank and Gaza Strip in the 1990s (Cervenak 1994: 308).

29. For years, UNRWA desired to radically reduce rations. They faced Arab government reticence and refugee resistance. By the 1970s, an improved standard of living among refugees in a booming regional economy had made rations less of a vital resource. Roll inflation and "ration merchants," who bought rations from refugees and sold them on the local market, and UNRWA's declining finances buttressed the logic of reduction. Refugees protested purported cuts less from the standpoint of need and more because of the symbolic nature of rations as an expression of an international commitment to the question of Palestine. The 1982 war in Lebanon was the momentous event that ushered in the end of rations as they were known. Subsequently, only refugees who qualified as Special Hardship Cases (SHC), families without breadwinners or living in extreme poverty, received rations. With the crisis in the camps in the mid-1980s and 1990s and the first *intifada*, emergency rations were once again distributed.

30. Mohammed Zaatari, "Palestinians Denied Rations in Saida Camps as UN Workers Go on Strike," *Daily Star* (Beirut), 18 February 1998.

31. "The Arab Development Society: Brief Historical Notes," no date. Musa Alami Files—IPS Archives.

32. "Hope in the Hashemite Kingdom of Jordan," Extension of Remarks of Hon. Francis P. Bolton of Ohio in the House of Representatives, Proceedings and Debates of the 87th Congress, Second Session, Monday, 5 March 1962, 5.

33. "Miracle in the Holy Land: The Arab Development Society Appeal, 25 Years On," no date. Musa Alami files—IPS Archives.

34. "Minutes of the Annual Meeting of the Musa Alami Foundation of Jericho," Washington D.C., 28 October 1989. (Musa Alami Foundation of Jericho was the U.S. support group of the ADS.) Musa Alami File—IPS Archives.

35. "American Middle-East Relief, Inc.," radio broadcasts, Cleveland, Ohio, undated, 30 seconds and 60 seconds. ANERA archives.

36. U.S. House of Representatives, Committee on Foreign Affairs, Hearings on Palestine Refugees, 81st Congress, Second Session, S.J. Res. 153, 1, 17 February 1950, 9. Washington, D.C.: USGPO, 1950.

37. The field director of the project was Alma Kerr, who had served with NER in Turkey (1919–21). During the depression of the 1930s, she had worked in the U.S. in emergency relief for the destitute and was an administrator with the WPA.

38. "The Marjiyoun Self Help and Small Industries Training Project," 4. AMER, Inc., New York, no date. ANERA Archives.

39. Letter from Corinne Hardesty to Colin Bell, 25 April 1949, 1. AFSC Archives.

40. Letter from Emmett Gulley to Howard Wiggans, 5 May 1949, 4. AFSC Archives.

41. Memo from Donald Stevens to Bronson Clark, Beirut, Subject: CICR and IRC Relief Operations in Arab Palestine and Trans Jordan, 7 December 1949, 1–2. AFSC Archives.

42. Holtz recalls that the Gazans "were worse off than the refugees. They were starving." Local destitution was sparked by the crush of refugees on local resources and the severe economic impact of Gaza's sudden isolation from the rest of Palestine and the Arab world. A local teacher "took me, and showed me six different places where people were hungry . . . the people were living in a little hovel and they didn't have enough food, except for the largesse they got from the refugees. So we invented a village. The Arabic word for the woebegone, the people that have been deprived. . . . I can never remember the word *muhamin.* And we created the village of Muhamin and registered about 15,000 people. . . . It was the right thing to do. . . . It was against the rules but it was the right thing to do" (Holtz oral history interview, 16, 27–28).

43. Report by Howard Wiggans, AFSC Geneva representative, to Brigadier R.H.R. Parminter, UNRPR, Geneva, 3 March 1949. AFSC Archives.

44. Operational Report of AFSC, December 1949, Annex I, "Population Figures," 25 December 1949, 15; Annex II, "Population by Village of Origin and Family Groups of Refugees Receiving UNRPR Rations in the Gaza Area," 31 December 1949, 16–23. AFSC Archives.

45. Biolsi describes the enumeration of the Lakota following military pacification in the 1880s: "census takers recorded some remarkable English translations of Lakota names . . . such as "Bad Cunt," "Dirty Prick," and "Shit Head" (1995: 28). The Lakota also padded their numbers by as much as 70 percent as a strategy to receive more rations. They would "file past the census enumerator, and then getting back in line—or lending their babies to people in line—to be

enumerated a second time using fictitious and rather imaginative names" (28–29).

46. Darwish's poem refers to enumeration and classification of the Palestinians who remained in Israel, but the meaning in the refugee camps was locally reinscribed. The poem portends the limits to what Palestinians would accept before they would strike back.

47. Another issue in the process of enumeration and classification with a productive quality as well as a managerial one was the Conciliation Commission's project to document Arab property in Palestine. The Commission established a Refugee Office to prepare an assessment of Arab property in the parts of Palestine under Israeli control since 1948 for the purpose of drawing up a program of Israeli compensation. According to Buehrig, it consists of the "identification and evaluation of every piece of Arab property in those parts of Palestine passing to Israel's control in 1948. . . . In all, some 450,000 record forms of properties owned by Arabs were prepared—now on file at the United Nation in New York" (1971: 24, 25). See UN General Assembly Resolution 1725 of 20 December, 1961 (b)); see also Fischbach (2003).

48. Charles Read, AFSC Field Director, Clapp Commission Questionnaire, 3 November 1949, 3. AFSC Archives.

49. Undated letter, Stanley Kerr File, American Middle East Relief, Inc. ANERA Archives.

50. Letter from Emmet Gulley and Delbert Replogle to Howard Wiggans, 1 March 1949. AFSC Archives.

51. See Cervenak (1994) for a detailed discussion of the gendering of UNRWA's definition of a Palestinian refugee, the delivery of aid, and the possible implications if a Palestinian state were to inherit UNRWA infrastructure and operations.

52. The gendering of rations collecting has often been overplayed, with consequent glossing over of instances where men do take possession of rations. Men did collect rations and this may have been connected to their urban status. In urban areas, it was culturally appropriate for middle-class men to do the household grocery shopping. This accords with greater female seclusion in urban areas.

53. Foreign Broadcast Information Service, quoting *an-Nahar* (Beirut), "Interview with Faruq Qaddumi," 18 November 1996 (FOFOGNET)

54. "Arab Refugees Self-help Project," *Arab World*, October 1959. ANERA archives.

55. Memo from Bronson Clark to Donald Stevenson, Beirut and Paul John, Cairo. Re: Conference with James Basten, 28 December 1948. Basten was chief economist to the Clapp Commission and on his own initiative undertook an economic survey of Gaza out of concern that it had not been given the attention it deserved.

56. At the end of the British Mandate in Palestine, the student population of 135,000 "was served by a total of 827 schools, of which 514 were public and 313 private." Thirty percent of school age children were in school (Abu-Lughod 1973: 103).

57. By the late 1960s, 85 percent of the school age children served by UNRWA were enrolled in primary school; about 45 percent of these were female. Gender imbalance was most marked in the higher levels as the female dropout rate increased with age. By 1969–70, the percentage of girls attending secondary school was 49.1 percent in Gaza, 35 percent in Syria, 23 percent in Lebanon, and 33 percent in the West Bank (Abu-Lughod 1973: 106–7).

58. See Beydoun (2000) for a poignant examination of this transformation and its implications for masculine identity in a Lebanese context. See Peteet (1994) for a discussion of the effects of militancy on Palestinian masculinity.

59. Stevens is quoting respectively Stewart Alsop, *New York Herald Tribune*, 25 November 1951; Dorothy Thompson, *Portland Oregonian*, 25 December 1950; "Despatch from Gaza"; and A.T. Steele, *New York Herald Tribune*, 15 March 1952.

Chapter 4. Producing Place, Spatializing Identity, 1948–68

1. For example, Afghan camps in Pakistan (Centlivres and Centlivres-Dumont 1988) were frequently sites for organizing armed resistance to Soviet occupation.

2. Damur is a small Christian town just south of Beirut on the coastal highway. During the early period of the civil war in 1975, rightist Christian militia staged innumerable kidnappings of Palestinian and Lebanese Muslims at checkpoints in the village, making travel between the capital and the south risky. The village was overrun by the combined forces of the Lebanese National Movement and the Palestinian Resistance Movement in January 1976. The population fled, taking refuge in Christian East Beirut. With the fall of Tel al-Zaʿter camp in August 1976, the resistance housed hundreds of widows and their children in the bombed-out ruins of the town. They remained there until the 1982 Israeli invasion drove them north to Beirut. Damur's original inhabitants began to move back to the village and renovate it in the 1990s.

3. Jounieh is a Christian suburb in East Beirut.

4. Um Fadi would point to her nephews and nieces as she referred to their parents.

5. Inhabitants of the Lake Hula or Ghur area of northeast Palestine, the Ghawarneh had somewhat darker skin and a lower socioeconomic status and feudal-like land holding system that distinguished them from other Palestinians. They have a consciousness of themselves as a relatively deprived group. Settled into Nabatiyyeh camp, they moved to Tel al-Zaʿter after the camp was destroyed in 1973, and then to Damur after the destruction of Tel al-Zaʿter. Many have migrated to Germany; the rest are scattered in Lebanon.

6. In the wake of the 2000 withdrawal of Israeli forces from south Lebanon, Palestinians rushed in droves to the border to gaze at Palestine and reunite with family and friends. Most had never been that close to the border given the restrictions on Palestinian movement in the area until 1967, after which it became a military zone.

7. Domestic disruption can be a predictor of the potential for violence in a camp. Rife with violence, the Hong Kong camps housing Vietnamese boat people in the mid-1980s are illustrative. Housed in prison barracks with little privacy, domestic units were accorded minimal spatial expression. Meals were taken in a cafeteria setting, and thus refugees were not in charge of when or what they ate, or the conditions under which it was eaten (Knudsen 1990; Donnelly 1992). In other words, the absence of a kitchen and hearth undercut domesticity.

8. The Brevet is the equivalent of tenth grade in the American educational system.

Chapter 5. Landscape of Hope and Despair

1. In 1969–71, Palestinian guerrillas in Jordan battled with the Jordanian Army and were routed in the now infamous 1971 Black September. In the aftermath, many PLO cadres went to Lebanon.

2. Sa'iqa was a guerrilla organization supported by and dependent on Syria's ruling Ba'th Party. Jebhat al-Tahrir referred to the Arab Liberation Front, an Iraqi-supported faction of the PLO.

3. See Mahmud Darwish's poem on Tel al-Za'ter (1978) and Turki (1978).

4. Quoted in As'ad Abu Khalil, *An-Nahar*, 13 May 1985.

5. *L'Orient-le Jour*, 26 September 1984, 2 (author's translation)

6. Abu Khalil, *An-Nahar*.

7. Um Taher was too shy to repeat the insults of the 'Amal militiaman. In all likelihood, he called her a *sharmutah* (whore).

Chapter 6. The Geography of Terror and Reconfinement

1. In the summer of 1999 there was an indication of a joint (Lebanese-Palestinian) public rejection of *towteen* in the context of external pressure on Lebanon to accept Palestinian settlement. In a speech at the Eighth Francophone Summit in Moncton, Canada, Lebanese President Emile Lahoud said, "Rejecting the settlement of Palestinians is no longer only an article in the National Accord. It represents an intersection of the interests of both the Lebanese and Palestinian people" ("Palestinians Not to be Resettled in Lebanon," Nicosa, Middle East Newsline (MENL), posted on FOFOGNET, Wednesday, 8 September 1999). A news report dated 1 July 1999 makes reference to a joint Palestinian-Lebanese memorandum that "rejects the prospect that nearly 500,000 Palestinians in Lebanon will receive citizenship" ("Lebanon wants Palestinians to retain Refugee Status," Nicosa, Middle East Newsline (MENL), posted on FOFOGNET, 1 July 1999).

2. In a communique during the first camp war, Etienne Sakr (Abu Arz), President of the Guardians of the Cedars, an extreme right-wing Christian organization and militia, contended that Lebanon's civil war was not a civil war but a Lebanese-Palestinian war. Palestinians were the "true enemy," and he called for an end to their presence in Lebanon. This interpretation of the civil war as not a civil war is a common refrain. The son of a well-known rightist thinker took pains to correct me at a conference when I referred to the civil war: "Dr. Peteet, you are mistaken. There was no Lebanese civil war. There was a Lebanese-Palestinian war." Such an analysis assumed a cross-sect cohesion in Lebanese *national* interests and coalescence in actions in which Palestinians were the enemy.

3. Television Interview with Michel Murr on "Kalam al-Nas," Lebanese Broadcasting Corporation, 5 August 1999.

4. "Qaddumi on Lebanese Court Death Sentence, Peace Talks," *al-Dustur* (Arabic), 6 November 1999, 16. FBIS translated text posted on FOFOGNET Digest, 8–9 November, 1999 (#1999–225), 1.

5. U.S. Committee for Refugees (1997: 159). When Selim El-Hoss became prime minister in 1998, he revoked this decree.

6. West Bank Palestinian villages with a history of emigration to the U.S. have long had village clubs and associations. The Ramallah Club, Beit Hanina Club, and El-Bireh Society, among others, are active in urban areas where a concentration of former villagers reside. Club social events are often sites where young people and their parents search for marriage partners.

7. In 1948, about half the residents of Saffuriyyah came to Lebanon. Many

others resettled in Nazareth in a quarter now known as the Saffuriyyah quarter. There is a Saffuriyyah Heritage Committee in Nazareth.

8. Fawzi al-Din al-Qawuqji, a Syrian with pan-Arab nationalist affiliation, was the self-appointed commander of rebel forces during the 1936 Great Revolt. He is credited with enhancing the "rebels' level of military organization and effectiveness" (Swedenburg 1995: 82).

9. See Bauman (1995) on the transformation of Saffuriyyah and its role in the local Israeli imagination.

10. On 26 August 2000, the Ibdaa Cultural Center was broken into. Computer equipment was stolen and the center was set on fire.

11. The early leader of the 'Amal movement, Iman Musa Sadr, disappeared in Libya in the late 1970s. With his disappearance, he achieved the status of martyr among the Shi'a community.

12. These are all sites of massacres. In April 1948, around 250 Palestinians were murdered in the village of Dayr Yassin by the Irgun and Stern groups, an act that precipitated the mass movement by Palestinians seeking shelter from violence. In October 1948, in Duweima 80–100 villagers were massacred after the village was occupied by Israeli forces (Masalha 2001: 47). In Qibya in October 1953, an Israeli military operation, supposedly a reprisal against murder and sabotage in Israel, resulted in a large number of casualties including women and children. In October 1956, Israeli forces imposed a curfew on Kafr Qasim village. Unaware of the curfew, men working in the fields were shot as they came home after work. In Sabra-Shatila in September 1982, Lebanese forces supported and coordinated by Israel entered the camp and engaged in a three-day massacre in which 800–3,000 civilians were killed.

13. For example, *L'Orient-le Jour* reported on 24 May 1985 (p. 1), that "Palestinian sources yesterday denied the fall of Sabra and Shatila as announced the day before by the 'Amal movement, whereas journalistic sources, while acknowledging the impossibility of confirmation while fighting continued, believe that 'Amal controls, in practice, Sabra and Shatila, where nevertheless, pockets of resistance persist" (author's translation).

14. In the 1980s, Afghan refugees rejected the label "refugee," preferring *muhajareen*, migrants in the cause of God. They did, however, find the term "refugee" useful and appropriate when dealing with international agencies that distributed rations and assistance to refugees (Centlivres and Centlivres-Demont 1988).

Conclusion: Refugee Camps and the Wall

1. See report by Jean Ziegler, Special Rapporteur of the UN Commission on Human Rights on the right to food: "Israeli policies hurting Palestinian children, UN expert on right to food says," which noted that "9 percent of Palestinian under the age of five suffer some form of brain damage because of chronic malnutrition caused by Israeli occupation." www.un.org/apps/news/story.

2. See "Are Jews Who Fled Arab Lands to Israel Refugees, Too?" *New York Times*, 11 October 2003, 18.

Bibliography

Abu el-Haj, Nadia
    2001   *Facts on the Ground: Archaeological Practice and Territorial Self-fashioning in Israeli Society.* Chicago: University of Chicago Press.
    1998   "Translating Truth: Nationalism, The Practice of Archaeology and the Remaking of Past and Present in Contemporary Jerusalem." *American Ethnologist* 25 (2): 166–88.
Abu-Lughod, Ibrahim
    1973   "Educating a Community in Exile: The Palestinian Experience." *Journal of Palestine Studies* 2 (3): 94–111.
Abu-Lughod, Lila
    1991   "Writing Against Culture." In *Recapturing Anthropology: Working in the Present,* ed. Richard G. Fox. Santa Fe, N.M.: School of American Research Press. 137–62.
American Middle East Relief
    1954   *Annual Report, 1 January to 31 December 1954.* New York: American Middle East Relief.
Anzaldúa, Gloria
    1987   *Borderlands. La Frontera. The New Mestiza.* San Francisco: Aunt Lute Books.
Appadurai, Arjun
    1998   "Dead Certainty: Ethnic Violence in the Era of Globalization." *Public Culture* 10 (2): 225–47.
    1996   *Modernity at Large: Cultural Dimensions of Globalization.* Minneapolis: University of Minnesota Press.
    1993   "Patriotism and Its Future." *Public Culture* 5 (3): 411–29.
    1992   "Putting Hierarchy in its Place." In *Rereading Cultural Anthropology,* ed. George Marcus. Durham, N.C.: Duke University Press. 34–77.
Aruri, Naseer, ed.
    2001   *Palestinian Refugees and the Right of Return.* London: Pluto Press.
Arzt, Donna
    1997   *Refugees into Citizens: Palestinians and the End of the Arab-Israeli Conflict.* New York: Council on Foreign Relations.
Asad, Talal
    1993   *Genealogies of Religion: Disciplines and Reasons of Power in Christianity and Islam.* Baltimore: Johns Hopkins University Press.
Aveni, Anthony
    1989   *Empires of Time: Calendars, Clocks, and Cultures.* New York: Basic Books.

Bammer, Angelika, ed.
  1994   *Displacements: Cultural Identities in Question.* Bloomington: Indiana University Press.
Barton, James L.
  1944   *Near East Relief Consummated, Near East Foundation Carries On.* Supplement to Barton, *The Story of Near East Relief.* New York: Committee of Trustees of Near East Relief.
  1930   *The Story of Near East Relief (1915–1930): An Interpretation.* New York: Macmillan.
Basso, Keith
  1996   "Places: Notes on a Western Apache Landscape." In *Senses of Place,* ed. Steven Feld and Keith Basso. Advanced Seminar Series. Santa Fe, N.M.: School of American Research Press.
Battaglia, Debbora
  1993   "At Play in the Fields (and Borders) of the Imaginary: Melanesian Transformations of Forgetting." *Cultural Anthropology* 8 (4): 430–42.
Bauman, Joel
  1995   "Designer Heritage: Israeli National Parks and the Politics of Historical Representation." *Middle East Report* 196 (September–October): 20–23.
Becker, Gay
  1997   *Disrupted Lives: How People Create Meaning in a Chaotic World.* Berkeley: University of California Press.
Behar, Ruth
  1996   *The Vulnerable Observer: Anthropology That Breaks your Heart.* Boston: Beacon Press.
Beinin, Joel
  1998   *Dispersion of Egyptian Jewry: Culture, Politics and the Formation of a Modern Diaspora.* Berkeley: University of California Press.
Benjamin, Walter
  1968   "Thesis on the Philosophy of History." In *Illuminations,* ed. Hannah Arendt, trans. Harry Zohn. New York: Harcourt. 253–64.
Benvenisti, Meron
  2000   *Sacred Landscape: The Buried History of the Holy Land Since 1948.* Berkeley: University of California Press.
Berdahl, Daphne
  1999   *Where the World Ended: Re-Unification and Identity in the German Borderland.* Berkeley: University of California Press.
Bermingham, Ann
  1994   "System, Order, and Abstraction: The Politics of English Landscape Drawing Around 1795." In *Landscape and Power,* ed. W. J. T. Mitchell. Chicago: University of Chicago Press. 77–101.
Beydoun, Ahmad
  2000   "Not the Man My Father Was." In *Imagined Masculinities: Male Identities and Culture in the Modern Middle East,* ed. Mai Ghoussoub and Emma Sinclair-Webb. London: Saqi Books. 263–72.
Biolsi, Thomas
  1995   "The Birth of the Reservation: Making the Modern Individual Among the Lakota." *American Ethnologist* 22 (1): 28–53.
Bird, Jon, Barry Curtis, Tim Putnam, George Robertson, and Lisa Tickner, eds.
  1993   *Mapping the Futures: Local Cultures, Global Change.* London: Routledge.

Brenner, Neil
  1997   "Global, Fragmented, Hierarchical: Henri Lefebvre's Geogra-
          phies of Globalization." *Public Culture* 10 (1): 135–67.
Buehrig, Edward
  1971   *The UN and the Palestinian Refugees: A Study in Nonterritorial Admin-
          istration.* Bloomington: Indiana University Press.
Bunn, David
  1994   " 'Our Wattled Cot': Mercantile and Domestic Space in Thomas
          Pringle's African Landscapes." In *Landscape and Power*, ed.
          W. J. T. Mitchell. Chicago: University of Chicago Press. 127–73.
Burns, Allan F.
  1993   *Maya in Exile: Guatemalans in Florida.* Philadelphia: Temple Uni-
          versity Press.
Calhoun, Craig
  1994   "Social Theory and the Politics of Identity." In *Social Theory and
          the Politics of Identity*, ed. Craig Calhoun. Cambridge: Blackwell.
          9–36.
Carter, Erica, James Donald, and Judith Squires, eds.
  1993   *Space and Place: Theories of Identity and Location.* London: Law-
          rence and Wishart.
Casey, Edward
  1996   "How to Get from Space to Place in a Fairly Short Stretch of
          Time: Phenomenological Prolegomena." In *Senses of Place*, ed.
          Steven Feld and Keith H. Basso. Advanced Seminar Series. Santa
          Fe, N.M.: School of American Research Press. 13–52.
Center for Policy Analysis on Palestine
  1992   *Facts and Figures About the Palestinians.* Washington, D.C.: Center
          for Policy Analysis on Palestine.
Centlivres, Pierre and Micheline Centlivres-Demont
  1988   "The Afghan Refugee in Pakistan: An Ambiguous Identity." *Jour-
          nal of Refugee Studies* 1 (2): 141–52.
Cervenak, Christine M.
  1994   "Promoting Inequality: Gender-Based Discrimination in UNR-
          WA's Approach to Palestine Refugee Status." *Human Rights Quar-
          terly* 16: 300–374.
Clifford, James
  1994   "Diasporas." *Cultural Anthropology* 9 (3): 302–36.
  1992   "Traveling Cultures." In *Cultural Studies*, ed. Lawrence Gross-
          berg, Cary Nelson, and Paula A. Treichler. New York: Routledge.
          96–116.
Coan, Peter Morton
  1997   *Ellis Island Interviews: In Their Own Words.* New York: Checkmark
          Books.
Cohen, Saul and Nurit Kliot
  1992   "Place-Names in Israel's Ideological Struggle over the Adminis-
          tered Territories." *Annals of the Association of American Geographers*
          82 (4): 653–80.
Connerton, Paul
  1989   *How Societies Remember.* Cambridge: Cambridge University Press.
Coon, Carleton
  1951   *Caravan: The Story of the Middle East.* New York: Henry Holt.

Curtis, Michael, Joseph Neyer, Chaim I. Waxman, and Allan Pollack, eds.
  1975   *The Palestinians: People, History, Politics.* New Brunswick, N.J.: Transaction Books.
Daniel, E. Valentine and John Chr. Knudsen, eds.
  1995   *Mistrusting Refugees.* Berkeley: University of California Press.
Darwish, Mahmud
  1995   *Memory for Forgetfulness: August, Beirut, 1982.* Trans. Ibrahim Muhawi. Berkeley: University of California Press.
  1978   "Ahmed al-Zaʿter" In *Collected Works of Mahmud Darwish.* Vol. 2. Beirut: Dar al-ʿAwda. 469–94.
Deshpande, Satish
  1998   "Hegemonic Spatial Strategies: The Nation-Space of Hindu Communalism in Twentieth Century India." *Public Culture* 10 (2): 249–83.
Dirks, Nicholas
  1992   "From Little King to Landlord; Colonial Discourse and Colonial Rule." In *Colonialism and Culture,* ed. Nicholas Dirks. Comparative Studies in Society and History. Ann Arbor: University of Michigan Press. 175–208.
Dodge, Bayard
  1973   Foreword. In Stanley Kerr, *The Lions of Marash: : Personal Experiences with American Near East Relief, 1919–1922.* Albany: State University of New York Press. ix–xiii.
Donnelly, Nancy D.
  1992   "The Impossible Situation of Vietnamese in Hong Kong's Detention Centers." In *Selected Papers on Refugee Issues I,* ed. Pamela A. DeVoe. Washington, D.C.: American Anthropological Association. 120–32.
  1994   *Changing Lives of Refugee Hmong Women.* Seattle: University of Washington Press.
Edidin, Ben M.
  1944   *Rebuilding Palestine.* Rev. ed. New York: Behrman House.
Eickleman, Dale
  1978   "The Art of Memory: Islamic Education and Its Social Reproduction." *Comparative Studies in Society and History* 20: 485–516.
Fabian, Johannes
  1983   *Time and the Other: How Anthropology Makes Its Other.* New York: Columbia University Press.
Feld, Steven and Keith H. Basso, eds.
  1996   *Senses of Place.* Advanced Seminar Series. Santa Fe, N.M.: School of American Research Press.
Feldman, Allen
  1991   *Formations of Violence: The Narrative of the Body and Political Terror in Northern Ireland.* Chicago: University of Chicago Press.
  1995   "Ethnographic States of Emergency." In *Fieldwork Under Fire: Contemporary Studies of Violence and Survival,* ed. Carolyn Nordstrom and Antonius C. G. M. Robben. Berkeley: University of California Press. 224–52.
Finklestein, Norman
  1995   "History's Verdict: The Cherokee Case." *Journal of Palestine Studies* 24 (4): 32–45.

Fischbach, Michael
    2003   *Records of Dispossession: Palestinian Refugee Property and the Arab-Israeli Conflict.* New York: Columbia University Press

Flapan, Simha
    1979   *Zionism and the Palestinians.* London: Croom Helm.

Foucault, Michel
    1980   *The History of Sexuality.* Volume 1, *An Introduction.* New York: Vintage.

Gabbay, Rony
    1959   *A Political Study of the Arab-Jewish Conflict: The Arab Refugee Problem.* A Case Study. Geneva: Librairie E. Droz.

Gasteyer, Stephen and Cornelia Flora
    2000   "Modernizing the Savage: Colonization and Perceptions of Landscape and Lifescape." *Sociologia Ruralis* 40 (1): 128–49.

Geertz, Clifford
    1988   *Works and Lives.* Stanford, Calif.: Stanford University Press.
    1996   Afterword. In *Senses of Place,* ed. Steven Feld and Keith H. Basso. Advanced Seminar Series. Santa Fe, N.M.: School of American Research. 259–62.

Ghannam, Farha
    2002   *Remaking the Modern: Space, Relocation, and the Politics of Identity in a Global Cairo.* Berkeley: University of California Press.

Giddens, Anthony
    1993   *The Giddens Reader.* Ed. Philip Cassell. Stanford, Calif.: Stanford University Press.
    1979   *Central Problems in Social Theory: Action, Structure, and Contradiction in Social Analysis.* Berkeley: University of California Press.

Gilroy, Paul
    1993   *The Black Atlantic: Modernity and Double Consciousness.* Cambridge, Mass.: Harvard University Press.

Gorny, Yosef
    1987   *Zionism and the Arabs, 1882–1948: A Study of Ideology.* Oxford: Clarendon Press.

Gulley, Emmett W.
    1973   *Tall Tales by a Tall Quaker.* N.p: the author. AFSC archives.

Gupta, Akhil and James Ferguson
    1997   "Culture, Power, Place.: Ethnography at the End of an Era." In *Culture, Power, Place: Explorations in Critical Anthropology,* ed. Akhil Gupta and James Ferguson. Durham, N.C.: Duke University Press. 1–29.
    1992   "Beyond 'Culture': Space, Identity, and the Politics of Difference." *Cultural Anthropology* 7 (1): 6–23.

Gusterson, Hugh
    1997   "Studying Up Revisited." *Political and Legal Anthropology Review* 20 (1): 114–19.

Hall, Stuart
    1996   "Who Needs Identity?" In *Questions of Cultural Identity,* ed. Stuart Hall and Paul de Gay. London: Sage. 1–17.
    1994   "Cultural Identity and Diaspora." In *Colonial Discourse and Post-Colonial Theory,* ed. Patrick Williams and Laura Chrisman. New York: Columbia University Press. 392–403.

Hannerz, Ulf
 1993 "When Culture Is Everywhere: Reflection on a Favorite Concept." *Ethnos* 58 (1): 95–111.
Harrell-Bond, Barbara, Efthia Voutira, and Mark Leopold
 1992 "Counting the Refugees: Gifts, Givers, Patrons, Clients." *Journal of RefugeeStudies* 5 (3/4): 205–25.
Harvey, David
 2000 *Spaces of Hope.* Berkeley: University of California Press.
 1993 "From Space to Place and Back Again: Reflections on the Condition of Post-Modernity." In *Mapping the Futures: Local Cultures, Global Change,* ed. Jon Bird, Barry Curtis, Tim Putnam, George Robertson, and Lisa Tickner. London: Routledge. 3–29.
 1992 "Social Justice, Postmodernisms and the City." *International Journal of Urban and Regional Research* 16 (4): 594–601.
 1989 *The Condition of Postmodernity.* Oxford: Blackwell.
Hayner, Priscilla B.
 2001 *Unspeakable Truths: Confronting State Terror and Atrocity.* New York: Routledge.
Heller, Yosef.
 1984 "Between Messianism and Realpolitik—Lehi and the Arab Question, 1940–1947." *Yahdut Semanenu* (Contemporary Jewry), a Research Annual (ed. Israel Gutman) 1: 225.
Herzfeld, Michael
 1992 *The Social Production of Indifference: Exploring the Symbolic Roots of Western Bureaucracy.* New York: Berg.
Herzl, Theodor
 1960 *The Complete Diaries of Theodor Herzl.* Vol. 1. New York: Herzl Press and Thomas Yoseloff.
Hirsch, Eric and Michael O'Hanlon
 1995 *The Anthropology of Landscape: Perspectives on Space and Place.* Oxford: Clarendon Press.
Hitchens, Christopher and Edward W. Said
 1984 *Blaming the Victims: Spurious Scholarship and the Palestinian Question.* London: Verso.
Hyndman, Jennifer
 2000 *Managing Displacement: Refugees and the Politics of Humanitarianism.* Minneapolis: University of Minnesota Press.
Jabri, Ahmed
 2003 "A Refugee Is a Refugee: 50 Years of Excluding Palestinians from International Protection." *World Refugee Survey 2003.* Washington, D.C.: U.S. Committee for Refugees. 40–45.
Jacobson, Laurie Blome, ed.
 2003 *Socio-Economic Situation of Palestinian Refugees in Jordan, Lebanon, Syria and the West Bank and Gaza Strip.* Oslo: Fafo Institute for Applied Social Science.
Jenkins, Richard
 2002 "'Imagined But Not Imaginary': Ethnicity and Nationalism in the Modern World." In *Exotic No More: Anthropology on the Front Lines,* ed. Jeremy MacClancy. Chicago: University of Chicago Press.114–28.
Jiryis, Sabri
 1976 *The Arabs in Israel.* Trans. Aneid Bushnaq. New York: Monthly Review Press.

Joseph, May
    1999   *Nomadic Identities: The Performance of Citizenship.* Minneapolis: University of Minnesota Press.
Kanafani, Ghassan
    2000   "Guns in the Camp." In *Palestine's Children: Return to Haifa and Other Stories.* Trans. Barbara Harlow and Karen Riley. Boulder, Colo.: Lynne Reinner. 129–33.
Keith, Michael and Steve Pile
    1993   *Place and the Politics of Identity.* London: Routledge.
Kerr, Stanley E.
    1993   *The Lions of Marash: Personal Experiences with American Near East Relief, 1919–1922.* Albany: State University of New York Press.
Khalidi, Rashid
    1997   *Palestinian Identity: The Construction of Modern National Consciousness.* New York: Columbia University Press.
Khalidi, Walid, ed.
    1992   *All That Remains: The Palestinian Villages Occupied and Depopulated by Israel in 1948.* Washington, D.C.: Institute for Palestine Studies.
    1961   "Plan Dalat: The Zionist Masterplan for the Conquest of Palestine, 1948." *Middle East Forum* (November): 22–28.
Khoury, Elias
    1996   *The Kingdom of Strangers.* Trans. Paula Haydar. Fayetteville: University of Arkansas Press.
Khuri-Otaqui, Salwa
    1971   *Family Service Center Program: Description and Analysis.* Beirut: Near East Ecumenical Committee for Palestine Refugees.
Kimmerling, Baruch
    2003   *Politicide: Ariel Sharon's War Against the Palestinians.* London: Verso.
Kleinman, Arthur and Joan Kleinman
    1997   "The Appeal of Experience, the Dismay of Images: Cultural Appropriations of Suffering in Our Times." In *Social Suffering,* ed. Arthur Kleinman, Veena Das, and Margaret Lock. Berkeley: University of California Press. 1–23.
Kliot, Nurit
    1987   "Here and There: The Phenomenology of Settlement Removal from Northern Sinai." *Journal of Applied Behavioral Science* 23 (1): 35–51.
Lefebvre, Henri
    1991   *The Production of Space.* Trans. Donald Nicholas-Smith. Oxford: Blackwell.
Leighton, Alexander
    1946   *The Governing of Men: General Principles and Recommendations Based on Experience at a Japanese Relocation Camp.* Princeton, N.J.: Princeton University Press.
Lockman, Zachary
    1995   "Exclusion and Solidarity: Labor Zionism and Arab Workers in Palestine, 1897–1929." In *After Colonialism: Imperial Histories and Post Colonial Displacements,* ed. Gyan Prakash. Princeton, N.J.: Princeton University Press. 211–40.
    1993   "Railway Workers and Relational History: Arabs and Jews in Brit-

ish-Ruled Palestine." *Comparative Studies in Society and History* 35 (3): 601–27.

Loescher, Gil
  1993   *Beyond Charity: International Cooperation and the Global Refugee Crisis.* Oxford University Press.

Long, Lynellyn
  1993   *Ban Vinai: The Refugee Camp.* New York: Columbia University Press.

Low, Setha and Denise Lawrence
  1990   "The Built Environment and Spatial Form." *Annual Review of Anthropology* 19: 453–505.

Malkki, Liisa
  1996   "Speechless Emissaries: Refugees, Humanitarianism, and Dehistoricization." *Cultural Anthropology* 11 (3): 377–404.
  1995a   *Purity and Exile: Violence, Memory, and National Cosmology Among Hutu Refugees in Tanzania.* Chicago: University of Chicago Press.
  1995b   "Refugees and Exile: From 'Refugee Studies' to the National Order of Things." *Annual Review of Anthropology* 24: 495–523.
  1992   "National Geographic: The Rooting of Peoples and the Territorialization of National Identity Among Scholars and Refugees." *Cultural Anthropology* 7 (1): 24–44.

Mamdani, Mahmood
  2001   *When Victims Become Killers: Colonialism, Nativism, and the Genocide in Rwanda.* Princeton, N.J.: Princeton University Press.

Manz, Beatriz
  1995   "Fostering Trust in a Climate of Fear." In *Mistrusting Refugees*, ed. E. Valentine Daniel and John Chr. Knudsen. Berkeley: University of California Press. 151–67.

Marrus, Michael
  1985   *The Unwanted: European Refugees in the Twentieth Century.* Oxford: Oxford University Press.

Masalha, Nur
  2001   "The Historical Roots of the Palestinian Refugee Question." In *Palestinian Refugees: The Right of Return*, ed. Naseer Aruri. London: Pluto Press. 36–67.
  1992   *Expulsion of the Palestinians: The Concept of Transfer in Zionist Political Thought, 1882–1948.* Washington, D.C.: Institute for Palestine Studies.

Massey, Doreen
  1994   *Space, Place, and Gender.* Minneapolis: University of Minnesota Press.
  1993   "Power-Geometry and a Progressive Sense of Place." In *Mapping the Futures: Local Cultures, Global Change*, ed. Jon Bird, Barry Curtis, Tim Putnam, George Robertson, and Lisa Tickner. London: Routledge. 56–69
  1992   "Politics and Space/Time." *New Left Review* 196: 65–84.

Menjivar, Cecilia
  2000   *Fragmented Ties: Salvadoran Immigrant Networks in America.* Berkeley: University of California Press.

Merry, Sally Engle
  2000   *Colonizing Hawaii: The Cultural Power of Law.* Princeton, N.J.: Princeton University Press.

Metress, Eileen
    1990   "The American Wake of Ireland: Symbolic Death Ritual." *Omega*
             21 (2): 147–53.
Mishal, Shaul and Reuven Aharoni
    1994   *Speaking Stones: Communiques from the Intifada Underground.* Syra-
             cuse, N.Y.: Syracuse University Press.
Mitchell, Timothy
    1988   *Colonising Egypt.* Cambridge: Cambridge University Press.
Mitchell, W. J. T., ed.
    1994   *Landscape and Power.* Chicago: University of Chicago Press.
Mohanty, Chandra Talpade
    1991   "Under Western Eyes. Feminist Scholarship and Colonial Dis-
             course." In *Third World Women and the Politics of Feminism,* ed.
             Chandra Talpade Mohanty, Ann Russo, and Lourdes Torres.
             Bloomington: Indiana University Press. 51–80.
Moors, Annelies
    1996   "On Appearance and Disappearance: Representing Palestinian
             Women Under the British Mandate." *Thamyris* (special issue on
             Gender in the Middle East: Transnational Connections and Con-
             testations) 3 (2): 279–310.
Morris, Benny
    1987   *The Birth of the Palestinian Refugee Problem, 1947–1949.* Cambridge:
             Cambridge University Press.
Mortland, Carol A., ed.
    1998   *Diasporic Identity.* Arlington, Va.: American Anthropological Asso-
             ciation.
Mouffe, Chantal
    1994   "For a Politics of Nomadic Identity." In *Travellers' Tales: Narratives*
             of Home and Displacement, ed. George Robertson, Melinda Mash,
             Lisa Tickner, Jon Bird, Barry Curtis, and Tim Putnam. London:
             Routledge. 105–13.
Myers, Fred
    1991   *Pintupi Country, Pintupi Self: Sentiment, Place, and Politics Among*
             Western Desert Aborigines. Berkeley: University of California Press.
Nagengast, Carole
    1994   "Violence, Terror, and the Crisis of the State." *Annual Review of*
             Anthropology 23: 109–36.
Natour, Suheil
    1993   "The Legal Status of the Palestinian Refugees in Lebanon." In
             Refugees in the Middle East. Nordic NGO Seminar, Oslo, 26–27
             March 1993. Oslo: Norwegian Refugee Council.
Nazzal, Nafez
    1978   *The Palestinian Exodus from Galilee 1948.* Beirut: Institute for Pales-
             tine Studies.
Norton, Augustus
    1987   *Amal and the Shiʿa.* Austin: University of Texas Press.
Paerregaard, Karsten
    1997   *Linking Separate Worlds: Urban Migrants and Rural Lives in Peru.*
             Oxford and New York: Berg.
Paine, Robert
    1992   "Jewish Ontologies of Time and Political Legitimation in Israel."

In *The Politics of Time*, ed. Henry Rutz. Monograph Series 4. Washington, D.C.: American Ethnological Society. 150–70.

Pappe, Ilan
    1995   "Critique and Agenda: The Post-Zionist Scholars in Israel." *History and Memory* 7 (1): 66–90.

Parmenter, Barbara McKean
    1994   *Giving Voice to Stones: Place and Identity in Palestinian Literature.* Austin: University of Texas Press.

Patai, Raphael
    1962   *Golden River to Golden Road: Society, Culture, and Change in the Middle East.* Philadelphia: University of Pennsylvania Press.

Peteet, Julie
    2000   "Refugees, Resistance, and Identity." In *Globalization and Social Movements: Culture, Power, and the Transnational Public Sphere*, ed. John Guidry, Michael Kennedy, and Mayer Zald. Ann Arbor: University of Michigan Press. 183–209.
    1999   "Points of Departure and Points of Return: Identity and a Palestinian Diaspora." Paper presented at Diasporas: Transnational Identity and the Politics of the Homeland Conference, University of California, Berkeley, 12–14 November.
    1997   "Icon and Militants: Mothering in the Danger Zone." *Signs: Journal of Women and Culture* 23 (1): 103–29.
    1996a   "The Writing on the Walls: The Graffiti of the Intifada." *Cultural Anthropology* 11 (2): 139–59.
    1996b   "From Refugees to Minorities: Palestinians in Post-War Lebanon." *Middle East Report* 26 (3): 27–30.
    1995a   "Transforming Trust: Dispossession and Empowerment Among Palestinian Refugees." In *Mistrusting Refugees*, ed. E. Valentine Daniel and John Chr. Knudsen. Berkeley: University of California Press. 168–86.
    1995b   "'They Took Our Blood and Milk': Palestinian Women and War." *Cultural Survival* 19 (1): 50–53.
    1994   "Male Gender and Rituals of Resistance in the Occupied Territories. A Cultural Politics of Violence." *American Ethnologist* 21 (1): 31–49.
    1991   *Gender in Crisis: Women and the Palestinian Resistance Movement.* New York: Columbia University Press.

Pile, Steve and Nigel Thrift, eds.
    1995   *Mapping the Subject: Geographies of Cultural Transformation.* London: Routledge.

Quigley, John
    1998   "Displaced Palestinians and the Right of Return." *Harvard International Law Journal* 39 (1): 193–98.

Rabinow, Paul
    1989   *French Modern: Norms and Forms of the Social Environment.* Cambridge, Mass.: MIT Press.

Reinhart, Tanya
    2002   *Israel/Palestine: How to End the War of 1948.* New York: Seven Stories Press.

Robben, Antonius C. G. M. and Marcelo M. Suárez-Orozco
    2000   *Cultures Under Siege: Collective Violence and Trauma.* Cambridge: Cambridge University Press.

Rodman, Margaret C.
    1992   "Empowering Place: Multilocality and Multivocality." *American Anthropologist* 94: 640–56.
Rosaldo, Renato
    1989   *Culture and Truth: The Remaking of Social Analysis*. Boston: Beacon Press.
Rouse, Roger
    1991   "Mexican Migration and the Social Space of Postmodernism." *Diaspora* 1 (1): 8–23.
Ruiz, Hiram
    1993   "Repatriation: Tackling Protection and Assistance Concerns." In U.S. Committee for Refugees, *World Refugee Survey 1993*. Washington, D.C.: U.S. Committee for Refugees. 20–29.
Rutz, Henry J., ed.
    1992   *The Politics of Time*. Washington, D.C.: American Anthropological Association.
Said, Edward
    1986   *After the Last Sky: Palestinian Lives*. Photographs by Jean Mohr. New York: Pantheon.
    1984   "Permission to Narrate." *Journal of Palestine Studies* 51: 27–48.
Sarup, Madan
    1994   "Home and Identity." In *Travellers' Tales: Narratives of Home and Displacement*, ed. George Robertson, Melinda Mash, Lisa Tickner, Jon Bird, Barry Curtis, and Tim Putnam. London: Routledge. 93–104.
Sassen, Saskia
    1991   "De-Nationalization: Some Conceptual and Empirical Elements." APLA Distinguished Lecture, 1998. *Political and Legal Anthropology Review* 22 (2): 1–16.
Sayigh, Rosemary
    1995   "Palestinians in Lebanon: (Dis)solution of the Refugee Problem." *Race and Class* 37 (2): 27–42.
    1994   *Too Many Enemies: The Palestinian Experience in Lebanon*. London: Zed Press.
    1979   *Palestinians: From Peasants to Revolutionaries*. London: Zed Press.
Schiff, Benjamin
    1995   *Refugees unto the Third Generation: UN Aid to Palestinians*. Syracuse, N.Y.: Syracuse University Press.
Scholch, Alexander
    1993   *Palestine in Transformation, 1856–1882: Studies in Social, Economic and Political Development*. Washington, D.C.: Institute for Palestine Studies.
Segev, Tom
    1993   *The Seventh Million: The Israelis and the Holocaust*. New York: Hill and Wang.
    2001   *One Palestine, Complete: Jews and Arabs Under the British Mandate*. New York: Metropolitan Books.
Shafir, Gershon
    1996   "Israeli Decolonization and Critical Sociology." *Journal of Palestine Studies* 25 (3): 23–35.
    1989   *Land, Labor and the Origins of the Israeli-Palestinian Conflict, 1882–1914*. Cambridge: Cambridge University Press.

Shami, Seteney
    2000   "Prehistories of Globalization: Circassian Identity in Motion."
            Public Culture 12 (1): 177–204.
    1996   "Transnationalism and Refugee Studies: Rethinking Forced
            Migration and Identity in the Middle East." *Journal of Refugee
            Studies* 9 (1): 3–26.
Shohat, Ella
    1997   "The Narrative of the Nation and the Discourse of Moderniza-
            tion: The Case of the Mizrahim." *Critique: Journal for Critical Stud-
            ies of the Middle East* 10: 3–18.
Shoufani, Elias
    1972   "The Fall of a Village." *Journal of Palestine Studies* 1 (4): 108–21.
Skidmore, Monique
    2004   *Karaoke Fascism: Burma and the Politics of Fear.* Philadelphia: Uni-
            versity of Pennsylvania Press.
Slyomovics, Susan
    1998   *The Object of Memory: Arab and Jew Narrate the Palestinian Village.*
            Philadelphia: University of Pennsylvania Press.
    1993   "Discourses on the Pre-1948 Palestinian Village: The Case of Ein
            Hod/Ein Houd." *Traditional Dwellings and Settlements Review* 4
            (2): 27–37.
Small, Cathy A.
    1997   *Voyages: From Tongan Villages to American Suburbs.* Ithaca, N.Y.: Cor-
            nell University Press.
Smith, Neil
    1997   "The Satanic Geographies of Globalization: Uneven Develop-
            ment in the 1990s." *Public Culture* 10 (1): 169–89.
Smith, Pamela
    1984   *Palestine and the Palestinians 1876–1983.* New York: St. Martin's
            Press.
Smith-Hefner, Nancy J.
    1999   *Identity and Moral Education in a Diasporic Community.* Berkeley:
            University of California Press.
Soja, Edward W.
    1989   *Postmodern Geographies: The Reassertion of Space in Critical Social The-
            ory.* London: Verso.
Spivak, Gayatri Chakravorty
    1994   "Can the Subaltern Speak?" In *Colonial Discourse and Post-Colonial
            Theory,* ed. Patrick Williams and Laura Chrisman. New York:
            Columbia University Press. 66–111.
de St. Aubin, W.
    1949   "Peace and Refugees in the Middle East." *Middle East Journal* 3
            (3): 249–59.
Stevens, Georgiana
    1952   "Arab Refugees: 1948–1952." *Middle East Journal* 6 (3): 281–98.
Stewart, Kathleen
    1996   *A Space on the Side of the Road: Cultural Poetics in an "Other"
            America.* Princeton, N.J.: Princeton University Press.
Suleiman, Jaber
    1999   "The Current Political, Organizational, and Security Situation in
            the Palestinian Refugee Camps of Lebanon." *Journal of Palestine
            Studies* 29 (1) (Autumn): 66–80.

Index

Acknowledgments

Many people have contributed their time, support, and critical vision to make this book possible. Among them are the Miari family, Rosemary Sayigh, Anni Kanafani, Mu'taz Dajanai, Suleiman Jaber, Awni and Jamal Elhaj, Shawn Parkhurst, Susan Slyomovics, Mia Fuller, Yvonne Jones, Lisa Markowitz, Ferial Salloum, Nina Dodge, Maher Yamani, Nancy Gallager, Shiva Balaghi, and my colleagues in the Mellon Seminar on Globalization and Social Movements at the University of Michigan (1995–96). Many others remain unnamed, as is usual in anthropology, but nevertheless contributed to the production of this ethnography. I extend my gratitude to the staff at the Institute for Palestine Studies in Beirut and Washington, D.C., and the American Near East Relief Agency for the use of their materials and facilities, and to the American Friends Service Committee librarian Jack Sutters for his hospitality and guidance in the archives at Cherry Street. My wonderful and hard-working research assistants Jessica Powell, Maryam Mirriahi, Luke Hall, Leslie French, and Morgan Taliaferro made the task of assembling this book much easier. My most heartfelt thanks go to the Palestinians in Lebanon, who never fail to make me feel at home and welcome and are always eager to participate in these ethnographic projects. I dedicate this book to those in the camps and those who have died defending them. My husband, Imad Elhaj, provided wonderful insights and support.

Research for this book, which took place in Lebanon throughout the 1990s, was made possible by grants from the Joint Committee on the Near East and Middle East of the American Council of Learned Societies and the Social Science Research Council, with funds provided by the National Endowment for the Humanities and the Ford Foundation, and the Graduate School of the University of Louisville. Preliminary writing was supported by a Mellon (Sawyer) Fellowship at the Advanced Study Center, International Institute, University of Michigan, Ann Arbor. Special thanks are owed to the Peter Agree of the University of Pennsylvania Press, whose encouragement and warm support were critical in publishing this book. I am grateful to Ellie Goldberg and Alison Anderson for their assistance in preparing the manuscript for publication.